# Finding Grace

## Through a Lifetime of Lies

KAREN WHISPERER

**BALBOA.**PRESS

A DIVISION OF HAY HOUSE

Balboa Press books may be ordered through booksellers or by contacting:

Balboa Press
A Division of Hay House
1663 Liberty Drive
Bloomington, IN 47403
www.balboapress.com
844-682-1282

Because of the dynamic nature of the Internet, any web addresses or links contained in this book may have changed since publication and may no longer be valid. The views expressed in this work are solely those of the author and do not necessarily reflect the views of the publisher, and the publisher hereby disclaims any responsibility for them.

The author of this book does not dispense medical advice or prescribe the use of any technique as a form of treatment for physical, emotional, or medical problems without the advice of a physician, either directly or indirectly. The intent of the author is only to offer information of a general nature to help you in your quest for emotional and spiritual well-being. In the event you use any of the information in this book for yourself, which is your constitutional right, the author and the publisher assume no responsibility for your actions.

Cover Design by Lisa Garcia

Print information available on the last page.

ISBN: 978-1-9822-7430-6 (sc)
ISBN: 978-1-9822-7432-0 (hc)
ISBN: 978-1-9822-7431-3 (e)

Library of Congress Control Number: 2021918882

Balboa Press rev. date:  09/13/2021

# CONTENTS

As I sit at my desk at my new home in Myrtle Beach, I start the first sentence of the first page of my book. This has been in the works for years. "You should write a book!" "Are you writing your book?" "I'm writing a book." "Do you have a book?" These have been the most asked questions and the most repeated words in the past 5 years of my 55. It starts NOW!

Here we are ~ January 15, 2021, almost two years later, a book that is 7 years in the making, I have now realized that it wasn't going to be fully written until I was "woke". Until I had those memories that began October 6, 2018 in Hawaii. I know now through therapy that I don't have to provide evidence. I don't have to convince the reader of the validity of my story. I don't need to prove anything. I chatted with my therapist about evidence of childhood abuse. I had put it in the Prosecutor / Defense outline. I don't need to do that. I know what I know. The evidence is in my memory and in my visceral response to several things and situations over the last 50 years.

The evidence in regard to my mother, is unmistakable, undeniable. I don't even create a defense questioning on that part of my story, it is a real as I am sitting there.

It's morning. My normal writing time. It's when I am most clear and can write undisturbed. As I sit here, nails clanking on the keyboard, I take a moment. This is a lot. I take a breath. I sit silent. I hear a quiet voice. A voice that I recognize. "Tell it, tell it all." It's my father's voice. Finally.

Last night I asked my deceased loved ones to help me be clear for the rest of the book. Today I got the message. Five words. "I don't need his permission." I am, however, incredibly grateful for the message. He has been forgiven. There is no reason for him not to contact me. My cup flows over with emotion typing those words. One more time, so I am sure I heard it right, "tell it, tell it all". A major energy shift just occurred. Why? Because this morning I did the internal work. The work my therapist asked me to do. A layer was peeled back, and I received this gift. This was no coincidence. No accident. Everything for a reason.

Today is also the first day I finished writing and then went back to it, as I was led to keep going. This is why.

Finding Grace is based on a true story. For the comfort, healing and respect of the author and her family; character names, places, and incidents in the book are used fictitiously and any resemblance to persons living or dead, business establishments, events, or locales is entirely coincidental.

On June 22, 2018 ~ I changed my name. I released all other names including my maiden name, Kendall. I was no longer attached to that name for many reasons. I thought I knew them all. I didn't know releasing that name would open a door to memories, and clarity that I would spend the next 2 ½ years sorting through. I am not afraid to tell the truth. I am afraid of what happens if I don't. The following is the truth as I know it.

Finding Grace ~ a story about finding grace in all situations in a traumatic. And also, finding Grace.

Enjoy!!

Hello ~ I'm Karen, pleased to meet you. Who AM I? Who is Karen? Well, Karen is someone who has had many names, many titles during her last 57 trips around the sun.

However, these are names I have been called, you will see some more throughout this book.

I am NOT "just a preacher's kid".

I am NOT just "his sister".

I am NOT "his wife" or "his wife" or even "his wife".

I am NOT "just a volunteer".

I am NOT "a healer".

I AM a "Motherless Daughter"!

I AM "the sister who took care of things"!

I AM "single and loving it"!

I AM "the one who went from Volunteer to DIRECTOR of Disaster Services, American Red Cross".

I AM "a Spiritual Advisor" who doesn't heal you, but guides you to heal yourself.

I AM THE QUEEN OF MY LIFE, MY BUSINESS, MOTHERHOOD AND GRANDMOTHERHOOD!

Welcome to my story, my life.

# THE MAN IN THE WHITE CAR –

Spring 2009 ~ It was a cloudy Saturday, a normal day, well as normal as could be after burying my father a week earlier. My daughter Tandy and her son Roman were at the house, as well as my brother-in-law (at the time), who happened to be using the facilities when the crash shook the house like an earthquake. We lived in a house on Wheeling Pond, on a class VI dirt road. As we ran down the hill to Route 125, straight ahead was the small white car facing north in the Southbound lane. Smoke was pouring from the engine, the car folded like an accordion. 50 yards north of the white car, still facing north but off the road, was the other totaled car. As frantic onlookers were running to the red car, I ran across 125 to the white car. Traffic was now stopped and the family in the van was yelling about the drunk driver in the red car. As folks approached the red car, they ran up upon what everyone assumed was a drunk long-haired man, hunched over the steering wheel, clearly deceased. We would later find out that it was a woman who had been treated and released from the local Hospital earlier. According to witnesses," he appeared to be having a medical issue all the way up Route 125." She had been rushing home to see her daughter off to prom.

As I approached the smoking car, I saw the little girl in passenger's side back seat, strapped firmly into her car seat, crying loudly for her "Daddy", while desperately searching to find her other shoe. She was 2, which she had carefully shown us by holding up her 2 little fingers. Next to her was an empty car seat, which left us with no choice but to think the worst. The front was demolished, the back folded, like an

1

accordion. Another child must have been ejected! We searched and searched and found nothing. "Brother", as the sweet child referred to him, must have been at home, that fateful day. The smells that day, car fluids, smoke, blood and freshly purchased food will be forever ingrained in my memory.

The daddy and his little girl had just left the grocery store, a mile away and were headed to their home, just a couple miles away from the scene. They had run out for some groceries; they were going to make mommy a nice Mother's Day dinner the following day. I will never forget the sights that day. On the ground sat, a gallon of milk, bread, ham, and bright orange crinkle cut carrots, with hockey gear hanging out of the trunk. A vision, I cannot erase.

Frantically questioning the two-year-old child, "who was in that car seat?" "My brother" she said. "Where is he hunny, where is your brother?" "Home with mommy", she cried. We found out he had asked to go that day but was told "not this time". That decision saved his little life. The damage was the front and back of the car, and the driver's side was bashed in. As my husband struggled to get her scared little body out of the car, car seat and all, just in case her little back or neck were injured, we finally figured out she was double strapped with seatbelts, and that they had locked on impact.

My brother-in-law ran to the house to get a knife, and she was successfully cut out of the car. Quickly wedging myself into the back seat in front of her while they worked, I blocked her vision line of daddy, so she didn't have to remember him that way. Right behind my back was her dad's face, looking straight at her. I knew he was still breathing ever so faintly; I knew his angels were on their way. I had checked his pulse while I was wedged in there. My husband carried her across the highway to my daughter, who would care for her and comfort her while I stayed with her dying daddy. Waiting there with a blanket and a stuffy, Tandy and she became instant friends. We would later learn that the little girl's dad had always been very safety conscious with the kids' car seats. He double belted and then he would get in and push on the seat with his feet to make sure it wouldn't move. He saved his daughter's life that day. She is now just about to turn 15, as her 3rd birthday was not long after the accident.

With the little girl safely on the side of the highway, and sirens beginning to make their way closer to the scene, there was nothing left for me to do, other than sit with this young, handsome man. His injuries were severe, his breathing almost stopped, his pulse weak. I managed to get into the glovebox to get his registration. His name and a NH city address were all I saw. At that moment, I had no idea his wife and three other children, all under the age of 12, had begun to worry about where he was, at their home less than 2 miles away. Just minutes prior to this accident, this now lifeless young dad had taken a video at the grocery store of him and his little girl. The last thing he would send to his wife before his passing.

"It's okay, she is safe. Please try to hang in there. She needs you." Words that I knew he would hear as his last. I called him his name, his given name. Not the obvious nickname associated with his name. That later proved to be the appropriate name, the one he went by.

The EMT made his way to the car, as I was now sharing the driver's seat with a man I had never known before that fateful day. I held him, and the EMT just walked away, as I assured him the young man was transitioning home. It seemed like hours. But I know it was minutes. He was gone. I didn't move. Not until I knew the medical team would come back and take him gently out of the car.

His daughter whisked away in one ambulance, as none of us were allowed to go with her, while a blue tarp was thrown over the white car, where my new friend's lifeless body now sat. There was nothing left to do. Reality set in. We began to search social media (which was much less advanced 12 years ago). We found what appeared to be his profile, but it was Lennox, NH. Our town, he was our neighbor. Things began to make a little more sense, as grocery shopping in Lennox and living in Manning, was not adding up.

Days passed and as we learned of the family in the media, we reached out and told them what had happened to their, daddy, husband, son, nephew. They became family. I must have described to them the last moments of his life 100 times. But I would have done it 100 more if they needed to hear it.

The wake, with huge numbers of decorated military on hand, proved to be one of the most difficult I have been to in my 50+ years of life. Just to see him lying there so young, so innocent, and his family so broken. It became so difficult to look at him. He wasn't the same man I had met. This man was in perfect order. The man I had met was broken. I later learned he had done two tours in Iraq. I learned three weeks earlier, that he had buried his best friend, who had given his life for his country. I learned he loved hockey. He had beautiful children, and a wife. He had a mom, who had to struggle through Mother's Day, just hours after her son passed.

It was a sunny Sunday in 2016. Seven years later. I thought often of the young dad whose life was taken, throughout those seven years. I, as I typically am, was doing a Mediumship Gallery at a friend's home in Merriman, NH. A year earlier, I had joined a direct sales company and had become instant friends with some of the women in the company. These women are some of my dearest friends to this day.

As Spirits came in with messages from the other side, I saw these two men, brothers, friends. One had shown me he was in the military and briefly described his passing. The hostess knew exactly who it was, a man she had known very well in school. Then he brought in his friend. I saw his passing. A white car. He had left 4 children behind. I started to choke up as I asked the hostess, "Where did this accident happen? Did you know him? I was there! I know this man." Through tears, I told the group the story. They had known someone was with him that day as he slipped away. That day, they found out it was me. Several times over the next few weeks, I was able to share what had happened to their friend that day, with his friends, who were now my friends. He was from Manning originally, he passed in Lennox. I lived in Anthem at the time of the Gallery, and we were in Merriman! I honestly believe he put us in each other's lives. No coincidences.

This year and every previous year, I have put a tribute to him on my social media. A couple years ago, the 10th anniversary of his passing, I was contacted by someone who happened to be "recommended as a friend" to me and had seen his prayer card as my profile picture. She too was his friend in school. She hadn't known he had passed. That was, until social media recommended that she "friend" me that day, the 10th anniversary of his passing. She asked several questions about that horrific day. How I knew him, or did I? She told the same story of what a great guy he was, just a real great guy. I think we both found some peace.

Father – Who art in Heaven - Let me tell you about the man. My father. Minister, English Professor and highly exalted in the church. The Exorcist ~ written Spring 2019

The looks on their faces when I tell them my father was an Exorcist, is priceless. Most people aren't aware that there truly is such a thing as an Exorcist, let alone meet someone whose father was one! Immediately they revert to the famous horror movie from 1973 that starred Ellen Burstyn and made the young Linda Blair famous.

Wikipedia refers to Exorcism as the "religious or spiritual practice of evicting demons or other spiritual entities from a person, or area that are believed to be possessed. Depending on the spiritual beliefs of the exorcist, this may be done by causing the entity to swear an oath, performing an elaborate ritual, or simply by commanding it to depart in the name of a higher power". For my father, this would have been done by the latter. "In the name of Jesus", "in the name of the Holy Spirit" or "in the name of the Father, Son and Holy Spirit, I rebuke this demon from this body!!!" I can hear him say it, as I write these words. This was not unfamiliar to me.

As kids, we spent a lot of time in our rooms, or outside, or in church. That was pretty much where you could find a Kendall kid. Or "PK", as we were often called, Preacher's Kid.

As I will discuss later in the book, there is, in my opinion, no difference with what he did as a "practice" and what I do. Yes, I work with spirits who are in the light and he worked with the lower energies. I didn't understand much about it as a kid. But I did think that everyone's dad must be like this, maybe that's what all ministers do? As an adult, I understand now that most people don't know exorcists. They may know Priests who have done exorcisms, but they don't know someone who is known as an exorcist. I remember being so proud when a New York Magazine featured a story about him, and I remember once making photocopies of the article. Where they are is beyond me.

I would often sit on the landing of the staircase and watch them in the living room. They .... what do I call them, patients, clients, customers...........were usually alone, very often women, and as I recall, they looked fairly normal to me. How many people can say that exorcisms took place in their living room or even in their house? I will say that I never saw their heads spin around or vomit coming from their mouths. I just remember feeling bad for them. Empathy would be a good word to use for what I felt. I would overhear my father talking about how they were possessed, voices in their heads, or was it all due to LSD? This was, after all, the late 60's and early 70's.

I have voices in my head. Am I possessed? Not at all. Am I different from most? Sure. I have Spirits, intuitive information, it all can be explained. I often wonder, "is that what was going on with these folks?" Knowing now what I didn't know then, did my father use a white light of protection?

Did he smudge? Did he clear out the energies? When the demon left the person, where did it go? Did the "devil" come get it? Side note: I do not believe there is an entity with horns, a pitchfork and fire all around him! I also, based on what the deceased have shown me, do not believe there is an actual hell.

By comparison, those in spirit show me that we are in a version of hell right now, here on earth. They are in Heaven. Heaven is a state of being. They walk amongst us, by our side.

While on the subject, I also need to visit what was so commonly known in our church as "speaking in tongues". I have to be honest, as a kid, this would scare the shit out of me! It is defined as a language(s) used unknown to the person. It is also defined as a "spiritual gift". Here we are again, with another reference to the work that I do, which is a "spiritual gift". I find myself, as do many folks, trying to understand the line drawn in the sand between what happens in a traditional church, and providing the gifts and services that I provide.

The point here being, what is the difference between an Exorcist, A Medium and someone "Speaking in Tongues"? More importantly, who defines it and who gets to say what is right and what is wrong?

Speaking in tongues as defined by Dictionary.com is, "a person who has what is known as the gift of tongues is usually in the midst of religious ecstasy, trance, or DELIRIUM." Well that truly takes the words right out of my mouth. When I channel, I channel Spirit. I have also channeled other beings on occasion, in which I was in a trance. The definition clearly mentions delirium. I've not been there.

When I was a child, growing up in a Non-denominational, Pentecostal church, this "speaking in tongues" was a quite common experience. If you have never experienced it, I would liken it to when Clark Griswold does the "drum roll" when he is about to light up the house with Christmas lights in my all-time favorite movie, Christmas Vacation. As a child, these folks "speaking in tongues" to me seemed possessed. I am not mocking any type of religious beliefs here. Just simply stating how I perceived this odd phenomenon. It was never explained to me, it just was a fact. One of the many "facts" a child was conditioned to believe.

As I write and examine my experiences, my forehead scrunched up, I am still a little unsettled. Perhaps it is the religious conditioning that I was, in a sense, brainwashed with, that everything that happens inside the four walls of our church is true and just and pure, and anyone or anything that does not agree to these exact followings, is a sinner and will go to hell. To save some heartache, (and hate mail) let me again remind the reader that I am referring to MY experience in OUR church.

We children were a secondary fixture in the church. Sure, there was Sunday School, and later on a teen group, which in my opinion was truly just a teen dating scene. Now, I am very aware that currently many churches have teen leadership and have gotten several kids off the streets, and on a path they may have never been on otherwise. However, once again, I am talking about my experience, in the 60's and 70's. Oh that anticipatory feeling of counting the days, weeks, months years till I turned 18 and NO ONE would force me into a traditional church again. No more twice on Sunday. No more Wednesday night prayer meeting, or Friday night Bible Study, although we did have some great refreshments after. Deserts were my reward for going. Fair enough. No complaints from me if there were maple squares.

Fear.

Fear was engrained in our being every, single day. As a small child and later as an adult, my father taught me fear. I was afraid of him. Afraid of what would happen after dark. I was afraid of being "put up for adoption", his words, not mine. I was afraid that if I swore, smoked a cigarette, or smoked anything for that matter, took a drink, or sinned in ANY way, that I was on the speed train to Hell. Although it sounds like a joke now, it was no joke. It is a wonder I was not riddled with anxiety throughout those formidable years.

The letter, ahhhh that letter. I am a sinner in his eyes. He even told me so. "You are going to hell", he told me in this neatly handwritten letter that I received in the mail from one town away. I shredded it and smudged the house and myself. His negativity and evil spewed out all over this letter that he had "felt moved" to write. (I despise that phrase)

Part of me wishes I still had it so I could shred it again and light it on fire. In his opinion, divorce was a sin, and I was a sinner going straight to hell and he wanted to tell me himself. Ahhhh, I was a sinner. Evil. It was now confirmed. I let it hold as much weight as the paper it was

9

written on. I valued it as much as I valued his negativity. ZERO value! Don't get me wrong. I always respected my elders. Now though, zero respect. Zero value.

"Felt moved" ~ Whisperpedia definition ~ a phrase used quite too frequently, that releases the user of this phrase from any guilt or blame, because they were "told" to take said action by their god.

# GRAPHOLOGY -

*Graphology, according to Wikipedia, is the analysis of the physical characteristics and patterns of handwriting with attempt to identify the writer, indicate the psychological state at the time of writing, or evaluate personality characteristics. It is generally considered a pseudoscience. *

Graphanalysis is the forensic examination of handwritten documents as a branch of questioned document examination.

Not only did my father practice the psychic phenomena of graphanalysis, or graphology, but he taught it. Telling things about a person from their handwriting, in my humble opinion, is an intuitive gift. I have met others who practice the same gift, talent or ability. One of them even works at a police station. So, I wonder, is handwriting analysis a learned profession? My gut says it is an intuitive gift, although it is taught. Yet not something that can just be learned. Mediumship, Intuition, Psychic ability; also, a gift. Not something that can be learned. Do many gifted folks go to "classes" to fine tune their abilities, sure. But one can't simply wake up one day and question, "shall I learn the art of cake decorating, or Mediumship?" It doesn't work that way. I was born this way. It sounds like my parents were too.

Exorcist – works with Spirits – Me, him, Mom?
Teacher – Me, him, Mom
Intuitive ability – Me, him, mom

It occurs to me that exorcism and graphology is non-provable in my opinion, which is no different from the work that I do.

I wonder… am I having a daily argument with a ghost, his ghost? Do I really need to prove myself? At the time of this writing, it is a full moon. Perhaps I shall visit it tonight so I can release this debate. If Dad were here, would I have the courage to have this debate with him? In the day, I don't know why I was ashamed of my work. How is my "God given" work any different from his?? In my day to day life, I find myself defending the work that I do. Stating quite often that I grew up in the church and I'm okay. My work is safe, and I am safe. Why must we be so AFRAID of this punishment from this all-loving being. Why would we be judged? It was all branded into my brain as a child. "Mess up in any way little girl, and you will go to hell."

I currently run in circles of people where this topic comes up often. Books, teachings and podcasts often mention this "evil being" typically called Satan, or the Devil, or a variety of names which I've known as long as I've known how to speak.

While researching "Satan" I found the following scripture. Stunned by how many times it mentions "Grace", as well as other references applicable to this book, I've decided to share it here as a reference point.

Ephesians 2 ~ BY **GRACE** THROUGH FAITH

"1 And a you He made alive, b who were dead in trespasses and sins, 2 c in which you once walked according to the 1 course of this world, according to d the prince of the power of the air, the spirit who now works in e the sons of disobedience, 3 f *among whom also we all once conducted ourselves in g the lusts of our flesh, fulfilling the desires of the flesh and of the mind, and h were by nature children of wrath, just as the others*. 4 But God, i who is rich in mercy, because of His j great love with which He loved us, 5 k even when we were dead in trespasses, 1. made us alive together with Christ (by **grace** you have been saved), 6 and raised us up together, and made us sit together m in the heavenly places in Christ Jesus, 7 that in the ages to come He might show the exceeding riches of His **grace** in n His kindness toward us in Christ Jesus. 8 o. for by **grace** you have been saved p through faith, and that not of yourselves; q it is the gift of God, 9 not of r works, lest anyone should s boast. 10 For we are t His workmanship, created in Christ Jesus for good works, which God prepared beforehand that we should walk in them."

In our scientific, rational age, spiritual beliefs are scorned as myth. While the book written that we refer to as the Bible, is considered factual. I am not on this subject to debate God vs Satan, Religion vs Spirituality. I am stating my opinions on this subject matter, which may or may not resonate with those reading this chapter. This is for those who have been tricked into believing the same ideologies that I brainwashed with as a child. Those who were led to believe that all 'men of God' are pure, incapable of evil or sin. I am not one of those people.

I truly honor each and every human's beliefs. My general take on spirituality, again MY belief, is that those of us who are "spiritual" welcome all beliefs of one's higher power, be it Source, Angels, Goddess, God, Spirit, I Am, Divine, Creator, Mother Earth, Father Sky, or any other term of endearment commonly used for our "go to" being.

Those who consider themselves "in Religion" or "religious" are known to honor God and all others are cast aside. With judgement. Yes, I said, "with judgement". Judgement that I have be subjected to from my very own former friends and my family. This leaves me the space to be able to speak to this subject. I have, and will, reference many examples of judgement against myself, by those who are "religious". As a matter of fact, I have zero family (that I was born into, not my own children) that have been without judgement towards me.

Is that fear? If they accept, without their church's approval, my spiritual work, will they go to "hell"? Oh, but what if they were to approve? Damned to the fast train to hell for certain? One family member in a condescending manor said, "were you doing that mediuming thing?" "I don't know, were you doing that churching thing?" Such is my life.

Matthew 7:2 – World English Bible – "For with whatever judgement you judge, you will be judged; and with whatever measure you measure, it will be measured to you." If you imposed standards on others, those standards will be imposed on you.

Simply said, I truly do not care who or what you believe in. I've shared this with so many friends and clients. Pray to a slice of cheese if you desire, but trust in a higher power no matter who or what it is.

In short, you do you and I'll do me. I don't think I could be anymore void of judgement against others. Are you? Let me say one last time. I have an abundance of love for ALL who go to church. I honor you. I went for 18 years straight. I am schooled enough on the subject to carry on an educated non-judgemental conversation in regard to religion and spirituality.

# LOCKED AND LOADED

A little bit about me. To know me, is to love me. I have worn many hats in my 50+ years, including the hat of mom. My children are all grown and have children of their own. Some people foster, some people adopt, not me.... I decided to add a pet menagerie to my repertoire. Here is a day in the life.........of a farmer girl.

It's a spring day in May, Laddon, NH, I am living in my 5 bedroom home on 8 acres, that I bought for myself, by myself. It is also a little farm. On this day I had one horse, 32 chickens, 1 calf and 1 dog. The most I have had in the past at any given time was 32 chickens, 8 ducks, 5 calves, 5 Rottweilers, 6 piglets, 3 horses and a partridge in a pear tree. Earlier, when I was married, we then lived in an 1100 square foot house on Wheeling Pond in Lennox we had 3 Rotties, and 2 St Bernards, totaling over 500lbs of dog. At our other house in Lennox, we had horses, not just little fun horses, but big ass Belgian Draft Horses. We also had 100+lb Rottweilers. Go big or go home, I always say, as I now sit in my own 3 bedroom house in Myrtle Beach.

On this particular day in May, however not an abnormal day, I just happened to have penned this one down, my day went as follows:

4:45am ~ Crows are here, that bitch must be back! I yell to myself and leap out of bed.

4:50am ~ First stop, potty

4:51am ~ Dawn is just breaking, and I can see him laying by my Escalade pick up. (yes, my farm truck was a Cadillac Escalade! Go big or go home, right?)

I am locked and loaded, no joke with my 22 in one hand and a rifle ready on the porch.

Walking through the house, I lose track of him. But the crows are circling, so he's still there, somewhere. Then I look between my house, and the stone wall, facing the house on the side street, there he is. Something in his mouth, I'm assuming it's one of my chickens.

At this point I can't get a shot without shooting my neighbor. As he flips it around, feathers flying by the hundreds, here comes fisher cat! The fisher is literally pacing back and forth on the stone wall, while fox works on the carnage and the crows continue circling. I am fit to be tied.

Some folks have a love - hate relationship with black crows, I have a huge respect for them. Many a morning, even in the evening, the crows would let me know the fox was near. I always thanked them for that. Their dedication and service saved many of my chickens.

Since my Rottie is a lover not a fighter, I bring Moscato in the house. The dog, not the wine. Although, at 5:30am, I already do need the wine.

As I stand at the kitchen sink, making warm formula for Cow, yes, he was still on baby formula, there he is. This fox is now in the horse pasture, directly behind Madeline, my 2000lb horse. Maddie doesn't care, she's too busy waiting for breakfast. Still, I can't take a shot at fox, not past my horse, not taking a chance. Fisher is gone, finally.

I figure that I probably looked pretty bad ass out there in my LuLaroes and tank top, complete with muck boots, with no socks.

I do a double take and lined up directly behind the horse, is the fox a few feet back. Then up the hill, directly behind them, at the tree line.......... DEER!! Which probably sounds like a pretty picture to you. But for deer to be at the top of the hill, IN the pasture, that can only mean one thing. They have broken through the electric fencing. Which now means my electric fence won't be working down the hill either, where ....... you guessed it, Maddie is right ready to get into some trouble. She may be big as an ox, but she is wise as an owl.

Cow formula is made, and I have to go out and feed at this point. Fox is gone, fisher is gone, I'm still locked and loaded, cow formula in one hand, weapon in the other. I look over at the horse and there she is, all tangled up in the electric fence. She must have heard it shut off, when the deer broke through, then she broke the bottom line, and got BOTH front legs hung up in the middle line. The top of her body is leaning out of the pasture to eat the fresh grass in the yard, which really needs to be mowed. Completely unphased by the events going on around her, she is now grazing and has found her own breakfast. Thanks to the deer that broke the fence, she could lean over the now non-electric wire, and have a snack!

I try to free all 2000lbs of her from the electric fence. She panics, moving forward, instead of back into the pasture. She's coming out!! The fence gets caught in her hoof and I am literally leaning into her, so she doesn't fall. If you've never seen a Draft Horse, picture the Budweiser Clydesdales. That's a draft horse. She is the size of a Clydesdale, so if she goes down, I am going with her.

This isn't the first time we have done this dance. Back in Lennox, I was in her stall saying goodnight. Hugs, kisses and an apple treat was the nightly routine. We lived near the racetrack, and at this very moment during our goodnight routine and tucking in, they lit off some fireworks at the track. Well, she zigged, and I zagged and crack, I was down for the count. Maddie is not very light on her feet. I re-broke an old break in my foot, from the night I jumped off the Hampton Beach wall. Another story, for another day. I didn't make a sound, but a little sqweeeee, if I had screamed, she would have lost it. I hobbled to the house and threw up from the pain.

Another time, we lived in Anson, NH, Marcus, my stallion had torn off his stall door, gone over and torn off the calves' stall door, and gashed his nose while doing so. He apparently wanted to play. As I worked on his bleeding gash, he jumped and landed guess where, my foot. Snap! Again!

Back to the fence.... It's only 6am and I am yelling horse commands in my stern farm voice! Gentle Animal Communication was not going to work at this point. After all, if she lands on me, there's no one but she and I who will know. By now I'm sure the neighbors are all awake. I manage to take the fence down, untangle her, she runs and at this point all the wildlife is gone too.

Now, to walk the entire fence line to see where the deer came in. Cow is fed, Maddie is fed, Moscato is fed, and I am off. Sure enough, the deer came in at the top, of course the furthest point from the barn or the house, which is where my tools to fix it are. Fixed the fence at the top of the hill. Fixed the fence by the barn. Fence is back on. OUCH, that first touch to the electric fence will get ya!!

I open the door to the coop, 25 chickens come out of the huge storage container now chicken coop, and I have one with a broken leg.

Mic drop, I'm out! What do you do before 6:30am??

*Side note, the chickens that the fox would keep coming for, were the last batch to come to live with me. They REFUSED to sleep in the coop. They slept in the barn instead. That did not serve them well. He got about one a day. Did you know a chicken's brain is the size of a peanut? *

About my Work ~ Communication with Departed Unborn Babies on the Other Side

Many folks have asked me, "well, if they aren't born into this life, then how can they communicate?"

I don't know "how", but I know without doubt that they do. I have received messages from unborn babies, whether they were miscarried, aborted, or still born. Even those who lived only minutes or hours. This is MY truth. This may not be what you will hear from another Medium. However, we don't all have the same stories. This subject may strike a chord with some. But again, this is what I KNOW to be true based on the work that I have done.

Case in point:

In a recent session, I connected with many passed loved ones, and had several "hits" of validation. But we got hung up on a couple things. I kept hearing the number 30. Nothing with it, just the number. We were a little stumped, but I told her to "take it with her" and I knew she would figure it out. Then I felt a "baby" boy in spirit's presence. The 30 got stronger. It was HIM! He was showing me 30. I asked her if her son was a twin. I was feeling twin energy!

My friend nearly spit out her drink as she put together the details of what had happened when she turned 30!

"She" had been doing In Vitro Fertilization for 2 years. She told me, "4 IUIs and 3 IVF's "and finally she was pregnant. There were 3 embryos implanted. Thinking just one had "taken", she had become extremely concerned when she started bleeding. She then recalled how she celebrated her 30th birthday in her pajamas, on bed rest, with her family. She also had only taken one picture, because she had been crying so much with worry. She was sure that she had lost the baby. They did an ultrasound, and her baby was fine. BUT there behind the baby was an empty sack!! The baby had been blocking it. After that day, there was no more bleeding and her surviving baby's heart was beating away!! She has a healthy son and had a healthy daughter a few years later.

I confirmed for her that the empty sack had been a boy baby, and she told me that she always knew that it was a boy. Now she had validation.

As she told me this story, I kept hearing the name 'Grace', over and over. Again, she wasn't sure what that meant, so I told her to 'take it with her'.

We went on with her session and she received great readings and information for her and her husband. We parted ways and before long I got a text, validating many of the things we talked about. BUT then she sent me a picture. It was a picture of "her" and her favorite nurse, GRACE!!!

Yes, babies can communicate even if they weren't born into this life or walked this earth. I believe.

# ADDICTION ....... IN MANY FORMS

Envision this ~ Waking up and reaching for your glass of water, only it is not water, it is Pepsi. Envision the last sip of anything that touches your lips before bed, also Pepsi. Every beverage throughout the day, Pepsi. This was my life.

Some of my friends know this, some don't. Some see me with my "Rtic" cool cup and think it is ice water, or god forbid …. coffee. SURPRISE!!

Rewind to over 8 years ago. I lived in Anson, NH. Everyone knew back then that I drank Pepsi. It was no secret. Although, I had over the years, converted sometimes to Diet Pepsi, but had always had one or the other in my hand. You see the thing about soda addiction is, you don't drink it when you are thirsty, you drink it all day. Sun up - sun down. At least that is MY experience. January 2013, NOT a New Year's Resolution, I just one day woke up and said, "enough". Well, that day, I had already had Pepsi as soon as I opened my eyes, so it would have to be the next day.

I took it all out to the trash, emptied it, and saved only enough for the rest of that day. The next day was "the day". I woke up, couldn't drink water, it made me nauseous. So I drank nothing. Finally, I was able to down a little bit of Ginger Ale. I was SICK! I had a headache. I wanted to just sleep, I literally couldn't move or function. I slept for almost 24 hours. This went on for three days, maybe more. But I NEVER gave in.

Fast forward, November 2016. YES, I remember the day. I had just put my house on the market, and I had a headache that lasted a few days, which was extremely abnormal for me. Many people said, "try caffeine, it will help". I knew that to be a fact because I had suffered from migraines, many years ago. Well go big or go home. I could have had caffeine in many other forms, but I said, "well, I will have just one Pepsi." I am addicted. I can't have just one. I was back on the "crack in the can", as I call it. I would drink Ginger Ale (flavored) in the morning and Pepsi all afternoon and evening, then take one to bed. Until slowly, but surely there was no more Ginger Ale. Just Pepsi, 24/7/365. I am addicted.

Tuesday, Dec. 5th, 2017. I had been back on the Pepsi a year. Although I literally plan errands, etc.... around making sure I have Pepsi 24/7, I woke up and had none! "Today is the day, I am done", I said.

I have suffered. The first 24 hours, the headache was unbearable. The second day, I thought I was coming out of it. "Maybe it would be easier this time, as I had been back on it only a year", I thought. I was wrong. Night two, day three. Not a drop of Pepsi still, lots of water, and MANY bathroom trips, as I clear out all the toxins, apparently.

I am alive and almost well. It won't be easy, but easy isn't my thing anyway.

Addiction comes in many forms. Relationships, self-destructive behaviors, sugar, food, alcohol, drugs, gambling, and more. It also comes in a soda can. Do you have an addiction? Are you ready to give it up 100%? Start today. Today is as a good of a day as any. Tomorrow there will be a new excuse. I know because I am an addict.

New update - not only is it 10/5/19 and I am on day 5 of sobriety, but I have started a Facebook group on addiction. I never know how many people have addictions of some kind!!

Update #2 January 2020, I am back on the "crack in a can", full time, in full effect.

Update #3 November 2020, down to 1 can a day. It's been a ride. But addiction is just that, a ride. A friggin roller coaster ride.

Update #4 March 2021, final update, I quit the 1st of December and am still clean.

Update #5 May 2021, I am clean and Pepsi sober!!

# WHAT IS A SLIDER, ALSO KNOWN AS "ELECTRIC PERSON"? -

Three years ago, I wrote this article and subsequently shared it on my Facebook Business page. It has had the widest exposure and response of anything I have ever written, to this day. I receive responses from all over the world, weekly still by many others who have been affected by this phenomenon. As of today, 11/28/20, the post has 213 comments and 89 shares all over the world. I wrote it while visiting a friend in Los Angeles, while staying in a penthouse in her bldg. and setting off the smoke alarm, as I often do, and doing some research.

A Slider is a term that refers to a high voltage person that has so much electrical energy in their bodies that it can cause electrical disturbances around them. They can cause strange electrical phenomena. For example, I drain batteries. Smoke detectors are a key example. It came to me today, that every time I travel to a new place, within 24 hours, the smoke detector goes off, either for no reason, or because my energy was so high it drained the battery. It often happens like today, during meditation, the last time was in Florida, same thing! Within 24 hours the smoke detector chirped, needing a new battery. It is a constant, not a coincidence. Last week I drained the battery on the key fob of the brand new rental car.

Sliders can pull energy from electronic and battery powered devices. This drain can cause batteries to die and cause things to stop working.

Batteries drain, lightbulbs blow, fuses blow, things won't connect ie: computers. Often your credit cards won't work due to the energy that zaps the card. Or a big one is streetlights going out.

They transmit their energy to other electrical systems, and they receive energy from them.

Supercharged bioenergy fields, (auras) seems to be an underlying cause. Everything in the Universe is made up of energy. When Sliders are super excited, charged, they are loaded with huge amount of energy.

Our bodies vibrate at a frequency of approximately 8 cycles per second, which is the same frequency as the earth's magnetic field. Should our frequency become abnormally high, unusual things, electrically oriented things will begin to happen.

Who is a Slider, and why?

There are many explainable causes: Near death experiences being one of them. Other sliders have been struck by lightning or suffered and electrical shock ... (defibrillator, perhaps).

Some theories say that Sliders can also be humans who lived on other planets in a previous lifetime, and they are born on this Earth with different energies and abilities. Something alters a Slider's energetic frequencies, causing unusual electrical phenomena.

My granddaughter, while being delivered, broke not one, but two monitors because her energy was causing the machine to read out at such a dramatic speed, that it literally zapped it. She is a perfect example of a Slider.

"Electric People" or Sliders typically have a high degree of psychic ability or related experiences. This makes perfect sense because "high energy" means "high vibration" which is the foundation of psychic power.

They are extremely sensitive to high energy situations and environments which can often be painful. This is not the same as being empathic. Fluorescent lights can make them uncomfortable, which absolutely makes sense for me.

A Slider has so much electrical energy that they can cause electrical disturbances around them. They often can't Skype. The energy causes disturbances. It can also be the cause of extreme "energy" headaches prior to a disaster or severe storm. The electrical energy of the storm which will often include lightning and high pressure, is so magnified that it causes the electrical or pressure headache, such as the one I had leading up to Hurricane Irma in 2017.

Sliders or Spirits?

The energy given off by a Slider often resembles the energy connection or manipulation noticed after a loved one passes, and Spirits are trying to get our attention. Working with nonphysical energy or electricity is the easiest way for them to affect physical reality. Have you seen the lights flicker? TV going off and on? Other electrical appliances having weird phenomena?

Spirits will use any existing energy when attempting to manifest "or show" themselves.

The skin is the boundary of a human in normal reality, when the human opens psychically, that boundary (aura) expands. The person extends outside the body (aura) and feels and emits things in an extrasensory way.

After all, we are a spiritual being having a human experience.

How to control "zapping" things as a Slider?

Yoga, meditation, grounding all help with creating a calm energy or stilling some of the electric charge. Deep breathing, centering and Chakra aligning can also assist as well as essential oils, Blue Lotus Lily or Rescue Remedy which a peace creating products.

Like any other phenomena, being a Slider is unique and has advantages and disadvantages. I chose to look at the advantages.

BEING STUCK ~ 2013

It is stifling to be in one place for too long. What is "spreading your wings"? Certainly not being attached to one place, one lifestyle, one situation.

I lived in the same house for the first 16 years of my life. We then moved down the street and I lived in that house for the next 2 years. Then I spread my wings. I think staying in one place throughout my childhood, is why staying dormant is so comfortable for me. This has been a constant battle for me over the past 10 years. I have tried to "stay put". I lived in one house for 7 years, and I had planned to live in my last house for the rest of my life. Wow was I wrong!

Now I joke and say I am "homeless". It is a very strange feeling. I guess a better way to put it is "in transition". I'm waiting for the next leg of my journey to take off. The gypsy life.

It's strange but true how the things we fear the most, the things we are constantly "bumping up against" are the things we are soon faced with. We give the potential situation that we fear, so much energy, that we actually draw that situation to us. The "law of attraction" comes into play.

"What we think about, we bring about" ~ The Secret by Rhonda Byrne

"I don't ever want to move, I don't want to move, I am never moving"! That is a lot of energy put into exactly what I DON'T want. And so, it is …. I move.

If we can't get past our fears, if we can't heal them, we provide them the daily thought and energy that they need to come to fruition. Hence the phrase, "my worst fears came true"

I always say to prepare yourself for transition or for the "next leg of your journey" it is time to "get out of the driver's seat, get into the passenger's seat, and hold on tight!"

The following came to me in a dream state 5 or 6 years ago:

~Being Stuck~

"It's like going to the beach.

When you are ready to leave, you want to clean off your feet.

So, you wash them in the ocean.

But how do you really get your feet clean ~ while you are still standing in the sand?"

# BARNYARD BANANA BREAD ~ NOW KNOWN AS BEACHSIDE BANANA BREAD

When I was young, I was not a big fan of banana bread. In fact, I didn't like it. When I was 18, I ate a banana and had a severe allergic reaction that earned me a shot of epinephrine. When my kids were young, I found a recipe for banana bread and would make it for holidays. It was a big hit. I once made it for a work Christmas party and two women ended up not speaking to each other, because one had gotten the last slice. Many people asked for my recipe. I did not oblige.

Christmas 2012, I made baskets for each family that came to my home. In it I put a mini banana bread. They were eating them right out of the baskets. A family member said, "the Irving sells slices of banana bread for $1.99 and yours is much better than theirs, you should sell it!"

I talked to a few people and asked around and decided to give it a shot. I would do my barn chores for the calves and the horses, come in, wash my hands and start making bread. It only made sense to call it Barnyard Banana Bread!

In April, I started by selling it at my son's restaurant. It was a big hit. In May, I started selling it at the local farmer's market. I had many repeat customers. I still do. In June, I had a booth at a festival in Sharon Springs, NY. It was hosted by a couple who have a TV show on the Cooking Channel. My banana bread was a hit! It had only been 2 short months since I started, and things really took off! That was just 3 months ago. Barnyard Banana Bread has grown and flourished so much in the past 5 months. The future will be amazing! I am blessed.

*Update ~ I have had to put the Banana Bread business on hold due to an overwhelming schedule with client sessions and public events*

*Update #2 ~ Barnyard Banana Bread is now called Beachside Banana Bread and is on a bit of a hiatus.

# CLEARING THE CLUTTER ~

We hear this phrase often and typically we feel it is "cleaning up our house or our home". While that is true, there are also many other places where we need to do some "clutter clearing".

Relationships ~ How many relationships do we have that are toxic? These don't necessarily have to be partner relationships; they can be family or friends as well. Do you have people that you continue to talk to, that just rub you the wrong way? Or they put out a lot of negative energy? Clear that clutter!

Another area we may not think of as often is our "spiritual house". Our spiritual house is divided into to two parts. First, is our beliefs. Are we hanging onto or vested in some spiritual beliefs that don't resonate or jive with us? Perhaps these are childhood beliefs that were instilled as we grew up. Or perhaps these are certain beliefs taught to us by the folks we "run with" or socialize with. The ones that no longer serve us, we need to let go of. We cannot grow and thrive off of someone else's thoughts or deductions, if we don't believe them to be our personal truth, for our highest good. We can only use what resonates with us, what feels comfortable, and what works in our day to day lives, spiritually.

The second part of clearing our "spiritual house" is clearing ourselves up physically. Many of our eating habits, food addictions, diets, etc......
stem from childhood. That doesn't make those ways of eating wrong, however some of these habits can clutter our "spiritual house", which is

31

contained in our "physical body". Reading and researching is a great way to learn how to clear your 'physical body clutter'. Start with eliminating sugar and drinking lots of water. Then go back to the way our ancestors used to eat. Many people turn to the Paleo lifestyle to do this. Soon you will see the benefits spiritually, as well as physically.

Finally, everything you dismiss, clear or send away, while "clearing your clutter", whether it is house clearing, relationship clearing, or spiritual house clearing, be sure to send away what is no longer of service to you, with LOVE.

## JOURNAL ENTRY – OCTOBER 16, 2017 – MOLOKAI HAWAII - MY FIRST VISIT –

*(At the time, I had no idea what all of this meant)*

"Serenity
What is the object of your desire?
Collective Oneness with Source.
Creativity.
Why are we here?
You have come here to learn. Stay open.
Storms will follow you, but not lead you.
Fear not.
Stay grounded
Stand firm
Serendipity = trust
Untangle. Unwind. Clear focus.
You know. The road less traveled.
The work won't always be pleasant. But this isn't about you, is it?
Huge opening / awareness in 2018
Don't fear the one, these folks live a life of fear.
This message is not that you are wrong. The message is stand in your own truth."

# THE REASON THERE IS A BOOK -

June 22, 2018, I was in Jersey working with clients for the month of June. But I had to make a swift trip up to NH to go into a court room to change my name. What would it be? Not Kendall, I didn't want to be associated with that name. It was my maiden name. I never liked it and something about it wasn't jiving with me. Perhaps the falling out with a family member, 3 months prior. I'd soon find out why I was led NOT to go back to Kendall. Not Ashton, it's simply weird, he's passed, and doesn't have a say. Husband #1 is deceased.

Not Henry. Husband #2 AND #3, Bob, is not deceased. Not Wheaton. Husband #4, Remmy, also not deceased ~ I don't want to do that, as we are divorced, and he has an amazing little girl who is now 6 and she would be super confused why I have her same name.

The only thing that makes sense is WHISPERER! So that I did. Karen Whisperer. It became official and legal that day. Also, on that day, I decided to get a tattoo to commemorate this self-empowering name change. I designed it myself. An arrow. An arrow can only be shot forward by pulling it back first. Huge statement for me. Inside the arrow, as part of it, an infinity sign, which is self-explanatory. In front of the arrowhead, <<<, the Viking symbol that signifies "create your own reality". Inside the circles of the infinity sign, in the left loop is "ehfar", which means Everything Happens For A Reason. The last piece, for the right loop, that ended up being the most prophetic, was a symbol for my favorite story, Alice in Wonderland. There wasn't much I could do in the tiny little loop space I had to represent it, so I chose the 10/6 tag that dangles from the Madhatter's hat. That would be my tattoo.

I'm not even sure how many tattoos I have, but it was the first one I really put my heart and soul into. It wouldn't be until 3 ½ months later that I would learn why.

October 1, 2018 With all intentions I should have been on the Hawaiian Island of Molokai, for two months, as I had been for my first year, the year prior. But then there was Florence! She had other plans. A Cat 1 Hurricane by the time she made landfall, she still forced the evacuation of Myrtle Beach, where my son had just moved a month prior, August 2018. I switched flights and made other arrangements and spent time helping with the grandkids.

I arrived in Molokai on October 4th. The trip, 13 hours in the air, plus airports and layovers, plus time change, plus island hopper planes that fly when they want, from start to finish ends up being a full 24 hour escapade. Then, by the time I arrive, I've lost 6 hours due to time change from Eastern Standard Time, 5 hours in the winter.

I did the same thing as the prior year, I went to my condo, made sure I had enough snacks and drinks and went to bed until the next morning in Paradise. October 5th, the following day, after travel day, is typically spent going into town, to the market, getting essentials, seeing what else is needed and ordering from Amazon, arranging the condo how I want it, checking in on island friends and preparing for my two month oasis.

October 6th ~ my first day to relax and release in Hawaii. I have had the same daily routine for the 3 months I've been there in the 2 years I have been going. This year, 2019, was my third year.

*Update this year is now actually 2020 and no trip to Molokai was made in October due to pandemic related travel restrictions. Later in the book, it will become apparent why I was not to travel to Molokai this year, aside from a global pandemic. Why I personally needed to be home. *

A typical day in Hawaii looks like this:

>5:30 am ~ up, shower, prepare for the day
>6:00 am ~ be on the beach (at the condo) for sunrise and meditation
>7:00 am ~ walk at least a mile out on the King Kamehameha V Highway
>8:00 am ~ swim at least a half hour
>8:30 am ~ breakfast
>9:00 am ~ off to explore
>noon ~ lunch
>12:30pm ~ read
>2:00 pm ~ NAPTIME

It is so easy to sleep on the island. The peace and nature sounds, along with the ocean air set the stage, for impromptu rest. Molokai is known as the Friendly Isle. Made up of many generations of families, the tourist population is small. It is 38 miles long and 10 miles across. Yet it is home to the highest sea cliffs in the world. A definite 'must see' when traveling there.

I was excited for my first nap on this trip. The sun, the breeze, the ocean, the swimming, the walking, reading, it all led up to this peaceful moment. I began to doze. But, not for long. I was jolted, sat straight up in the lawn chair on my lanai and cried out loud. Fortunately, it was mid-day and locals were off at work and tourists were off at play. "I can't be awake! I must be still in a nightmare! What the fuck is happening? Is this a dream or a memory?" I had been alerted by my subconscious mind of a horrific situation and this was no nightmare.

As I sat there, tears streaming down my face, it was as if a waterfall of memories had just been let loose. It wouldn't stop. It connected me to this one memory I have had my whole life of me as a child around 6 or 7 years old. I had seen this in my head over and repeatedly throughout my childhood, my adult life, for about 50 years. But I thought it was some weird dream. Like something I conjured up in my head that was so vivid, the "dream", now known as a memory, was exactly the same, no matter what day, week, month or year that I saw it in my head. FIFTY YEARS and it was the same, every single time.

Running to the ocean out front of the condo screaming in my mind, "Nope, can't go in deep enough, without walking a mile out." "Pool", I thought, "next best thing" ....... just someone please make this go away. "Spirit, Universe, Water Element, please take this ....... please?"

There wasn't enough water. There wasn't enough peace. There was nothing but a little girl, curled up in a ball. This day, 10/6/2018, would change my life forever. "Wait, what? 10/6 ! My arm! My tattoo from 3 months prior! NO WAY!!!!!!!! I am in some sort of fictional horror film. I must be."

I am Spiritual. I believe in a Higher Power. MY particular Higher Power does not consist of one man who has a beard. While I was raised in a church, by a father who was the minister of his church, the conditioning and the rhetoric stuffed down my throat has actually brought me to where I am today in my journey. I believe there is a collection of entities who guide me daily. The Universe, Source, Angels, Archangels, they are all part of my team. These beliefs are solely mine. They do not belong to you, or anyone else. I have no room in my life to be concerned with who or what you 'believe in', or as in my former church, "worship". Imagine worshiping someone, something. That thought throws me way off balance. But this is a subject for another day.

I would eventually, months later, tell my Intuitive Mentor about these memories that changed my life that hot and sunny, peaceful October day. Yes, I have a mentor too! I will never forget the words she spoke during the conversation we had, in which she would be the first person I "told". I still haven't told many folks yet and it is now over 2 years later.

Of course, I thought the book would be done before now. Little did I know that day, what was left to still be uncovered.

But this day, 10/6, the same "date or numbers" that I had tattooed on my arm less than 4 months prior, would be the beginning of what was so horrific. What is now a blessing in disguise.

"I'm sorry. So sorry. You didn't know? I thought you knew. I've known all along. I just knew you'd talk about it when you were ready", my mentor said

Although this book has taken over 2 years to write, it has needed the time for the rest of the events to unfold. This would have been only half of a story, had I published it back in 2019, as I had planned. What's that saying, "we make a plan and 'God' laughs"?

## JOURNAL ENTRY – OCTOBER 6, 2018 – MOLOKAI – THE DAY I REMEMBERED

*(This was not part of the recordings. It was in my evening meditation and journaling)*

"Apparently there is something so deep I have hidden it for 50 years. It absolutely explains the disdain I had for this man and why he liked the other kids better. I will cry! I will scream! I will heal! Please help me!"

## JOURNAL ENTRY - OCTOBER 9, 2018 – MOLOKAI

*I went into a channeling meditation.*

"Do you need to know everything? What purpose does that serve? Because that is the 'traditional way' to do it? You are far from traditional. You are original. Take in all that you can so you can help others. You never knew this was part of your story. You never knew you would have another way to help people. Can you look at it this way? Can you accept it? It is possible. You have the power to use it. Use the water to charge you up."

## JOURNAL ENTRY – OCTOBER 16, 2018 - CHANNELING

"It's been 10 days since my awareness happened. Plan a title. Write a book. Change the title, change the book. Just record whatever you are thinking. The good, the bad, the ugly, the sad. It is part of your healing, you must do it."

ONE YEAR LATER - 2019 ~ I'm here, in Hawaii again. A year has gone by and nothing, or no one could have prepared me for the inconceivable things that have happened over the past year. Things that help me understand now, what the book is really, truly about. I am still trying to process all of this, as it is constantly unfolding. But first…. I am going to listen to and transcribe into this book, what I recorded into my phone a year ago, as my memories of my childhood came rippling into my mind unexpectedly, here in Hawaii.

10/6/18 ~ Recording #1 ~ Recorded 10/7

"I don't really know what's happening", I whisper, barely being able to catch my breath.

As I listen to the first 30 seconds of the first recording, tears fill my eyes. Little did I know when recording this, that life was about to get even crazier!

"October 6, here in Hawaii, I realize that I was molested as a child. I can't even say it 'molested as a child'. My voice trembling. "From what I can figure right now, this went on from age 6 to age 10 or 11. I can't even believe I am saying this out loud. So many things, so many things over the past 24 hours, 36 hours.

I woke up during a nap October 6 with this sick, sick feeling. And all my life I've had this memory of a person in my life, who I am not ready to say who he is. *reminder, this is a transcript of the recording that I made, the day of the memories that came back. * And he is in his pajamas and I hated those pajamas. And they are a light, light light light light green and I hate the color green. Yet, I bought a bathing suit to wear in Hawaii that's green. It's all so weird, green with blue stripes down them and I hated those pajamas, and I know now why.

So much has come rushing back over the past few hours, even the past day, the past few hours, it's making it hard to concentrate, it's making it hard to think. But I can't go any longer without at least recording my thoughts, feelings, memories. Yesterday, I couldn't find a ride back from the parade. And while I was walking, I did my 'okay, the next one of the next ten cars is going to pick me up. I don't want to walk any further, I don't want to walk any further.' And then suddenly, suddenly a *white dove* flew down in front of me and I said, 'oh my goodness, okay, I guess I needed to see that today'.

*Author's interject: The dove's soft graceful looks, white plumage, and gentle cooing calls all make it a symbol of* **grace***, peace, gentleness, and divinity. Dove symbolism, as we all very well know, is peace. But, apart from peace, the dove actually represents many other things.*

*Universally, dove bird meaning is purity. It is the living thing of the three-dimensional world that has been chosen to represent the human concept of enormous quality: sacredness. Across cultures, the dove represents purity, gentleness, devotion, beauty, and faith.*

*On an international level, peace dove represents hope and peace, and that has resonated well across the vast majority of religions and cultures.*

*It fits into the cognitive framework that allows for global optimism to be shared by many people. Dove symbol is also love. This symbolic representation of the dove has been seen in many major works of literature and art.*

*This bird is also considered as the dove holy spirit. Pigeons and doves have carried messages for thousands of years. People believe that this bird is very close to the Gods. It has, therefore, come to represent the worship of the deity.*

*In many motifs and artworks, white doves are seen flying out of depictions of warfare and **bomb blasts**. Perhaps, in these cases, apart from peace, the dove represents the martyred soldiers' soul. The dove is also a **symbol of protection**.*

*It can represent the agent of God sent to protect humanity from violence. The dove always snuggles close to its partner. It is a gentle-looking, rounded bird, and for these reasons, dove significance represents femininity and love.*

*Doves also represent the **Goddess of Love**. They were also used for **delivering messages**. Since the early times, the dove delivered messages to humans from God – including dove and olive branch in the Bible.*

***The Native Americans, therefore, believed doves to be the Great Spirit's deliverance and the symbol of forgiveness.***

*What do doves represent? All dove encounters symbolize peace. But this theme of peace can be very broad in the sense that it has to be connected with **communication, understanding, and sympathy**. When doves appear, it is a sign of your innocence and **grace**.*

*Know and trust that your loved ones are watching you always. Dove totem animal brings peace, joy, and harmony. It tells you that new beginnings and ventures wait. The gist of dove symbolism is **grace**, love, beauty, and peace. It can also mean innocence and femininity.*

*Dove Symbolism & Meaning (+Totem, Spirit & Omens) Updated on November 13, 2020 / By Garth C. Clifford* (updated only 2 weeks before my research)**

*Recording #1 cont.* "Little did I know how much was going to come rushing back. There's just so much, so much, I guess I'll just piece meal it. So just now I was in the pool 2 hours, nobody around for 2 hours. Suddenly after 15 plus years of not having a bathing suit or wearing a bathing suit, or going swimming, suddenly I am obsessed with water. I've always been obsessed with water. Being near it. But I hated to hear it running. I never understood. I understand now. I know it has something to do with it. Water running from a faucet, that I can't stand to hear. The trickle of a waterfall, the trickle of a river, that's fine. But water running out of a faucet, I can't stand it. It makes me wanna...............I don't know why it makes me tear up, but I don't like it." (I'm now sobbing on the recording)

"So far I've been just in shock that I haven't been able to cry, like there were no tears. Not able to cry. It's been 10 years he has been gone and its now coming to me at age 55. It's been, it's been almost 50 years since it started and I'm remembering now, why? Ya know many healers told me that, many healers told me that a lot was going to happen in Hawaii. That I was going to become a new person. That I was going to go through a healing. I didn't know this was it. I didn't know I'd be alone. I didn't know I'd be alone. (sobbing) Everything is just so synchronistic in the past 48 hours. It's...

I stumbled upon a Gabby Bernstein interview where she says she is a Medium, which I did not know. I don't know much about her. I never

43

really listened to her until this one. And then she talks about how less than a year ago, she realized that she was molested as a child. Is that why we are all healers? So much. Just so much. The cards I pulled this morning, I just pulled two more cards.

Ya know, I did the, I did the um, Inner Child Workshop for everybody, I did the Inner Child Workshop for everybody at the Women's Retreat last weekend. And while I was participating, kind of in my mind, I was still leading the workshop. And I kind of feel like that's where it all started. Like everything flows.

And so ........I was just out by the pool and things and things and things, and more things are coming back. I don't think I need to, I don't think I need to tape record all the evidence, because now that these memories are back, I don't think they are ever going to go away. Even down to the memory of............ (author deleted due to sensitive nature)

And so just now as I was walking on the beach, like I feel like can't even focus. I have clients who want sessions. I have. I just have to work through this. This is going to be the speediest working through anything I think ever.

But just now as I was walking on the beach because as I decided to get up from the pool after 2 hours of being out there, because I knew I had to start recording things. I went down and I walked on the beach, and it started pouring, but the sun was out. And I said (sobbing) 'maybe I'll get a rainbow. Maybe I'll get a rainbow.' And I looked and I didn't see a rainbow and it was pouring and the sun was out, and I was just running in the water. Literally just going as fast as I could in the water. No rainbow.

But then I looked down and there was a walking stick. It was a walking stick. It's got a handle on it. I took a picture of it. I've got pictures of it. And I walked past it and the beach isn't very long here. I walked past it. I turned around at the end of the place where you can't walk anymore, you have to turn around. I started back down the beach. And I looked at it and I heard this voice that said 'Pick it up' 'Pick it up! We're going to help you walk through this. We're going to help you walk through this. Pick up the walking stick! Take it with you!' I instantly started to worry. 'How am I going to get it home? How am I going to get it home? But maybe I'm not going to need to get it home. Maybe everything that is going to happen, is going to happen here. And maybe I don't need to take it home, because maybe I'm just going to leave it behind." (sobbing uncontrollably) "It doesn't mean that I'll get fixed. But it means that the worst is gonna end, and it's gonna end here. But no matter what I know, no matter what I know, I WILL rise above. I'm gonna rise above. And I'll keep recording.'"

"And I knew there was going be a book here. (in Hawaii) I knew it. I had no idea. Now I think back to my hysterectomy and I think back to so many things that I refused to do [in the bedroom] (details removed by author) So many things that I didn't want to do <in relationships / marriages>. And my hysterectomy. And Louise Hay always said when you had issues in that area that something had happened to you. And I said, 'not me, not me, nothing happened to me. It must be cause my mother died. Everything I've chalked up, everything I've chalked up to, 'it must be cause my mother died'. That's not been it the whole time. That's not been it.

I know that Hawaii. I know that this island, I know that Molokai, I know that the healers are going to support me, it's why I'm here. My friends at home are too, but they don't do this, no offense to them but these people are my sacred Native Hawaiian healers. I will rise up. I WILL rise up!

My tattoo! My tattoo!!!!!! I got my tattoo June 22nd (2018), the day I changed my name to Karen Whisperer. The day I became my own identity. I changed my name. Nobody knows. But I changed my name June 22nd. Drove home from Jersey to do that. Why? I don't know why. June 22nd. And I looked at the clock when the judge hit her thing and said that my name was officially changed. And it was 11:22:33. Because they record the seconds there. It was unbelievable! (OMG as I write this, I am stunned even more by the number sequence, as 123 is my current address, and more) So, then my tattoo came that same day. Yep, my tattoo. My tattoo came. My tattoo, which I've always been attracted to Alice in Wonderland. I said,' what will I get for this tattoo that connects everything about me, Alice in Wonderland, where I've been, where I'm going? Like this is an important day. I changed my name!' I had NO idea, no idea what was coming. No idea. No idea. So, I said, "Alice in Wonderland, I'll get the Mad Hatter, the little thing that's hanging off there. 10/6, 10/6, 10 over 6. 10 over 6, I'll get. And the arrow. And the Nordic sign. And the EFHAR, Everything Happens For A Reason. And the 10/6 and the infinity. And I created a tattoo. And in that tattoo is 10/6. 10/6, the day that I became aware that I had been molested and my life has now changed forever. 10/6, you can't make this shit up. You cannot. And so, I'll heal. While being a healer. Right? I'll heal while being a healer. I can do this. That's it for now.

RECORDING #2 ~ 10/7/18 ~ 5pm

"And then the rainbow came. It's currently 5 o'clock pm on the 7th. The rainbow came. I knew it would. The rainbow came. And so many more memories came flooding back when I was trying to take a nap. Things I will never forget now. I will record them later."

RECORDING #3 ~ 10/9

"It took me a while to even be able to reflect back on the regression that I did yesterday. So that would have been 10/8. So, 10/8 regression in regard to current life stuff and actually went into a past life. So, I've got some current life stuff, I've got some past life stuff. I know that, I know that my soul was trying to protect me. Um, I know that I keep getting, every time I close my eyes, I get more and more memories and more and more things brought to my attention that are starting to make sense. For instance, my first 'intimate relations', um for some reason I knew that I wasn't a virgin and I also… the person knew as well. And I couldn't compute that. I just couldn't compute that. Um, however now I can compute that.

Ya know yesterday I wasn't able to talk about it and today I think I can so. I also learned that I just remember in the bedroom my mother's favorite plaque being on the wall and when I close my eyes, I can see it and it said, 'may the road rise up to meet you, may the wind always be at your back and may the good Lord keep you in the palm of his hands.' And I remember just seeing that, as I was and after I was, ........... And I feel like I am more mad than anything else. The thing is, is that I am NOT confused, I'm actually clear.

And I remember seeing that plaque also when I was being paddled with a wooden basically paddle. It was one of those paddle toys. (with the red ball and string). And I remember having to take my pants (and underwear) down (or off) and be lying there naked over his or her (the other adult often in the house) lap and being paddled on my naked bottom. And as far as I remember, I was the only one who had to be paddled like that. Like who does that? Who does that? Rarely was it a bare hand. (when I think of this, and I think of it often, it literally makes me nauseated! I cannot imagine ANYONE thinking it was okay to allow a little girl to be completely exposed naked from the waist down while another watched the brutal humiliating force that was referred to as a spanking)

Don't get me wrong. My children were spanked. A tap on the CLOTHED bottom! No nakedness, no embarrassment of other adults watching. No private parts being exposed. THERE IS A HUGE DIFFERENCE!!!!

Imagine an adult forcing a child to pull their clothes down to the floor and exposing their little girl parts while someone watched another adult inflict pain on their nakedness. I could puke!! That was excused as "spare the rod, spoil the child" as quoted from the "Bible". Imagine their "God" telling them to go ahead and shame a little girl by making her get naked from the waist down and then causing her pain, redness and bruising till she cried for 'no more'!

*Author's note* Please do not write to me and want to debate the interpretation of that scripture or any of the Bible at all. Also, I do not judge or rebuke whatever punishment you use in your home. To each his own. Yes, I do know and abhor the fact that children are beaten every day and "have it a lot worse" than me. I work with Domestic Violence victims and advocates. However, this is MY story, MY memory and MY assessment of how wrong this "man of God" behaved at home. In short, this is MY book. I don't portend to know what your book will be about. Just mine. *

But I also remember always having to wear a nightgown to bed and I also remember not being allowed to wear underwear because 'girls don't wear underwear under their nightgowns, you just wear a nightgown.' And now it's all making sense.

And I just get madder and madder and madder and madder. And I know that... Soon I will need to forgive. Soon I will need to forgive. Soon, I will need to forgive. But for right now? I am pretty mad. And a couple of reasons.

First of all because I don't want to tell anybody, and it's not so much the shame that it happened to me, or the thought that nobody'd believe me. It's more the 'tarnishing his reputation', which people always thought, 'he's so innocent' and I, I remember thinking "why do they idolize this man so much? Why do they idolize him?' Now I don't know if this happened to him, hence the strained relationship with his parents. I don't know and I don't think I need to know that. But as (my dear friend across the pond) Toni Riley says, "fuck it!" Which is weird that I created the "fuck it bucket", over the weekend at the Women's Retreat.

As I start to piece the things together, the tattoo, the 10/6, the Everything Happens for A Reason, like the tattoo is so symbolic that day that I changed my name, the tattoo is so symbolic of my newly found freedom from all of it and I didn't even realize what I was going to be free from. I mean, who knew that my attraction to Alice in Wonderland and the 10 over 6, the Mad Hatter, like I would use that in a tattoo and then 10/6 ends up being the day that I'm awakened to what happened in my life. And, and things that I was using to protect myself and now water, I can't get enough water. I still don't like to hear it running from the faucet, but I just want to be in the water, in the water. I just want to be cleansed. I want to be free from all of it."

## RECORDING #4 ~ 10/15/18

"After doing a full regression meditation, I realize that there is so much more to the picture that I don't remember. The picture that came or started becoming aware to me. It's interesting because I can go through the regression and be angry and I can go through the regression and be in control? But damn it!

My hysterectomy, like all these troubles, there's no family history but me. All these troubles, my thyroid, like for not speaking up for myself. My hysterectomy obviously from the abuse. Like, what??? It, I mean it all makes sense, but it doesn't make sense. It is unbelievable, I think is the word. Not…. I don't even want to say unbelievable, because it is believable, when I think. I think I'm nine days into this and I think little bits and pieces keep coming back. So many bits and pieces. Ya know I think about the paddling, like having to have my pants down to be paddled. Like what? It's hard to even wrap my head around it. I can't imagine taking a child's pants down and exposing their private areas so you could paddle them. What? Are we even thinking, ya know? And always being watched during that? Like that is just fucking creepy!

And now through the regression I had this morning, I have memories of being locked in the closet. Um, ya know, sometimes these memories are so vivid, I think I'm making them up but there's no way because I remember every inch of that closet. I don't know if I locked myself in there, or if I was being locked in there, but what I do know is that I was definitely locked in there.

I feel like it was a punishment of some sort. And I do remember there being a lock on that bedroom door, which I'm not even comfortable saying what bedroom it was. And (sigh) I remember sitting up, I remember being in a horrible position. I remember not having underwear, I remember something about my throat, my neck. It all makes sense. And yes, I keep saying that, but it all makes sense. 10 over 6 …. From the age of 6 to 10. Like there are no coincidences, this is all so, so bizarre.

I remember the TWO hour conversations in his study. His study where he was supposed to be writing sermons and, and correcting papers. But we weren't allowed in there? Always having to prove myself. Always having to be the best one.

We weren't allowed in there for these two-hour conversations with Mrs. H, with PY. And I can remember being taught to make fun of her because of her weight. Like it's not that we were doing it and we were told not to, like her weight was a thing. And I remember this now. And she was made fun of for it, by the adult in my house.

And I remember going to I believe it was Bow Lake, thinking we were going to have……… My father needed some time away, he needed time away, he needed time away, ooooooh had to go work on this, that and the third. And come to find out Miss M was there!!!!!!!!

(author's note: He claimed to us that she would never be his girlfriend because she was FAT!) Ya know, this this man, who was a leader of this church? No wonder, no wonder I spun on my axis and said, 'get me the fuck away from this church!'

Like not only did they think that our household was authentic, and everybody would want to be in our household like it was magical? There was nothing magical about our household.

It explains why that even in his death, I didn't even want to sit in his room with him by myself. It makes perfect sense! All these things I have felt like, why am I this person, why am I that person? Why have I done this, why have I done that? And now I know. And it's not an excuse. It's an explanation. Those are two completely different things. Completely different.

Like I feel like I want to run in the ocean and just wash off again. This is what's happening every time I am getting a memory. It's that I want to run, and I want to get in the water, and I want to cleanse myself and I want to clear myself. And I wanna fix this and fix that and it's gonna be a slow process, but ya know I've been working 45 years to fix that and fix that and never knew where it came from. And now I know.

And so, like my dear friend, Toni Reilly says, "you've already lived the shit, now it's time to release it and let go." I release and I let go. I release and I let go. I release and I let go. And I can wash it away. Had I been anywhere else when this happened? Like I got here on the 4th and all this happened on the 6th. 10/6, it's tattooed right on my arm. EHFAR, everything happens for a reason. 10 over 6. 10/6 which was MY connection to Alice in Wonderland, which comes back around, and it is actually the date of my awakening.

See I thought my awakening was when I became awake to my abilities or when I knew that I was spiritually gifted. Or things like this. But my awakening is learning this. I never knew. Learning this.

And I'd always wondered about that scene. Where I saw something that I wasn't supposed, not that I thought I wasn't supposed to. Where I feel like I reached to touch something, and I was told "not now". And THAT was the one memory that stayed in my mind clearly. Like in my conscious mind. Not in my subconscious. Not dug way back there, but in my conscious mind. I reached out touch a private part (on him, in his bed) thinking that's what I was supposed to do, and I was told, "not now". So now I know. NOW I KNOW! But see the part I did NOT remember, is that I was 'supposed' to do that, just not right at that time. And all this time that's haunted me, like why would I have done such a thing as a (6 or so) year old? But now I know. Now I know.

Other things that have popped up again …………(author edited this part out to protect another). All my life since I'm a kid, I've wondered was it the bicycle. I've always wondered that. There's a reason as a kid, that we question things. There's a reason. Because somewhere, even in our child mind, we know. We absolutely know. That something's not right. We absolutely know.

And as the rain starts to fall, the same as my card this morning, I pulled rain, and the cleansing healing water. Don't like it coming from a faucet cause there's so many memories surrounding that. But I must take one day and actually just put the memories out there.

But this Mrs. H thing, Miss M, PY, um Jane....... these people knew. These people knew. It's too weird. It's like he had a harem. *harem - Websters Dictionary – noun – the women occupying a harem; the wives (or concubines) of a polygamous man. A group of women sharing a single mate. * No wonder they didn't get along with each other. I understand it in my adult mind now."

"But you don't need to give a church person two hours every day of counseling or what? And no money exchanged. Like, no, this is too weird. And there were no boundaries. Like people were just allowed to come to our house. No boundaries. And if they weren't right, they were possessed. And he'd be an exorcist. Weird that he'd be an exorcist when I feel like maybe the devil was working through him.

I know it's part of my journey but so much of this doesn't make sense. The apology before he passed, now makes sense. I thought it was for not being there, for neglect. And come to find out, here I find out, what, almost 10 years later what that was all about. It all makes sense now. Everything that's happened. Everything. And as more memories come to mind, and more correlations and more understandings, I realize that this is so much bigger, so so much bigger. And yet I just seek for answers, seek for answers because I know that....... people aren't gonna like to hear this. They aren't gonna wanna hear this. But it needs to happen. It needs to. It needs to. It needs to happen. And so, it is.

*Note: Recording #5 – I just rambled on about chapters for this book, so I pulled it out.

Recording #6 ~ 10/26/18

I just needed to record this quick, it's 10/26 I just did something I swore I would never do. I just apologized to somebody for asking them to pay for their session they had 4 days ago. Like I'm honoring myself and the fact that I provided a service, and it needs to be paid for and when they got pissed or appeared pissed and said, "it's on my list today!!!" I went back and said, "I'm sorry" Like I'm sorry for charging you for services rendered? Like most people have to pay before they get a session and I allowed this person, I went against my rules and I allowed this person to have a session without paying for it and it came around to bite me in my ass. Because I have had to ask them 4 times to pay. Their session was Tuesday, this is Friday afternoon. That should not ever, ever, ever happen!

Recording #7 ~ 10/26/2018

Because here I am sitting in my bed. I have been sitting here for an hour. I have been, to say the least, avoiding and ya, just avoiding and I am done avoiding so here we go. I have so many thoughts that I don't know where to put them and I know that I have to work on one chapter at a time. So, let's call this chapter Aloha. (note – this piece brought me joy when I thought I would fall to pieces) *

*Author deleted part of this transcription of the recording, due to its lack of relevance. What it symbolized was the little child in me trying to think of something pleasant to write about, to deflect from reliving childhood trauma. It was a beautiful chapter about Molokai. But will end up in another book*

Recording #7 cont.

"Ya I definitely need help. This is hard. I don't know if the tears I am having right now is because this is hard or because of what it's opening up and I've been protecting myself from this. Even though I can talk about it all the time, I just don't know. I don't know.

All of this, all of this, all of this, brings me to where I am today. Each and every little piece. Each piece plays a part in the puzzle that we call me. I'm collecting my thoughts and I don't ever want to be portrayed as a victim, because I don't look at it that way, I look at it as that's what brings me to 2018. It's just one piece that brings me to 2018.

I remember when I worked at Red Cross in Disaster Services, I remember a lady coming out and she had just had a small fire, I don't remember it being much of anything. I don't know if we offered her services, I don't know what it was. But I remember her, and this has stuck with me for 30 years, I remember her looking at me and her saying "you're an angel" and me saying "awe that's nice, thank you, but it's my job or whatever. "And she's like "no, I mean it you're an angel, I don't think you know it, but you are, you're an angel." That always stuck with me. It's one thing to say, "oh you're an angel for A, B, and C," but it's another thing to insist that somebody's an angel. That's always stuck with me and I get it now.

It's very similar to what my older brother said, his dying words telling me that I'm different. That he can see right "through me". Was he able to see me as a spirit? Was he able to see me as an angel? "I can see right through you". He didn't mean like "I can see right through you" like I'm up to something. He meant "I can see right through you." Because he said to me, he was able to see the TV that I was sitting in front of. He was able to see the TV screen. I know that there's something there. I know that I'm different. But I know that I am here to teach people and teach people how to heal. I know that I'm here to teach people how to catch their dreams. To get their dreams and not just chase them but to capture them. Capture them. Ya know? To capture them. Right? We can't chase our dreams forever and ever. We gotta capture them.

I have so much in my head, and I think I'm getting frustrated (sobbing) because, I can do this, I just, I'm frustrated. I don't know if it would be better just to type it into a computer. I thought this would be the easy way just to record my memoire' and then turn it into a book. But I'm finding that my head gets cluttered with so much content, ya know? Past, present, future. I mean I need this book to be a teaching / feeling book as well as how I got to where I am.

People look at me every day and they say, "you're so lucky, I'm so jealous." How am I lucky? Like which part of my life has been lucky? What brought me to today, has nothing to do with luck. It's got to do with manifesting, it's got to do with following what I'm led to do. It's got to do with being of service. It's got to do with, this is my journey not anybody else's. It's got to do with, I've earned where I am today. I have earned it.

I am collecting my thoughts again. So many thoughts. I just. I gotta learn how to do this. This book isn't going to write itself and I know that it needs me. I've just got so much. I can teach all day long; it's remembering this that and the other that is so difficult for me. I think I am still blocking so much out. I don't want to force it. I guess I just need to ask (my guides) for more help.

Maybe I am recording more thoughts, less book. Energy flows where attention goes. If you don't believe that, post on your Facebook wall that you're sick and see what happens. Even saying, "I'm not sick", the Universe doesn't know "not". You put out "I" speaking of yourself and speaking of "sick", it's just, God how many times do I have to say the same thing.

I know now that bigger things are around the corner. I don't know what they are. I know that it's easy to get out of the mindset to receive. I think that's common for everybody. I think that it's hard for us to let go of control and let money, abundance to flow to us. Not that we can lay in bed and watch it come, but more so is knowing what right action to take.

Well, I have been recording for 21 minutes. I don't know how much is useable. But I have been recording for 21 minutes. Sometimes I look around and I wonder how people cannot be grateful. Or not 'not be grateful' but how do people go through life without manifesting, without gratitude, without just being the best version of themselves. Like how do people just float along? I don't get it, but I see so much of it. (author's note ~ I noticed the same thing this year 2019 in Hawaii)

I think maybe morning is a better time to do this instead of night. Maybe morning will be clearer. Today I think I just get caught up in the little bits and pieces of what happened during the day and that's not productive book writing. But hey the funny news is that there is somebody who lives here, already thinks I'm a famous author. People think I am independently wealthy when all I simply did was line things up and set my intention and the Universe did the rest! People just don't get it! Especially around here. I need to have a chapter called houses, houses everywhere, but no one will write a loan. Or something cuz people don't like to give loans to people who don't have jobs on paper. It's weird but it's true. I will end this for now. Namaste'

Recording #8 ~ November 2, 2018 (author note ~ deflecting from talking about the "business at hand")

Remember this. The more money you play with, the more money sticks to you. That's especially important as far as manifesting goes because it is so true. If you have this fear of not having enough money and you hang onto every dollar and you stare at it. I'm referencing one-dollar bills. Put those away and stare at $100 bills. It's absolutely true.

From the book, "Are You Dumb Enough to be Rich?" by G. William Barnet II, this is a revised edition. "Our third responsibility in taking care of the poor is to tithe. Yes, tithe. Tithing is the single greatest money management principal I have ever learned."

So, to 'take care of the poor', it doesn't necessarily mean give your 10% to the church (as was drilled into my head). It means to help others. Women, children, animals; the poor. It doesn't have to go to your local church. It needs to go to someone who needs it, and quite frankly, your church doesn't need it.

Another quote from the same book, "I don't own anything. Most of the wealthy are ready for war. Not because they have little or nothing to lose. But because they don't own anything. They have it in a trust."

"The wealthy use a lot of water. To make your lawn grow it must be watered. The wealthy know how to make a fortune grow. They must water it. They must water their fortunes with investments. The wealthy all know how to weave the fruits of their success back into circulation. A man named 'Cavett Robert', founder of the National Speakers Association, used to say, he's passed now, 'you've got to circulate if you want to percolate. The wealthy know how to make their fortunes circulate. They understand they must give back. The wealthy I know are some of the most generous people you'll ever meet. I'll also tell you that the wealthy people I know are some of the happiest people I know. The wealthy understand, 'the truth of give it back, it's yours'. Giving it back can happen in a variety of ways. The most basic way the wealthy give back is through their tithe. They tithe it back to their church or synagogue."

I personally don't follow that ideology, because the church and the synagogues have more money than anyone else, and the ministers make more money than anyone else. The ministers make a whole lot of money. (in my educated opinion) So I would suggest that the wealthy give back to their communities, their favorite charities and their professions. So, for instance if they were in the National Swimmers Association, maybe give back so that less fortunate swimmers could be part of the program, or something to that effect.

There is also giving blood. You can also give "in kind" too. Gifts of items or time. Same book: "Sit down in the next 48 hours and write 10 letters. Ten handwritten letters. They don't need to be long, but they need to be to the point. The point of this challenge and of these letters, let the 10 most influential people in your life, let you know how feel about them." (KW- They could be famous, not famous, they could be writers they could be actors or singers, they could be anything, or the 10 people could be family and friends, neighbors.) "Take a few minutes out of your busy life and write a letter to these people. They must still be living. Tell them point blank that you love them. Thank them for the example that they have set for you and for others. Tell them about at least 3 specific ways they have influenced you. But tell them and tell them in writing. Do not use email or phone. This needs to be a letter. A handwritten letter. Make this part of your life each year. You will never regret it. If you want to become wealthy, you need to act like the wealthy."

I do want to mention that 11/1, last night I did see a shooting star while I was out floating in the pool.

It's interesting to me, how people like to claim their illness, first thing when they meet you. I met a woman the other day and the first thing she did was talk about her autoimmune disorders. "I can't do this, I can't do this, I can't do this. She was telling me how when she's home she goes into the hotdog position and lays in bed. That's crazy, it's insane. I don't understand how that is a conversation opener?

So today I am in the pool with some people I met last night, and the first thing the woman did was talk about how many strokes her husband had, and now he's on A fib, something to that effect. Then this morning they go to get into the pool and she's talking about how she has asthma, and she can't go in the pool up to her chest because it will cause her to have an asthma attack and her husband also validated that for her. Then I said something how I HAD asthma. But I look over now and she's in the pool up to her neck. It's just weird how people, even coming to a beautiful place like this of peace and healing, come to this place and that's what they do. They talk about their problems. Not their problems but their illnesses. It's hard for me to wrap my head around. (recorded on Molokai, Hawaii)

*This now completes all that I had recorded during my stay in Hawaii, while discovering horrific memories on 10/6/18 about my childhood*

# HAWAIIAN HEALER ~

Monday, I had a healing with a man here on Molokai that I had seen 3 times on my prior visits. It is the best thing I do for me when I am here. He did huge body work and energy work. He told me I WAS a leader. "Do not be a follower. You are a leader!" He explained it's why my journey has been the way it was been for the past 50 years. When I said I was lied to, he validated that.

My root chakra is totally blocked. Not a surprise! That's the energy system in your body. There are 7 chakras. The root is the lowest. Protects the sexual organs. While doing the work on me, he got a vision of several dark cloaked beings with hoods. These spirits were on the edge of a cliff. They were getting ready to leap, due to their indiscretions. He saw flames or heat below. Which to me represents everything I was ever taught in my childhood about "hell".

While on the table, I was told there wasn't one it was more like a dozen. Not a dozen who abused me, but that must be the dozen who knew the secrets, the lies. I may not be the only one abused in the church, he told me. The cloaked beings were on the edge. It wasn't my forgiveness that they needed; they need me to forgive myself! I never looked at it that way. He went on to explain that when I forgive me, they will be able to go all the way to the light. WOW! This is a huge discovery for me.

I have been doing forgiveness work, root chakra work, and new breathing exercises to bring healing to my lungs, kidneys, and liver. For 3 days.

Today I have another healing with him. So excited to see if he can tell the difference. I am so blessed to know him.

While it tears my heart out, it was total validation, AGAIN!!! While having NO idea of my family life, he was able to see what I knew. He saw all the lies. The abuse connection with the church. All of it.

How did I get this blessed? OMG!!! This is so amazing, having a healer right here in Hawaii.

He said, "you've had to do this alone, haven't you"? "Yes, yes I have".

Tears are so cleansing, aren't they?

Today with my Hawaiian healer / energy worker / body worker, overall shaman / guru..........we touched on so many things that make writing this book a day-by-day adventure of discovery. He asked me about genealogy. Had I done any research. Well, as a matter of fact, after our session on Monday, I got an email from Ancestry, with a lot of new docs that were found. I found it quite interesting that he asked. Also, this morning 20 minutes before I left for my healing, I got another one! I don't believe in coincidences. I will definitely look into that. He said watch for patterns that I will need to heal.

"You are a link a chain of causation that stretches before and after your life for a thousand generations" Rev. Chris Michaels, Center for Spiritual Living, Kansas City, MO.

That said, and from what I learned but I think I already knew, my life has taken a different trajectory because of the choices made by those who came before me. Today he said to stop this. I must heal the four generations before me, the two that are here now, and the two after that. Four generations in each direction. Seems like a huge job. I am a mom, and gamma, who would never want their children or grandchildren to suffer the things they have suffered. So, explore I will.

I want to know who my grandfather's first wife was. Not my maternal grandmother, who bore only my mother, but the woman he married before her, the one that passed away. And before that?? I need to explore this. The pattern, as it stands currently, is my mom leaving us when I was 5, what I was told was her death, but either way, she was gone. She had 3 biological children and one apparently adopted. (I often use the word "apparently" due to the discovery of so many lies in my family.

My first husband passing away when our kids were little. He had 3 biological children, and my other daughter who he always joked was his. And now one of my children is in a similar situation, no one died, in that sense. They have 3 biological children and one that my child has raised. WOW, as I lay out the pattern, the similarities of the overall picture are uncanny. In addition, again my mother's oldest is adopted, and she had 3 biological children. I raised my non-biological oldest from a baby with his dad till he died, and I have 3 biological children. My child is helping raise a non-biological child and three biological children. Bonus child, a much better name.

Let's see where this is a similar pattern before my mother......... As research continues to some of the hidden parts of the family, watch for a second book.

Today my healer also wondered if my mom was caught in the crossfire when my father would do exorcisms in our home? In those days, as he gently reminded me, "you were either sane or not". If not, you went to a facility.

Mediums, yes more than one, have said to me, "he shows me that he thought he was protecting you by taking her away." But why the lies? I must forgive the person, not the action. But most of all, I know now that I must forgive myself. I didn't make her go away. I didn't make him violate my childhood. I didn't purposefully marry and have children with a man who would die when they were little.

Had my mom ever gone to any of the houses of these possessed people? I cannot imagine, although I hadn't thought of this until today, not doing proper protection or clearing for the safety of your home and family while doing this work. In my work, I clear, smudge, light candles, open the door......all of it. Especially now that my four grandchildren live with me.

He did none of this. No candles, other than on the dining room table when we were trying to impress someone. Often addictions are not a secret. And me, well as you learn throughout this book, I've got my own set of issues! Today, I learned to use my heart to heal everything else. Everything is centered there. Let my heart tell my brain how to be. I will continue to use the 6 healing sounds, for the lungs, kidneys, liver, heart, spleen and balance. All of this taught to me by my Hawaiian healer.

# LOSS –

*It's important to remember that his was written 2 years ago in 2018*

So, my story as I remember it, again this is as I remember it, doesn't mean it's exactly how it happened but this is how I remember it. I went to bed. Now, I remember only my mother being sick maybe one time. I remember her laying on the couch I remember her drinking out of that funny straw. (author's note, now that new information has been uncovered ~ was she DRINKING?? Is that why she couldn't walk??) I believe she wore wigs, and I remember my father would carry her to the bathroom or the bedroom. Do I remember all of this, or was I told this? That question burns in my mind, daily.

I was 5 years old, and it was Christmastime. I will never forget the last Christmas she was "alive." I had asked for play money, with this cute wallet. I was only five. Go figure, I asked for money. I had wanted this specific wallet and the play money. I sort of remember it being a little child's wallet / purse set, go figure. We can't go without the purse, even at five. Some things never change. I had wanted this specific one, I had asked for it. (I always knew exactly what I wanted)

Now, we only got to have $40 worth of gifts for Christmas. So, we had to figure it out as to what we asked for and what we could get. I had this little wallet kit that I wanted so badly. I remember getting this kit and it not being exactly what I wanted, and I remember being really upset, because yes it was the same idea, but it wasn't the exact one I wanted. I remember being a little rotten child at that point and saying something like it wasn't the one I wanted.

That has stayed with me all these years because instead of showing gratitude for even getting the gift, even at the young age of five, I still think I was a naughty child. Even then I remember thinking I had hurt my mother's feelings and I thought someone else had gone and bought the presents, but I found out later in my life that my mother had gone shopping that Christmas.

I don't know why all of us children were so sheltered from all of this, but I seem to be the only one who feels this way.

That's like the last real memory I have until the day she "died". I woke up in my bed, went down (stairs) like any normal day, and Mrs. H was standing there, and I just remember her acting weird or sad, something was off. Then my father got home, only hours after he had left. He just blankly, with no emotion, told us that our mother had died. She had apparently gone to the hospital. If memory serves, and again, memory may not be serving but, she apparently went to the hospital for x-rays that day. Chest x-rays? Now I don't know if that is the truth, I don't know if that is a LIE, because we were never really allowed to know the information. I didn't know until I was older. It's like this was a big bad secret.

That's the whole entire story. No funeral memories. We weren't allowed to go. Enough said.

This is not easy. It's easier for me to instruct people, than it is to bring up the past.

# THE CALL ~

I sat there, in the living room at home with my daughter, Tandy. This house I lived in for a noticeably short time with my second husband, after he became my 3rd husband for less than a year. I did say previously that I had my own set of issues, case in point. The real point is, I had lived there for less than a year. The year, based on the timing of my marriages, would have been 2000. The cordless house phone rang, and naturally the teenager ran to answer it. "Mom, it's for you." "Who is it?" "I don't know, an older lady."

Karen: "Hello?"
Woman: "Karen?"
K: "Yes, who's this?"
W: "Oh Karen, (voice trembling) it's your mother."
K: "What is this, a joke?!!! My mother is dead!"
W: "No! This IS your mother. I am your mother!"
K: "Okay, if you are my mother, what's your name?"
W: "My name is Grace. I am your mother."
K: "Please, my mother died when I was 5, this isn't funny! If, you are Grace, if you ARE my mother, WHERE are you?"
W: "I'm in a home, a......."
*CLICK* the phone went eerily silent.

A couple days later. (no caller ID again)
K: "Hello?"
W: *same voice* "Karen?"
*CLICK*

That was the beginning of where we are today. But I didn't know.

You see when you have been told from age 5 to age 35, your formative years and all of your adulthood to that point, that your mother is dead, there is not one little weird call that would REALLY make you think differently.

After all, my father the "god like", "definitely honest" minister, told me she was dead. How could she not be? "What a cruel joke", I thought at the time. Always wondering who or how that call happened. But I was raising my four kids, and we had all been through enough trauma.

At the time, I was active in the Disaster Services of the Red Cross. Oh my gosh! THAT'S how she found me! As I sit here in Hawaii, writing this book, it is 8:17pm, Hawaiian time, on 11/22/19 and I just realized now how she would have found me. Through the many articles in the news about my Disaster work. Or did she have my first husband's obituary from just 2 years prior? Either way, I know she had help making that call, as several Mediums, all in different states, have validated in our sessions.

The few people that I have shared this story with, and quite honestly myself included, wondered if it in fact WAS her, "how did she find you"? At the time, I went along with that line of questioning. After all, my father the minister, told me she was dead. So how would that even be possible? It had been THIRTY years at the time of the bizarre call, of consistently being told she had died. Now just one call would leave so many questions.

However, thirty years of conditioning, believing that she had died, led me to tuck my investigation of this call away for later. This childhood conditioning had been a regular practice in my home, and in his church. Conditioning, brainwashing, persuading, convincing, stuffing things down a child's throat, whatever your choice of words is for manipulating a child's mind, they all fit.

Do I wish I had handled the call differently? Absolutely. But the timing wouldn't have been right. He, my father, was still alive and remarried, and if my mom were truly not dead, he would then be a bigamist! I was not on my Spiritual journey or any journey for that matter at that time, other than trying to keep my children, and myself quite honestly, alive after their father's death. He was my best friend, and we raised our kids together. We just couldn't be in the same house. A fact that I now understand, four marriages later, and take FULL responsibility for. An understanding that came only after the discovery of my childhood trauma.

After reading this book, you will understand too. Anyway, life was happening. I would be divorced again soon after, determined to never marry again. Although that changed in 2002, and my fourth marriage would be my longest, ending in 2013.

And so "the call" came and went. It was tucked away in my memory somewhere while I navigated another almost 20 years of my life. That is, until March of this year 2019. The beginning of my exploration into "what really happened to my mother".

This exploration began shortly after the realization that I had been traumatized by the man who was supposed to have been my protector. Currently exhaling through that statement, and feeling into my heart, as my heart now tells my brain, "it's okay. She knows." According to my healer, the heart and the brain will soon come into sync and I will be writing about it in this book. Update: he was right!

# CHILDHOOD TRAUMA –

What defines it? Who has had it? Who has it? Or, the bigger question, who hasn't? Since the discovery that my mother may not have died when I was 5, I have been hyper aware of similar stories. None as bizarre as mine, but odd, none the less. I currently see many clients who have struggled with not knowing who their parents are. Or finding out their parents aren't who they thought they were. Looking for parents, family members, always searching, never complete. I can't look for her anymore. It seems all bridges have been crossed. All clues have been hidden, and the facility that I thought she was at, is since closed and I believe demolished. So, I have no hope. No chance of finding her.

I play with the notion of childhood trauma daily. What defines my trauma? The thought that your whole life has been a lie? Nah......that's not childhood trauma since I just figured it out. Death? Well yes death would be a childhood trauma. It's one I struggled with. Many days, many nights. As a child, no one could explain to me how a God who was supposed to be so loving could take a mommy away from four children ages 3 to 9. I understand now why they had a hard time explaining that premise. It never happened, that's why. Not that this situation fulfills the answer to the question, but it brings clarity as to why I never got an answer. I was always the one of the four children with all the questions. That would end up being my downfall. Or would it?

I would define childhood trauma as an extraordinarily unpleasant event that can take away a child's innocence and leave long lasting scars for life. I said earlier that my whole life has been a lie. The lie didn't have the capability to traumatize me until I discovered it. I sit here in disbelief, thinking that I could never have imagined that phrase to be in a conversation about myself. Ever. Yes, "my mother died" or so I was told. That would be the day the trauma began.

# MEMORY AND MEMORIES -

I genuinely believe that we have the innate ability to block out anything and everything that our heart, our soul and our mind cannot comprehend. Especially as a child! We store these memories in a place that we never intend to go back to. It's called self-preservation. Our mind knows how to do it.

It's my understanding that at least 80% of women (and men) have zero recollection of abuse in their conscious mind. Especially sexual, until an event or trauma later in life happens to trigger all the feelings and emotions around the initial trauma. The trigger is often in one dream, or in a repetitive dream or vision. Kind of like that saying, "you don't know, till you know".

"School Girl" / "Brat" - In a recent reading with a local Medium, I asked her who else was involved in the abuse that I was subjected to. At this point I was now aware that there were more church members involved. I had an idea of one, but no memory of the other until I talked it through.

To protect anonymity, for no other reason than the sake of not having to hire a legal team for this book, the one where the truth is finally exposed, I will use the name Frank. Not their real name. The Medium had said that there were two "Franks".

I remember the first "Frank", now deceased. I remember his appearance, his sour smell, his infatuation with me. I was only six years old. Seven

71

years old. A child. He lived in Seacook, and when he would come to our house, unannounced, I always had to sit in his lap. No visitor ever had to call ahead, therefore we would never know when our day of play would be ended by a church member, any hour of the day or night. No boundaries. No family first.

"Come sit in my lap". Please, no! I would look past him, look at whatever other adult was closest, and look down at the ground. I'm sure these uncomfortable times are when I started the practice of not being able to look people in the eye. I still won't, to this day. Especially with men.

Yet there I was, at the encouragement of the presiding adult, my head down, nauseated and wanting to vomit, slowly walking over to where he was sitting on his motorcycle. The walk from the back door of our house, to where his bike was parked by the garage, felt like some sort of walk of shame. I dreaded those words, I wanted to run away. I didn't get to say "NO", that would not have been polite. "School Girl", he would call me. "You're my schoolgirl". After I sat in his lap, because that was the "polite thing to do", he would give me money. Usually, a dime and a nickel. Gross. I was probably between 5 and 9 years old. I can picture this in my mind and my stomach now turns thinking about it. I remember the walk over, the walk back, nothing in between.

The Medium described his face as having a mole and him being scraggly. She's got that right. He always had drool. If I were to see him today, I would know his face. I just found his obituary online, and even that turned my stomach. So, I guess I won't see him today, or ever, for that matter.

As the minister's daughter, these things were not out of the ordinary. As I start to have some recall of these times, I realize how wrong it was, is. Today in our society if you force your child to sit in someone's lap and he has a pet name for you and gives you money, I believe that would fall under the auspices of pedophilia.

I literally have the feeling in my throat like I am going to vomit right now. I know that I have also blocked out much of what happened with

Frank #1. But I do know for sure, his visits were NOT supervised. He went to our church, on a Harley. How bad could he be? In these current days, he probably would be considered slow, or mentally challenged. This makes it all the worse.

I know I have nightmares about him and now I know why. Until the Medium mentioned his name, and actually it was the mole or wart on his face that gave him away, I had all memory of him buried somewhere. Somewhere deep down in a dark place. I don't remember much of my childhood, but I see him clearly in my mind.

There was another "Frank". This one thought he was much better than many people. He was always borrowing money. At some point in my younger years, I must have pissed him off. Imagine that! I'm a kid. A preacher's kid. What in the world could I have possibly done to be called "Brat"? He called me that all the time and was never stopped by my father or any other adult, for that matter.

I learned in those days that I could never count on a man to protect me. I should never expect a man to defend me. I was a child and adults were permitted to call me names. In the church. Yes, I said "in the church". I would love to interject here and say, "awe, my father did the best that he could".

But nah, I'm not feeling that. He may have been the best English Professor he could, he may have been the best Minister that he could, but neither of those two accomplishments made him the best father he could be. It is common sense, it is a feeling, and emotion, a natural state of being, NOT to let other adults bully your children or abuse your children.

What happened? Why did that not come naturally? I don't know at this point, I do however, know Frank's involvement at least in the verbal abuse of at least one child, me.

This same man had the audacity to come to my work around 10 years ago. It was quite interesting because my then ex-husband who had no idea who he was, got super defensive when this man came into MY place of employment. Yes! Ten years ago, he resurfaced and walked into my office, referred to me as Brat and my ex did exactly what I would expect a man to do. He ushered him away from me. He protected me.

I had to have gotten a look on my face that what had just happened was not cool. I probably looked super disturbed. We have never spoken of it to this day.

NAME CALLING - I might as well uncover all the names I was called. Around the same time that I was forced to sit on Frank #1's lap against my will, was being called Brat by Frank #2, I was an avid cookie lover. May I mention, I get this from my father. Someone was always making cookies. My father loved his sweets. I loved to try to get seconds, as any child would. They are cookies, for crying out loud! He always was sneaking cookies. Anything more than the two we were allowed after dinner was subject to name calling. But only for me. I was "the Pig".

So, at six or so years old, I was called PIGGY! Not once, but all the time. Not by my siblings or friends, by adults! How do you feel when you read that? It was unkind and demeaning. A joke? Maybe in their minds. But in my mind, I wanted snacks even more. You want to call me PIGGY? I will show you piggy!

The name calling never stopped until as a teen I said it was ENOUGH! I was tall and skinny. I was a cheerleader. But I loved and still love my snacks. All food, as a matter of fact. I used to cut out pictures of food and make booklets by gluing them to paper. It was like my food Vision Board. Deprivation can create these kinds of issues. The more I was called names, the more I wanted to fit the bill. Maybe that sounds strange to you, or maybe it struck a chord.

Were you called a little pet name? Do you remember it like I do? How did it impact your life? Wanting or desiring food was gluttony, a sin. For me, not for him. Oh, my goodness, a sin! WOW! Show me a kid who doesn't want another cookie! I was never called dumb or stupid, which can clearly impact a child's self-esteem. I was called Piggy. To simply say it has impacted my life, would be an understatement.

Our developing ego as a child is so fragile. I often wonder if there are adults who were called names that did not stick with them. I doubt it. But ahhh, the little blonde minister's kid being called names by the minister and the elders. Powerful, God like leadership! Yes, that is sarcasm.

Since I am on a roll, I may as well continue! Hmmmm name calling.... Oh well, let's see. There was an exceptionally large woman in our church. Her size was always being pointed out. She was one of the many women who had a serious crush on my father. When I say many, I am not exaggerating one bit.

I won't say her name here, but the middle of her last name was "_____ phan___". We were not only allowed, but echoed others, when we replaced the "phan" with "phat" and called her that behind her back. And not "phat" in the pop culture definition of today. We said FAT and we meant it. Ah......." thou shall not judge".

I will bring up a story later in the book under another subject matter, where a plus sized parishioner was referred to as being "too fat" to be someone he would "date".

I don't claim to have all the answers. I don't think our childhood defines us. I believe we need to let things go as adults. But I also think these things have the potential to shape us. I think name calling and shaming around food can affect someone for their life. The fact that a family member suffered with a food related disorder is proof of this, as well as my own issues.

Many times, we don't know where certain behaviors and habits come from. We can't identify their source. We are disempowered by thinking we are broken or damaged goods. Or a PIG or a BRAT. That cannot be allowed to be our truth. We often search our whole lives trying to figure out eating patterns or addictions and their source was. Sometimes its name calling. Sometimes its unhealthy lessons around food. Can you imagine taking away a child's meal as punishment? A parent has a couple jobs. The first is to keep their child alive. That means nourishment. You want to keep away dessert? That's one thing. But "you misbehaved, no food for you" to me seems a bit twisted. So, if we are good, we get food as a reward?? I am always good. I like rewards. Do you see the pattern here?

# WOMEN ~

The greatest distraction of them all for him. As I sit here writing today, I have a picture of my father sitting right next to me. Not because I want the distraction, but because in some way, it shows that I can look at him, after everything. He's my father and I love him. I forgive him. These words will shock you as the book plays out. How can she? Love? Forgive? What's that they say? "Not forgiving is like drinking poison and expecting the other person to die." I'm not ready to die. I am ready to forgive. Which is why there is a book. Which is why you were drawn to read it. Which is why you will begin to transform in your journey. Which is why....... which is why....... which is why.........it just is.

Ahhhhhh women. The bane of my existence. These are some things I do remember. Interesting, I don't remember any fun times, I am sure there were some. I remember hearing the phone conversations. As children with no mother, we had this inherent desire to sit outside my father's study door and hope he'd be off the phone soon. Hence my lack of patience these days and my disdain for the phone and phone conversations. One of the women, married to an elder, would speak to him on the phone a minimum of 2 to 3 hours a day! Without fail, daily. Imagine being outside his "study" door for that long! Imagine how long that amount of time feels to a child. He would only come out for a bathroom break or cookie break... After that call, there would be others, but none so long as this one woman. Imagine if you will, being a husband, out working your own business day after day, while your wife was home on the phone with another man? Oh, I see, because he

77

is the minister it is okay? They had several kids, he had 4. So, between them, quite a few kids were being ignored for these daily conversations. "Oh, it's your dad's job to help people." "You know he needs to counsel people". WHAT? "That may make sense to all you adults, but it's not sitting right with this little girl". The best part, well maybe not the best part, but imagine needing a ride home from school, or being hurt at practice, or wanting to know if a friend could come over?? Beep, beep, beep.....who remembers the busy signal from yesteryear??

There wasn't just one. There were many. The extent of their relationships was unknown to me, so I can't speak to that. What I can speak to is what it looked like and what it felt like. I used to call them his girlfriends. I was so jealous. SO, SO JEALOUS! Take all of that from my childhood and then imagine being married to me as an adult. My poor husbands!

One church woman was either on the phone or at our door around the clock. They ranged from married, to unmarried, divorced, widowed, moms, and wives of other parishioners in the church. I would love to assume every one of these women being counseled was on the up and up with pure and right intention. My guess, however, is no. I always tell my children and grandchildren, "it's not what you ARE doing, it's what it looks like you are doing!" I wonder how it looked to the rest of the congregation. Did we ignore it? "Oh, he's the Pastor, so no harm done." I wonder how many church husbands wondered if this crap would ever blow over. I don't think it ever did. It did stop however, when he got married when I was a teen. Or at least it appeared to. But after that, there was just so much more lunacy, that I am not sure it's worth the read.

I remember a while back someone I know being extremely devastated when she found out her married pastor was having an affair with someone, also married, in her church. To me? That didn't seem so far out of the realm of belief. Again, not to bash him on this matter, but to reiterate, "It's not what you ARE doing, it's what it looks like you are doing". Two-to-three-hour unprofessional phone conversations with a married woman of the church, while your children wait, definitely seems inappropriate to me.

In the current times, folks blame children being ignored due to their parents' cell phone use. Although I agree, I also know that this didn't just start with cell phones. As I sit here now, reliving those long days of waiting, I feel that hole. I feel that just wanting attention from my only parent. I feel the rejection. I feel the emptiness. The feeling of being an orphan to the church. Disrespect comes to mind. Ignorant does too. At least if he didn't have enough sense to put an end to this nonsense, why didn't the women? Yes, I do blame the women too. Most of them were moms, as well as wives.

For example, picture this, we sit down at the kitchen table, it's dinner time. The phone could ring. The doorbell could ring. A knock could be heard. It NEVER failed. I bet you're thinking, oh he surely didn't attend to the church folks needs first! Yes, but they "needed him". Those are his words! Apparently the four children with no mother, didn't need him? He would rise from the table, like a king from his throne. Who needed him? What did they need? It was always a woman. Always. Gone, not to be seen from again, for the evening.

There was the one day, and this one is engrained in my memory. We thought we'd make a picnic basket and go visit our father who had gone alone to pray and write sermons at someone's camp or something or other for a week or whatever, I don't remember exactly. What I DO remember is his face as he rushed out the front door of the camp when his children arrived, excited to finally spend time with him, only to find out he had a female parishioner with him inside the camp.

Had she been there the whole time? Sleep overs? Was this planned? How did she know where he was if he hadn't invited her? It's not like he "checked in" on Facebook! It was that day that I lost my trust in men. Right, wrong or indifferent. It was that very day. We never went away on vacation. We never went on any of his trips. But this woman got to, why? Oh, that's right, because she belonged to the church. That makes it okay! *sarcasm again* But the best part of this story is he had previously told us that she would never be his girlfriend. "She's too fat!" "Thou shall not judge" ~ Luke 6:37. Thou shall not covet another man's wife." Commandment #9

I don't write these things or say these things to mock another person's religious beliefs. This is about the real life of a preacher's kid. The title that many kids in my childhood wished they had. I wouldn't wish it on anyone. Not then. Not now.

Then there was the day that he did get a girlfriend. She was single and it wasn't a secret. I've not decided if this subject is worth going into. But I will share this one story. Standing next to my father as he greeted the people when they left the church was a thing, we did every Sunday.

I was almost always there, as it was expected of me. However, one day she decided to squeeze in between us. He said nothing. Not one word. Nothing.

As I stood firm in the position next to him that I surely had earned, she told me to "bug off!" "Bug off"!

I will NEVER ever forget that phrase nor will I use it. But still, he never said a word. Never defended his child. Nor did he say a word when she took down my mother's things in our house and eventually went on to insist that he sell our childhood home and move. Just down the street, but she wasn't about to live with the "ghost of my mother". Later, she would convince him to throw me out of the house as a teenager. He never stood up for me, but I didn't leave!

Ah, reduced to rubble again. We surely have a pattern going here. Can't trust the men, can't trust women. Who can I trust? I would then spend the next 40+ years trying to answer that question.

My father, he wasn't a laborer. He wasn't a clerk. He wasn't a painter. He was a minister. By taking on that responsibility, he had a duty to behave like the man of God that he was. And I still believe him to be a man of God, I do. But while he was walking around portraying this godliness next to holiness, all hell had broken loose in his home and NO ONE KNEW!! Just us kids. We each have our own issues, but I will speak solely about myself.

My other sibling has done nothing wrong and may never remember the disruption in our childhood home. They will always live in a protected state of fear. Not my journey. Not my problem. I'm only responsible for my journey and how all this disfunction affected me.

One has since died; one is now blind. I'm just over here writing books. Writing books and helping people. Sound familiar? Here in lies the difference. My kids, my grandkids, will always be first. They will never sit outside a door for hours, while I carry on inappropriate conversations with married men.

As I type this, my three-year-old granddaughter, donned in full Mini Mouse attire, is asking me to put my laptop down on the coffee table, because she has her pretend babies in her hand. I need to climb off my soap box and say I was not perfect either. I surely was not. I am not. But what I do know is that I don't appear to be one thing in front of a congregation and run a completely different life at home. I consider myself to be 100% transparent. And now it is time to play babies.

I always wonder why no one noticed. Why did no one in the church spot what was going on? Or did their needs come before ours? Afterall we were to be seen and not heard. Oh, what's that you say? "No one had a perfect childhood"? Agreed. But this book isn't about "anyone". It is about me. It is my story.

As I write in my quiet Myrtle Beach home, my grandmother stands before me in spirit. Well, she is over by the bookcase in front of me. This is an absolute first for me. I feel her. I see her. She just told me to "tell your story little girl, you tell that story. You let them know the truth!" I definitely got my spunk from her. I would truly like to pretend this treatment by my father ended when I was an adult. It didn't.

March 4, 1998 — and again this is not a story for a pity party. I do not want or need any pity. It's been a tough life, but many have had it tougher. I was home, asleep. A call came from my oldest son. I will not ever forget every minute of that day.

"Mom, daddy won't get up for work. His alarm has been going off since 5:30 and he's not up." "Okay well run upstairs and tell him mom says to get his butt up for work!" "Mom, no!" he screamed. "Something is wrong. I know something is wrong." "Yes, he's lazy", I said," that's what is wrong", assuming he had stayed up too late watching cartoons or WWF. (my heart still races as I tell this story, 22 years later!)

"Ok son, switch to the 'cordless' and take me up there with you. I will tell him to get up."

Just a couple months earlier Brayden had bought his parents' house, and had been doing renovations on it, to make it good for our kids. It was a traditional cape. The boys had made bedrooms in the finished basement, the first-floor bedroom was a junk room, and the second floor had the traditional, walk up the stairs, bathroom in front of you, bedroom to the right, bedroom to the left. Brayden's room would be to the right, my daughter's room to the left.

Exactly one month earlier, February 4th (the pic is date stamped) he had saved his money and bought the kids a yellow lab puppy, Sasha. I found out months later that he had intended to get a second puppy, eventually. He would have named it Miesha. That never happened. What did happen though is 6 years later I bought my 3rd husband a Rottie puppy which he unknowingly named "Miesha". No coincidences.

Their life was full. A house with a pool, a puppy and their own rooms. What more does a tween need? Their dad.

My son went up the stairs with the "cordless" in hand, me on the line, and stood in the doorway of his dad's room. "Wake him up!" "Mom he's not moving". "Go over and wake him up". Phone in hand he walked to his dad's bed and touched his arm. His scream was blood curdling!

82

"Mom he's cold! Mom!" "Okay, okay please just try to wake him up." I was dressing while talking and trying to hold my shit together. "You have to hang up this phone and call 911. You MUST!" "I can't!" he cried. (I felt the touch just now, I know you are "here" Brayden) "Okay I will do it." I said. I hung up the phone. I picked it back up to call 911, he was still on the other end of the phone. "You have to hang up, son! I can't call 911."

"911 what's your emergency?"

"My husband, no, my kids' dad, there's something wrong with him. My son said he's not moving!"

"Okay is he breathing?"

"I don't know."

"Well, can you check?"

"I can't. He's in Hampton and I am in Exeter." I gave them the address and hung up.

I don't remember the time frame, but I do know I got from my house to his in 7 minutes. I left the house half dressed in my Mustang, not a cop in site. Three minutes later I called the Hampton PD.

"We can't tell you anything ma'am, you are not next of kin."

"Oh really, well those children there, those are MINE!"

"How many are there?"

"Three, I said. THREE!"

They had found my younger son who had in that short period of time at barely 13 years old come up the stairs from his basement bedroom to over a dozen EMT's, Firefighters and police in the house. The same house that not so many hours earlier was as quiet as any other night that they were at their dad's house.

They hadn't found my daughter. Yet.

"I'm sorry we still can't tell you anything."

"Okay well I will be there in 2 minutes!" CLICK!!

"You cannot fucking do this! Don't you dare leave me to raise our kids alone." I screamed at the top of my lungs!!! "DO NOT DIE!!!!!!!!!!!!!!!!!!!!!!!!!!!!!!!!!!!!!!!!!!!!!!!!!!!!!"

There was nowhere to park. Emergency vehicles parked everywhere! Two ambulances, police cars littered the driveway and front lawn. Fire trucks. I squeezed the Mustang in between something and something else. I have no clue. It all became blurry at that moment. This has to be a nightmare.

A brief check as to who I was, don't get me started, and I was in the house. There were our sons. Each flanked by an officer. I rushed to them, dodging cops and EMT's. My youngest son looked like his world had just ended. It had. I will never forget his face. Ever. The puppy barked like it was her job. It kind of was. With both sons accounted for, I begged for my daughter. She was just 11 at the time.

"She's upstairs."

"WHERE?????" Knowing, of course, that her dad was also up there!

"She's asleep."

"Of course she is." Only HIS daughter could sleep through a dozen First Responders in her house, even upstairs where she lay innocently sleeping, unaware that her father never woke up that morning. Her life, her entire life was about to be destroyed. How did I know this? Because mine was when I "lost" a parent at age 5!!

"I'm going to see him."

"No, you can't."

"Well, I am. So, arrest me if you must, but I am going to see him."

Although the sun had risen, his room was kind of dark, it felt cold. If death has a smell, that was it. Two police escorts stood by while tried not to collapse. Looking at it now, I'm sure what I could have done wrong, but they had me covered like a criminal.

A full questioning of my whereabouts would ensue not long after. His lifeless body, part of him with rigor mortis set in, lay there as if he was sleeping. Peacefully on his back, he lay there untouched by the EMT's, it was way too late. 5:30 am was way too late. His blood was settled in his back near his rib cage. To my left, a picture of me on his dresser. His plaid shirt on the bed. His raggedy sweatshirt on the floor. Nothing out of the ordinary to me. I was now in a constant state of losing my shit. Yet I still remember it all. I picked up his sweatshirt, smelled his cheap aftershave, that sweatshirt would become mine. I yelled some more. "You cannot do this shit to me, Brayden! What the fuck"!!!!!

I hadn't realized when I got to the top of the stairs that to my left, in front of my daughter's bedroom was a female officer in uniform. As I saw her out of the corner of my eye, I was like an arrow shot from a bow. I left Brayden's side and stood in front of the officer.

"I am going in."

"Okay", she said, "I am going with you."

"No."

"Yes"

"Well then stand where she can't see you. She is not going to open her eyes to see a cop standing over her."

I would describe the next 10 minutes of my life as some of the hardest minutes a mom could endure. "Hunny, your daddy, well he got sick and during the night and he died."

How was this happening?! NO ONE had ever told me, oh go ahead and have kids and don't forget to practice how you would tell them their daddy is dead at age 37, just in case!

We powered through it. The officer was kind. She asked her a bunch of foolish questions while I just held her. I am fairly certain, being woken from a sound sleep, she didn't understand. She was definitely in shock. She, to this day, does not like to be woken up in the morning. Not even by me.

At this point, it dawned on me that my two sons were literally downstairs with all the police and that time had to be standing still for them, while they waited for me to come down with their sister. Outside neighbors were strewn throughout their yards, tattered bathrobe, coffee mug in hand. Never imagining the scenario inside that little brown cape.

"How can I do this? Tend to all their needs right now? How? These kids cannot watch the coroner take their daddy's lifeless body out of this house. They don't need that. As it was, the oldest had seen his father dead. He was only 17.

"I know, I will call my father", I thought. "He can come sit with them for me." He lived 3 miles away and would be there the quickest.

Every move that each of us made was under constant scrutiny by the officers. I get it. But it sucked. So, for me to make a call, an officer would have to stand there with me. It went something like this.

"Dad, I need help. It's B, he's dead. I need help with the kids. You've done this (now the conversation seems such bullshit because he hadn't had do to this). You know how to help them when a parent died. I can't help the officers, coroners, etc.... and answer questions and protect the kids at the same time! They're going to move his body. The kids can't see it. Please come help me, dad. Please!"

At this point it must have been 9am or so. I surely wasn't watching the clock. What happened next, although it fell in line with my life 30 years earlier and for many years after that, will NEVER leave my memory.

And I quote, "oh no, Oh dear lord."

"How long before you can be here?" I asked.

"Oh, I have the men's breakfast today. I can't come there." my father replied.

"WAIT WHAT????? Brayden is dead. Your daughter just lost her kids dad. Your grandkids just lost their daddy. And you what??? You have the Men's Breakfast?"

I handed the phone to the cop that was guarding me and got my sea legs for the first time that morning. Wobbly and unable to breathe, it all came back to me. The loss, the loneliness, the abandonment of the only "living" parent I had. In my deepest darkest hour, the "Men had a breakfast."

He would go to that breakfast, only to call me after and see if I still needed help. At that point it was past noon and I had real family (ie: friends) helping and surrounding us all.

I handed the officer the phone and for the first time that horrific morning, I felt compassion coming from someone. As he held me, he told me that his dad would have done the same thing and he completely understood how I felt. Well, aside from Brayden dying, he understood.

It didn't stop there. I often wonder why me. I wonder why I was not accepted. I always had the biggest mouth, maybe? I always asked too many questions? My own father couldn't stand to look at me, knowing what he had done to me?

And then there was the absolute fake persona that began that day, the day we were told our mom died. Maybe it was fake before then. Maybe the whole thing was a lie. From the start.

Did the lies start the morning that I woke up, at five years old, to see a church lady in my house and not my mother? Coincidentally, the woman in my house that morning that we were told mom died, was the same lady from the three-hour phone calls, in his study. It's not what you ARE doing, it's what it looks like you are doing.

# POSTPARTUM DEPRESSION

Now I believe Postpartum Depression is absolutely a thing. Although I was never one who suffered from it, I know many a mom who has, and I honor and validate that to the absolute fullest. That said, let me tell a story.

Circa 1998, shortly after Brayden's death. Weeks prior to his death my nephew was born. From the day Brayden died, I had been in a fog. That night he died, I collapsed in the doorway and was taken to the ER by ambulance, as my oldest watched, thinking he was losing another parent.

The phone rang. Now at this point, getting out of bed for the second time in a day after getting the kids to school was quite a feat. It was mid-day. I was in bed.

"Hello?"

"It's your father."

"Yup I know."

"How's it going?"

"Um let me think. Not good."

"Oh, oh no. Well, I was wondering."

"Okay, what?"

"Well, I talked to your sister (she's 3 years older) today and well you know, she's got that Postpartum Depression thing. Well, I was wondering, could you call her and talk to her and maybe see if you can help her?" He asked.

"Okay, I will calmly remind you that I am trying to keep my children from a nervous breakdown. I am trying to get out of bed every day. But most importantly I am doing so with no help from any of you! None! So no, I can't help her!!! Goodbye!"

My sister, bless her heart, has since (many years ago) apologized for being so absent during the weeks and months that I had just needed at least a sister. I said it was okay. That's what we are taught to do. Say it's okay. Absolutely no reflection on her, she was definitely in emotional trouble with her second baby. But my family was not there. Not for me. Not for my kids.

You see I am the glue. I'm in the 3rd position in the 4 of us. Now the middle because my oldest brother died 10 years after Brayden. When the glue breaks down, the fixing breaks down. The fixer was broken, and no one ran in to help put the pieces back together. The sad truth.

## THE EXORCIST – The Article

Let me note that between the time I started this book and today, I had told the story of my father being an exorcist. I have told many people that I remember some New York magazine doing a story on him. I searched and searched. I Googled; I did all I could to find this article. I knew of it. I remember it.

Well, the door has opened. I have the article. I'll tell the story later. I believe everything happens for a reason; I know I was meant to find it. I know it needed to be in this book.

"A Day in the Life of an Exorcist" ~ By John Stephenson ~ July 1977 ~ Psychic World Magazine ~ (I was only 14 when this was published)

The following will be excerpts and quotes from the article, complete with my personal thoughts, feelings and reactions. Right, wrong or indifferent, this is how I feel, it's my beliefs. Which is great because it's my book!

The cover of the magazine is classic 70's. It advertises "The Healing Ministry of President Carter's Sister". – Ruth Carter Stapleton was a spiritual healer in the 70's.

Also on the cover is an article called "The Cayce Legacy Lives ON -...." Edgar Cayce was one of the first authors I read when I was seeking out my next part of my spiritual journey. No coincidences.

As I read this article, I can't even get past the byline "Teacher, minister, exorcist, Dr. Roland Kendall......." Someone forgot to put his most important job. Whenever I have stories done on me or my social media profiles, I am a mom first, Gamma second and a whatever, third. As a matter of fact, nowhere in the interview does it speak of his children.

In the article he speaks of doing over 50 exorcisms in the past EIGHT years! Oddly enough .... that is since I was 5 or 6!! No coincidence there! My mother was taken from me when I was 5!

According to the story, in this instance, he got a call at 1:30am and ANSWERED the phone! "He told the young girl to come to his house immediately", the article states. (Out of complete disregard to the fact that his 4 young, motherless children were asleep in the home he was having the "possessed" woman come to. I cannot wrap my head around this concept! Cannot!)

Do I connect with passed loved ones in a home that my grandbabies and my son now live in with me? Absolutely. Do I do it with them here? NEVER! Not that I am afraid, but for many other reasons. I protect them with white light. My home is protected, I am protected. I smudge with sage and palo santo, I clear, I meditate. AND I only allow in love and light and higher energy. No lower energies are allowed in my home or around me.

Do ministers sage or smudge? This one sure didn't! I knew that, but this article, as I pick it apart, 100% confirms it. The devil's mistress, energies or has he said it "evil spirits" were cast out of these people in the living room. Directly below my bedroom. Sick. I remember sneaking to the landing on the stairs to watch. So yes, as a child, I watched an exorcism in my own house. The place where I was supposed to be safe and protected. The "sacred space" that I grew up in. Did it affect the four of us children? You decide! Well definitely not me, quite on the contrary.

The article goes on with his story......... "the 20 year old girl and her boyfriend shared that he had long periods of despondency (depression). 'as if some outside force was driving him into his gloomy spells' (depression?) That's when she suspected he was possessed. She went on to 'try her own exorcism', she said, and then an intelligence besides her own 'forced its way into her mind'. She had taken a demon into herself."

Let me remind you again after this actual occurrence in our home, that we were all fast asleep in our beds, above this room!!

"The man lay sweating and shivering on the sofa" (my living room) "He then performed an exorcism on him." "Kendall likes to explain psychic phenomena in religious terms." "Satan opposes the Christian and the Godly people in this world." He goes on to reference people under the influence of drugs or alcohol who 'give themselves up' (to the demons).

Demons vs. Spirits –

I really want to jump in here. Mainly because as wise as my father claimed to be, and he was a highly intelligent man, I felt he always took the stance, and the article confirms, that the inexplicable was always demons.

A home with what I would refer to as housing either your deceased loved ones, or someone else's, he would refer to as possessed. I clear out unwanted spirits in a home with sage, protection and my voice. He cleared out "demons" with his voice. No sage, no protection. So, what you may feel is your little Grammy visiting the baby that was born the day she passed, he was shooing Grammy from the house. It is not an exaggeration. That is the long and short of it. Exorcism vs. house clearing 101!

"I ask them about their involvement with the occult as this is often the source of their problems." the article continues.

The definition of Occult; "noun – supernatural, mystical, or magical beliefs, practices or phenomena." Hmmm, is that my problem? No, no it's not. I am not involved with the Occult. I have a God given gift that my father now 'understands from the other side', is what I have been told more than once.

1 Samuel 28: 1-10 "6- ........the Lord would not answer, either in a dream or by a priest or prophet" "8 -10 ...........Saul went to the woman and asked, 'will you bring up the ghost of someone for us?' ....'I swear by the living Lord that nothing will happen to you because of this.' Footnotes *Bible Gateway.com – 1 Samuel 28: 1-3 "Many people believed that it was possible to talk to spirits of the dead, AND that these spirits could tell the future."

Hosea 12:10 "I have also spoken by the prophets, and have multiplied visions; I have given symbols through the witness of the prophets"

2 Chronicles 20:20 (that reference number is not lost on me) "..........believe in His prophets, and you shall prosper."

Numbers 12:6 "Hear now My words.... make myself known to him in a vision. I speak to him in a dream."

Ephesians 4:11-13 (another sequence not lost on me) ".... He Himself gave some to be apostles, some prophets, some evangelists, and some pastors and teachers.........."

Joel 2:28 "………. Your sons and your daughters shall prophesy, your old men shall dream dreams, your young men shall see visions"

Matthew 7:22 "…… have we not prophesied in your name" (ME)? "Cast out demons in your name" (DAD). "And done many wonders………."(ME).

1 Thessalonians 5:20-21. "Do not despise prophecies. Test all things; hold fast what is good."

Prophet – noun – "an individual who is regarded as a being in contact with a divine being and is said to speak on that entity's behalf serving as an intermediary with humanity by delivering messages or teachings from the supernatural source to other people."

At this point, I feel fairly confident that I have stated my argument with evidence. The same argument I would be having with him if he were alive.

"Lust or Fear" …… His own words in the article…WOW! It just hits me so hard because he would have judged me for what I do. I know that because I have this article. I know that because I have heard his words myself. I know that because some "family members" have made some nasty comments to me and about me. It does not bother me one bit. Not one bit. I don't even want to discuss the word lust when it comes to the church. FEAR, that will be discussed in another chapter.

Poltergeists – the article goes on to talk about Poltergeists. I won't be taking a stand either way on this subject as it really has nothing to do with what I do, and I don't feel educated enough to support either view.

The article goes on to speak of another incident that "Dr Kendall" went to do an exorcism because the radio seemed to "turn off and on by itself", shortly after her husband died. Hmmm……. Thoughts anyone? Sound familiar. Spirit visit, maybe?

"Poltergeist activity stopped in Ms. Newton's home but started again a few months later. The woman refuses to see Dr. Kendall or attempt another exorcism "I just don't believe in it anymore" she said "It's all phony. It doesn't last. "Well then dad, I guess we all have our share of skeptics, don't we??

The minister refers later in the article to a woman who is weak and falls victim to her anxiety and fears. (the reference point is she must be possessed if she is anxious or fearful.) She had been taking anti-anxiety meds and seeing a psychiatrist for years. He did an exorcism, but she later became a victim of anxiety again and returned to the psychiatrist and refused to accept deliverance through exorcism.

"When I asked the girl why she continued the psychiatric treatment she stated she had faith in it. What kind of logic is that? His explanation of her problem is no better than mine!" (a quote from my father)

I think I have no words at this point.

After several more examples of his work my father goes on to say, "she spoke of lights being switched on and off." (a perfect example of passed loved ones saying 'hello') "A woman hanging her wash, approached by another tenant in the building describing a woman who she had seen outside with the other woman. The woman told her she was alone out there". (passed loved one, obviously) "I woke up and saw a man standing at the end of the bed. I looked at him for a minute and then he was gone." "Perhaps, Kendall says, Spirits and Demons are beyond science."

The comparison, in all fairness, is not about who is/was right, or is the Bible right. It speaks more to the one sidedness of my father and his religion. He worked with Spirits and I work with Spirits. His were dark, mine are light. I never judged or disbelieved what he did. I was actually proud. People who are close to him judge me quite often. He judged those like me. That would not have changed. Even in life. I do hear it's changed now in death though.

Blind -

Several years ago, during a semi routine visit to the eye doc for what my brother was told was "floaters", it later would become the biggest mistake the doctor would ever make. I'm assuming that to be true, anyway.

November 18 several years ago. I will never forget this date, among others, as long as I am alive.

"Karen, call your brother, he is trying to call you, but he can't see!" A phone call from my now ex sister-in-law that I was never expecting, would change my life, his life, and our relationship forever.

Although he and I are now estranged, I tell this story with confidence, as it is my story too. I was there for him 100% of the time. Above and beyond what any other person in his life was.

Late October, one of my brothers was complaining of pain in his left eye, "as if someone had punched" him. His vision was blurred, and I convinced him to see his eye doc. After he gave a complete explanation of what had been happening physically in the prior weeks, including severe leg cramps and hiccups, along with all the eye pain and vision issues, his eye doctor dismissed all the symptoms as "floaters that you often get as you get to be about this age". She would then suggest a specialist, but he was in Portland, Maine ....... Oops, she forgot to call him. A series of mistakes, including a neurologist who looked at his optic nerves in November, would lead up to this early morning call, November 18th.

"Okay don't do a thing, I am on my way". I picked him up and from that day on, I would be caring for him and his business, full time. After a series of local doctor visits including my eye doctor, we were told to rush to Mass Eye and Ear in Boston, and from there we transferred to Mass General. Little did we know, it had now become our home away from home.

My life as I knew it came to a screeching halt. There was him, his family, his care. The businesses, and although I currently worked for him, I would be left to make decisions about the future of the business.

I would go on and on about this time in my life, but there has since been a break down in our relationship, and although it affected my life all day every day, I also don't feel comfortable sharing the ins and outs of the hell this disease took him and took me through.

Although this part is my story, it is his life. If I hadn't cut him from my life, a much-needed separation after a very scary day, I would let him know that I am writing this. Not so much for his permission, as this is mine to tell, but just to not do him wrong, in case he ever writes a book, or takes more legal action against the doctors involved prior to his blindness. He's still my brother, and I feel I he deserves that much. I don't know why, but that's what I feel. I have taken care of him since we were kids. So, it just comes naturally.

How does someone wake up blind? How does an eye doctor, specialist, and a neurologist miss what is going on? He was so specific about his symptoms. He told them everything. I was there. I've seen the doctors' notes. They left out major symptoms in their notes. After days and days of impatient testing, and teams of doctors, led by one of the top Neurologists in the country, we had a diagnosis at Mass General.

Neuromyelitis Optica (NMO) a rare, yet severe autoimmune disorder that attacks the central nervous system, including but not limited to the demyelination of the optic nerve, causing optic neuritis. It can also attack the spinal cord, causing paralysis of all the limbs. In short, it can cause sudden blindness, as well as quadriplegia. Although this condition caused only blindness for him thus far, I worried constantly that he'd become wheelchair bound, as well as blind for the rest of his life.

Neuromyelitis affects only 4000 people in the United States and can be fatal. Neuromyelitis Optica cannot be cured. It can however, go into periods of remission. IV steroids can slow the Optic Neuritis (blindness due to inflammation of the optic nerve). Unfortunately, due to the lack of competent medical care prior to his waking up blind, the steroids finally given at Mass General would save only the smallest fraction of the optic nerve in his right eye. His left optic nerve was dead at this point. Just days after his visit to the neurologist who inspected the nerves, and "loved them".

Plasmapheresis, "the removal, treatment, and return or exchange of the blood plasma or components thereof.........", although suggested, would not be an option because it was "too late" as they say, the damage had already been done. Eventually, chemo would be the only treatment. Did it help the condition that had now destroyed everything he'd ever known, including his marriage? (the disease isn't solely to blame) It didn't make one bit of difference. It may have held the paralysis at bay, however, there is no way to know for certain.

In my simple mind, when given the symptoms, pain in the eyes, loss of vision, weakness or numbness in the arms and legs, uncontrollable hiccups, and more (hiccups being the strangest of symptoms, yet it helped diagnose) a little Google search would have given a diagnosis. As a matter of fact, I did come up with NMO while sitting alone at his bedside in Mass General.

"MS and Neuromyelitis differ, in that the symptoms of MS attacks are less severe. Early and aggressive treatment is important in reducing the harm caused by NMO." (healthline.com)

MS vs NMO – Years ago NMO would have been diagnosed as MS. However, research found NMO – IgG (anti-AQP4 antibody) separated it from MS. It now stands on its own. The antibody is not found in people with MS but IS found in 70% of NMO patients. His occupation, his business, which he'd owned since he was 20, was a business where you would need eyes. This would eventually be the beginning of the end.

It would also mean the closing of the business, just 6 short months after I bought my first home, as a single woman.

Full time Mediumship practice, stage left.

Everything for a reason, not sure what the reason of the closing is for him, but I absolutely know what the reason would be for me.

As far as my younger brother goes, I haven't had a conversation with him for about three years. And it's okay. My work for him is done. My taking care of him is done. Onward and upward. I cannot be around his life. That ship has sailed.

# STORAGE –

After my 3<sup>rd</sup> husband and I split, I was looking for a change, a big one. So I rented a small apartment in a little town called Sharon Springs, NY. It was only a 4+ hour drive from Anson, and I could just stay there on weekends to get away from it all.

I fell in love with Sharon Springs after attending a Garden Festival in the quaint little village, once known for their Sulphur Bath Houses, and immediately meshing in their community. I was selling my wares, then known as Barnyard Banana Bread, at their festival, and immediately "sold out" after the famous Beekman Boys tried my bread and subsequently sang it's praises about it on social media.

Sharon Springs is a small village, currently widely known for the Fabulous Beekman Boys, winners of the Amazing Race reality TV show, and their 1802 Mercantile, as well as the late great Sharon Jones, and several Broadway stars, who have made, or currently make their home there. Visitors over the years include Rachel Ray, Martha Stewart, Mindy Cohn and many more. Rodger Hazard from the show, "Sell This House", and his husband made Sharon Springs their home for a short bit. I won't share the escapade he and I went on one day looking at a house for me to buy, (sorry about the arm, Roger).

The Mayor of Sharon Springs and his husband own the American Hotel, a gorgeous well appointed hotel, and dining room. My dear friends own a contemporary restaurant, 204 Bistro, where many famous people have enjoyed their well loved Schnitzel and house made daily, crusted bread. I am very familiar with what time the Chef begins the bread making in the morning, as my little apartment was right above the kitchen. No complaints here.

You may know by now, when I visit a place and it calls me in, I instantly move on that vibe. And it did, and I did. Two friends and a U-Haul on a weekend and I was moved in, not long after my first visit to this amazing town. But I had moved out of a 2200 sq ft house into a small apartment. It didn't all fit. I was fortunate to find a storge facility for the rest of my stuff, a couple towns over.

My NY residency was cut extremely short, when I had just returned from a weekend at my apartment, and the call came saying my brother couldn't see. I tried to get to NY on the weekends, but my entire life was consumed with his care, many visits to Mass General, and running his business. Eventually, I had to move out. My furnishings, all my memories, my family heirloom dining set, all just made their way into my NY storage unit. I left. As fast as I moved in, I moved out. I was able to find a small apartment very close to the business and my brother's house on the Seacoast of New Hampshire.

My divorce was final in 2013, and I was going to have to rebuild financially following that. The first bill to be ignored would eventually be the storage unit. I tried, I really did. But I got to the point where I had to accept that I couldn't pay everything, and I didn't have the time or resources to get my things out of storage in New York.

I eventually forgot about the storage unit and stopped paying. I had inadvertently said "goodbye" to the things that were so dear to my heart, realizing that they wouldn't bring back Brayden, my brother, or my mom. Every now and then I would wonder if when they auctioned off my storage unit it would be like the TV show "Storage Wars", and whether the highest bidder would be super excited or disappointed when they won my unit.

# MORE ADDICTION

There are not many things that scare me. Typically, things that I fear have to do with my children or grandchildren. The kids running out in the street. Or falling off their bikes. My adult children, well... those fears are bigger. The biggest fear I have had regarding my children, is the fear of addiction. The fear of overdose. I deal with drug related deaths every day that I am with clients. From sobriety to death in less than 24 hours. Addiction is the biggest pandemic in this world. Bigger than Covid, in my opinion. But people don't want to talk about it. If it's hidden, it isn't happening.

Such was my life. Although the booze didn't take my brother Tim's life, it certainly wasn't an innocent bystander. It's so easy to laugh at some of his antics now, but the night he scaled the roof and banged on my bedroom window in our 2nd childhood home, I surely was not laughing. I was sound asleep, counting sheep, and heard a loud bang, bang, bang. It was admittedly a good thing at this point that I hadn't been allowed to watch violence or horror movies on TV. I would have gotten under the bed, instead of going to the window.

My teenage twin bed was the one I had my whole life. My sister had the exact same bed. Mine was always in a pink, hers was boring. This was my first official bedroom alone. Or so I thought. Our typically designed New England Cape home made his climb up the back of the garage to the dormer where my window sat, an easy accomplishment. After all, he had legs like any other track star. Tim was an all-star for the State of NH, representing Winnacunnet High School in the pole vault jump.

But not this night. He was not winning any medals. No, there he was .......... drunk and bleeding. Glass impaled every few inches in his skin. There I was, pulling glass out of his cut-up body. Although I was horrified by his condition, be it the booze or the bleeding, the minor surgeries commenced. Irritated, but surely didn't want to get him in trouble with my father, I fixed all his wounds in the silence of the night. He passed out in his room, my younger brother, completely unaware. I'd later learn that he had been up in the White Mountains and was shot at. Who knows what he was up to, or why someone would be shooting? I did go up to the National Forest parking lot weeks later see the bullet holes in the dumpster that he had described to me. I was a curious teen, to say the least.

# LIES – THE MYSTERY BEGINS
# – THE CEMETERY

"She is not dead" … "Your mom is very much alive!"

A phrase I have heard from most, if not all, mediums I have connected with. Most recently from a friend of a friend. How is this even possible?

Positioned in front of the KENDALL gravestone, untouched by visitors. No flowers, no plants............. essentially a forgotten resting place. I am up in New Hampshire, seeing clients and doing events, July 2020. I find myself with a partial day off. I am between hotels and needed to entertain myself, as napping wasn't an option. Anyone who knows me, knows that I don't believe that the cemetery is where we really connect with those who have passed. We connect with them in our minds. In our hearts. My visit this day is more of a discovery visit. I can connect with those I wish to connect with, in my mind and heart. So, my purpose here still kind of escapes me.

First up is my kids' dad. My first husband. He's on the way in, off to the right, and still, 22 years later the grass has still not grown on his plot. I joked with him a bit and then it was almost a straight shot to the Kendall stone. A small white angel leaned against the stone, most likely place by a little girl who was missing her daddy. Briefly stopping there for a minute and for the 20th time trying to size up, what grave is where? How many people are actually buried there? Two. That's the answer, two. Since she's not there............it felt weird this time. It was my first visit since I learned that she's not there, it seemed almost blasphemous! A lie. Fake. False. Bullshit.

On that chilly April day in 2008 when they laid my brother's body to rest, even through my grief and tears, I could not figure the plots out. I still can't. Details. I guess they don't matter. We have bigger issues.

A short ride in the car, truthfully would have been an easy walk, and I am quickly at the Howes stone. Checking dates and names, it felt more like a history lesson. They've all been gone a long time. With a total time of 20 minutes inside the cemetery......I was on my way.

My fear of getting locked inside those gates, is not unfounded. After a long visit at B's grave 20 years ago, I drove towards the exit and found it locked. My navigation of the Hampton Cemetery consisted at that point of over 30 years .........walking, biking and eventually in my first car. Afterall I was a girl who believed her mommy was there, then her Grammy, then her kids daddy, then her brother, then then then...... The list is never ending. But the "mommy" grave, that's where it all started.

For a July day in New Hampshire the temperatures were extremely high, and I was anxious to get back in my rental granny van and run that air conditioning full blast. It was close to the temperature at home that day. In Myrtle Beach air conditioning is a staple, in the car, in the house.

The exit of the cemetery faces my Junior High school. Hampton Academy was also my mom's school and as I stared at the building, I envisioned a young little Grace, happy and carefree in the hallways of that sturdy brick building. Little did she know at that time, her fate several years later.

Left, or right? What seemed like hours sitting there staring, was actually a minute or two. Envisioning, imagining, all while making the decision, into town or towards 222 High Street. A left turn and I was headed towards the house. Where it all happened.

The lights at Mill Road, the Smith's, the Sullivan's, Mr. Andrews, and then Grammy's. The bungalow, 217 High Street, Grammie's house. Ohhhhhhhhh the memories came back like a freight train. I was always happy when I was there, whether I was learning piano, or watching one of the many students that banged away at the keys of the upright piano in Grammie's living room. Always knowing that when we finished, we got to have some of the M&M's that always sat on the corner of that old piano. Or would we get to have steak? Something I believed we were 'too poor' to have at our house.

Between 217 High Street and 222 High Street, sat the biggest of the three houses built by my grandfather. 219 High Street was my aunt and uncle's house. I thought they lived in the fancy house when I was young. As I sized up the houses today, it really WAS the fancy house, it still is. The fanciest of the three anyway. They didn't really care for us four kids, or so it felt. But their house is where the steak would be cooking. My uncle would make a "steak for Timmy", as if he was an only child. We always got a bite though. The steak was just one of the things that would be special for Timmy. Why was he so favored? We had no idea. At least not until one evening when Timmy was 16, my younger brother was 10, my sister and I, somewhere in between.

Next would be my home. 222 High Street. No memories come up, none. At least some good memories? None. I'm not mad or sad. I'm not confused. Numb, just numb. Not emotional. No feeling at all. In awe that the garage that could barely house one car, was still standing, forty years after we had moved.

After a quick ride around the streets, I know so well, including Howes Road......named for my grandfather who built many of the houses, I made my way west towards Epping.

Being a Medium, I often feel that I've seen it all. All the bargaining, the pleading, the conversations. But something came over me and I spoke out loud, "if she IS alive and I am supposed to find her, there will be someone at my Mediumship Gallery tonight whose name will be Grace.

I left that challenge right there on High Street, downtown Hampton, got in my zone and never thought of it again.

As always, I had everyone go through their names, Amanda, Abby, Jessica, 17 people and not one Grace. Which was fine, at this point I wasn't even thinking of my challenge that I had spoken aloud to my father not long before this Mediumship Gallery group event.

The night progressed...amazing messages and beautiful connections as always when Spirit is right there among us. Nearing the end, I had a mom in spirit who wanted to connect with a daughter there. A hand quickly raised, and a sweet young girl claimed this Spirit as her mom. The mom in spirit who was just so eager to let her young daughter know that it was really her, showed me the daughter tripping over her own feet. This clumsiness was apparently a regular occurrence, as the mom in spirit showed it in several different forms. "Would you understand the reference of your mom showing me you are tripping over your own feet, in a clumsy type of way?" "Haha, yes I would. I am a dancer and I'm always so uncoordinated. My mom had a nickname for me. She would call me GRACE."

As I said, I don't do these challenges often, if ever. A part of me was my very own skeptic. But my gut believes in me and the work I do. And if the work I do is true, and I expect others to believe they can do similar tests with their loved ones, then why was I so shocked when it happened? But I did the challenge, and I got my answer! Now what would I do with it?

If only............if only I had my mom's few belongings, and Tim's mementos, articles, and whatever else I had tried to salvage over the years that I had abandoned in that storage unit, 6 years earlier. Maybe I had clues I didn't know about. Maybe I had something that would prove my mom did not die, and I didn't even know it.

# IF ONLY –

"In life we spend so much time 'shoulding' (said fast, sounds like shitting) ourselves", I often tell my students. 'Woulda, coulda, shoulda", are all words we waste so much energy on. We cannot change the past. It's the past for a reason. But yet we try. We long to have a second chance at making a certain decision, albeit a good or bad decision. I wanted desperately to change the fact that I left everything that was really important to my heart in storage unit #109, in upstate New York, back in 2013. (yes, I sure did remember the unit number)

I had gotten those horrific memories back in October of 2018. Through a series of readings with Mediums that I didn't know, and others, I was awakened to the fact that every one of them saw my mother alive and either in a facility, or memory care type place.

It was now almost a year later in September 2019. I was getting ready to leave for Florida. The pain of wondering how my mom could be alive, how I didn't know all these years, and where she was, was becoming unbearable. I couldn't sit on my hands any longer. But how, how could · I find out the truth?

Packing has become such a repetitive habit, that I do it with little thought and the speed of an athlete. My mind is typically somewhere else. This day it was on finding whatever I could to lead me to my mother.

"Maybe I could try and figure out the name of the storage facility. Maybe when they auctioned off my unit, the buyer left behind all my personal effects, things that would mean nothing to them. Maybe the owner felt bad and stuffed it in their garage incase I show up 6 years later and want it. Maybe. Maybe I am just wishful thinking. Maybe I was hanging on a wish that made absolutely no sense. I remember the dumpster on the property. Too convenient to just toss it all. Okay, I'm being silly. Goodnight."

I shot out of bed early in the morning. I remembered the storage owner's name was Troy. "Surely if I Google 'Troy, storage, New York', SOMETHING will come up," I thought. I had no idea the name of the town. It was about 30 minutes from Sharon Springs, and I could definitely drive there, but I was at home in Myrtle Beach, SC, getting ready to leave for Florida. I was being silly again.

"It's a long shot, but let me Google 'storage near Sharon Springs', after all, that's how I found the storage facility in the first place. Now I only have to be able to recognize the facility name after 6 years of not knowing it," I grumbled to myself.

That area in upstate New York, is mostly country. Massive working farms are home to the locals, including the Amish. They are often seen in their horse and buggy as folks travel those back roads. "How many storage facilities could there be in that area anyway?" I asked myself, trying so hard to stay positive. There were a lot!

"SHIT, that's it! There it is!" I screamed. I had been leery on some of the names I saw, but when I saw it, I knew Google and I had found it. Although, now what? "It has been SIX years, Karen. Six years. You need to relax," I reminded myself. I slowly slid down the wall to the floor, heart racing, tears quickly filling my eyes, as I read in bold red letters. *"Permanently closed"* "Stop this roller coaster, I want to get off!" I shouted to my phone. But I wasn't done.

"There is a phone number. Maybe if I call it, I will find out someone bought the facility with a new business name. Maybe that someone found my personal belongings in the corner of the truck garage they had there. Maybe they kept it in case I came back SIX years later," I fantasized, refusing to give up at this point. Afterall, my celestial team of guides MUST be working on this, or I would never have remembered Troy's name.

Before I knew it, my fingers were slamming out those digits on my phone. "You have reached ABC Self Storage" her familiar voice said, "please leave us a message and we will get back to you." NO WAY!

Jan was so sweet when she would call me for late storage payments faithfully during the first few months of my default. Once she stopped calling, I knew the unit was gone. The words "permanently closed" dashed any hope I had of taking my search any further. But now I was listening to Jan's voice asking me to leave a message. "I've come this far, I may as well oblige." I thought.

Beep............... "Um, um, um, okay, well I know you don't remember me, but I rented Unit 109 at your facility, your place, well the storage place that is now closed," I stuttered with my tongue glued to the roof of my mouth due to sheer panic. "Anyway, I know you don't remember me, but I have a story. You see, since 1969, I have been told since I was five years old that my mom, well, that my mother was dead. And I know this sounds so crazy, but in the last few months, I found out she's really alive, and has been for the past 50+ years. And I don't know where she is." I cried. "And, well you see, everything I had of hers, it wasn't much, but any clues or information in what little I had, well it was in that unit. And I know I didn't pay it, and you had to auction it off. But I just HAD to contact you to see if maybe, just maybe, I dunno, maybe whoever bought it, tossed my personal memories boxes to the side. And maybe you picked them up and saved them. And I know, I know I sound crazy. But I had to try everything I could. And this was one thing I needed to try, to know for sure that anything I had that may help me is gone. Well, I am sure you already think I am nuts, but if there was even a notebook or anything that fell out and you picked it up, can you please, please, please call me? Please? My number is 603-.......... Okay

110

well thank you for listening, bye." And I hung up. "Good Lort, what have I done," I chuckled to myself and finished packing.

The flight to Fort Myers, Florida was uneventful. Check-in was a cluster, but I finally made it to my hotel room. Setting up for sessions in my room the next day, I had all but forgotten the message I had left in hysterics the day prior.

I have been traveling to Florida to meet with clients 'one on one' for several years. An ad that a friend of a friend put in a "Mom's Facebook Group" had soon filled two weeks' worth of client sessions.

I would sell out my entire schedule for every visit since that initial post. They told two friends and they told two friends and so on and so on. I now have over 300 clients in the Fort Myers / Cape Coral area. I see some of them faithfully every time I am down there.

I typically take a day off after two or three days of back to back sessions. It was my day off and I had a book to mail out to a client. Fortunately, there was a Post Office within walking distance. Juggling all my belongings, I began to cross two busy lanes of seasonal traffic to get to the plaza across the street.

Only my children are allowed to text me, well and a couple close friends are too. As I am trying not to drop anything while crossing the road I heard my text go off. I finished crossing, knowing that if one of my kids had an emergency, they would call first.

Leaving the post office, I suddenly remembered my text had gone off. It was almost lunch time, so I figured I would sit for lunch at one of the little cafés nearby. The hostess quickly sat me, and I settled into my booth for four, by myself.

"Just ice water", I said, as she asked me for my beverage order. I would definitely be having tacos since the smell of Mexican food was permeating my entire being. Afterall, I was in a Mexican restaurant. With my lunch order stored to memory, I began to scroll.

The text from an unknown number read, "Karen, it's Jan from ABC Storage. I got your message, and I am sorry it took so long for me to text you. We closed the storage facility a couple years ago." It read. Ready to puke, I looked up and mumbled my taco order to the waitress who I hadn't noticed standing right in front of me. Returning to my screen, I scrolled to get back to Jan's text.

"About 5 years ago, my whole life changed suddenly. It's a long story." She went on. "Okay, get to the point", I whispered, staring at the screen, wiping tears from my face, so as not to cause a scene. Due to this, I have *good news!*" Now hyperventilating, salty dried tears on my face, I sat up straight and continued through the long text, speed reading, as I often do.

"I fell behind on everything, and your unit is *exactly how you left it six years ago.*"

"Okay, I am speed reading. Slow down Karen and read it right. It really said, 'bad news' not good news," I convinced myself. I slowly read it again. "….your unit is exactly how you left it six years ago" "What the hell! No way, yes way." "Waitress……I will have a Grande' House Margarita, I am celebrating!!" "Coming up" she said, glancing down at her watch. Hey, don't judge, the bar was full of snowbirds with their dirty martini's, so I was in good company.

I read on. "I went over there this morning just to be sure, as I haven't been over there in a long time, and it is as if you just left it." She said. "I never got to cleaning it out. Over five years ago, at age 45, I had an 'oops'. I got pregnant. My kids are grown, and Troy and I now have a 4 year, almost 5 year old. I am too old to have a toddler. Many projects fell behind. Cleaning out your abandoned unit was one of them."

To this day, I still don't know how I didn't pass out before I began day drinking. I didn't know what this would mean. It might mean nothing. But what I did know, is that the few memories I had of my mother, were NOT in a landfill. To this day, I still say, "you can't make this shit up!"

By the way, this particular story is one hundred percent fact. Aside from the name of the storage facility.

"OMG, I cannot believe this!" I texted with shaky hands. "This is a miracle. OMG, thank you so much!" Quite honestly, I did not have a plan in place for my unit to still be full. I had no plan at all, actually. "Okay Jan, I am working in Florida. I will be home in a few days. I want to pay you and come retrieve my things from the unit. Is that even possible? How much would that be?" I asked. Looking at my calendar while waiting for her to respond, I quickly remembered that I would be leaving in a few weeks for Hawaii for a one month stay in November. "I will have to ask Troy, I will get back to you soon." She replied.

Two or three days passed, I was seeing clients, so time was passing quickly. A text came in. "Karen, Troy says '$500 and you can come clean out the unit'. Can you do that?" "What's your Paypal?" I replied, before I even thought about it for a second. She then sent me a picture she had taken of my unit, and I sobbed, as I could see my mom's dining room set, dressers, and the bins that held all my memories.

I would later do the math. $110/month X 12 months X 6 years. They could have charged me thousands.

When I came to and realized I was not dreaming, it dawned on me that I had already scheduled a trip in October up to New Hampshire and Massachusetts. So, driving to New York, picking up a U-Haul and driving home to South Carolina, following my sessions and events, was an absolute probability. And it would all have to happen before I left for Hawaii on November 1st.

I met the little boy in New York whose birth ultimately saved my storage unit contents for me for six years. I thanked him in my mind, as Troy and his adult son so graciously loaded the U-Haul. I don't know where those angels came from, but I will never forget them.

While the men were loading, Jan settled her toddler and walked over to me, as I supervised. "I have a confession" she said. "I had come over here once years ago and just opened up your unit, to see what would be needed to empty it. There was a box with some books and a movie called, 'The Secret.' I can bring what I can find back if you'd like." "Of course you did," I said. "Obviously, you needed it more than me. I would never have noticed. But thank you for telling me. No I don't want it back, it's the least I can do." "The Secret movie was so good", she replied. "Oh, I know," I said. "I know".

"If Only......." The title of this chapter. I got you, didn't I? I **did** have mom's things. I still cannot believe it!

# IT'S JUST STUFF -

When I retrieved the contents of my storage, much of it was connected to my grammie or my mom. I had hung onto it for all these years. I'm not just talking jewelry or a music box. More like, dining room set, dressers, etc.......Whether it had been my mom's or her mom's, I had spent thousands of dollars over the years to store it. Storage units down here in Myrtle Beach are nearly $200/ month. A year here had cost me almost $2500. It made no sense. And that certainly wasn't the first time I had stored the dining and bedroom sets during the decades that I have had it. I had no use for so much of it.

Pictures, jewelry, albums, those things have proven to be so valuable emotionally, but to hang onto large items, is something that is inside me. I didn't need the furniture. At one point I was using the dining set and the sideboard, as well as the dressers. Not now. Life had changed. The dynamics had changed. I had to let go. And that I did. I remember hearing one morning when I was journaling, "it's just stuff". That has been my motto since that day.

But is it "just stuff"? Stuff can bring us comfort. It can temporarily fill a hole where a loved one used to be. But at the end of the day, it's still just stuff. In a case where you have no physical memories, the things that serve you best are writings, pictures, mementos, scrap books, etc. Things help you feel. Maybe you don't remember that day, or it was before you were born. Create a story with those pictures. Savor the look in your loved one's eyes. Or a souvenir. What were they doing? Did they enjoy it?

Creating a memory where there is none, can fill your heart with joy, even if your memory is skewed from the actual event.

Writing this I am thinking about all the silverware I have up in the attic. Today if a piece of silverware ends up unnoticed in the garbage while a child clears their plate, no harm done. But my ancestors took their serving and dining pieces quite seriously. Have I hung on to too much of it? Probably so. But the pieces with initials so painstakingly carved into them, they have energy. I know who touched them, I know who held them. That ....... brings all the feels. Especially the piece that says "Grace" on it.

It is no secret that I am narrating this book, in real time as I go along. Why? Because it is my story, and I chose to tell it this way. I finished the above paragraph and a couple others following it and went out to check the mail. Yes, it is important to come up for air when writing a book, and I often forget.

As I crossed the front yard in my bare feet, because well, it is January in South Carolina, the sunlight shone on something glistening on the ground under the tree. I walked over and it was, and I swear, none other than one of my grandmother's spoons! This is when I am reminded that the original title of this book was "You Can't Make This Shit Up"!

Seven or eight years ago, when I was moving and contemplating yet again if I wanted to keep lugging this stuff around with me, I got the crazy idea to make something out of some of the silverware. My friend's husband took my grammie's candy dish, and some flatware and made it really flat, turned the candy dish upside down hung the silverware, and viola' a windchime, making good use of just a couple of the pieces of silverware that I mentioned above. That windchime has hung everywhere I have lived and been through some major storms. It has never had a piece fall off. That is, until today.

So many things crossed my mind. Fix it? Keep this flat spoon? Or, after writing this chapter, toss it. I am proud to say, I tossed it. Knowing full well in the back of my mind that I have plenty more up in the attic.

I will never hug my mom; I will never know what it feels like. But there is nothing missing in my life, that hanging onto a dresser will replace. In my uneducated opinion, this must be how hoarding begins. I am not wise to a lot of issues regarding this effort of replacing someone(s) with stuff. I don't relate to it. But it's real. I write this chapter from a place of compassion for anyone who has difficulty with any issues associated with loss.

Mayo Clinic provides the following information on their website:

"Hoarding disorder is a persistent difficulty discarding or parting with possessions because of a perceived need to save them. A person with hoarding disorder experiences distress at the thought of getting rid of the items. Excessive accumulation of items, regardless of actual value, occurs.

Hoarding often creates such cramped living conditions that homes may be filled to capacity, with only narrow pathways winding through stacks of clutter. Countertops, sinks, stoves, desks, stairways and virtually all other surfaces are usually piled with stuff. And when there's no more room inside, the clutter may spread to the garage, vehicles, yard and other storage facilities.

Hoarding ranges from mild to severe. In some cases, hoarding may not have much impact on your life, while in other cases it seriously affects your functioning on a daily basis.

People with hoarding disorder may not see it as a problem, making treatment challenging. But intensive treatment can help people with hoarding disorder understand how their beliefs and behaviors can be changed so that they can live safer, more enjoyable lives."

Those who have suffered a traumatic loss may be more likely to become hoarders than those who haven't. Some people develop hoarding tendencies after experiencing a stressful life event that they had difficulty coping with, such as the death of a loved one, divorce, eviction or losing their possessions in a fire, according to The Mayo Clinic.

When someone is taken from you, you want their things. There are huge holes to fill. In my work, I see many moms who have lost a child, whether 5 years or 25 years old. Throughout this time of grieving, they have kept their child's room completely intact. While this is not considered hoarding, I certainly can see the correlation between the two. When all you have left is things you can see, feel, touch, smell, why would you do any different? On a rare occasion, not only with a child's passing but with other loved ones, often spouses, relatives are immediately invited to take what they want and before the actual funeral, the home is cleared out, property sold or donated. The surviving loved one, wants nothing.

The difference between the three scenarios; increased hoarding, keeping everything as is, or getting "rid" of everything, would in my humble opinion, depend on the survivor's ability to navigate loss at that time. We all grieve differently.

As a child, we get stuff. If we are good, we get a reward. Often that reward is food. I will address that later. We don't typically have to toss our things out. We start accumulating stuff.

Our toybox fills, our stuffed animal collection flows off the bed and onto the floor, and although we always tend to rip the pages out, our bookshelves are continually filled with more books.

We get stuff. It makes us feel good. Since birth. More stuff than we need, but as an infant or child, that's not in our control, it just comes. Birthdays, Christmas, good grades, you name it, here comes more stuff.

Do you have a blanket or teddy bear from your childhood still? Why? That is not a judgmental "why", it is meant to be thought provoking. The answer is because it causes you feel some kind of way.

Often as a child, the first human we lose is a grandparent. We are taught 'they went to Heaven'; they are in the clouds; they have angel wings. Not for me though, I was told my mom was dead, then 5 years later, my Grammie, her mom, actually did die. Then less than 10 years later, my Nannie, who I don't think I really knew, died. I think she had throat cancer. One grandfather was already passed when I was born, and my father's father, I know nothing about. I've seen him, had meals with him, but I know nothing.

Then some of us lose a pet. We are told they have crossed over the rainbow bridge and are frolicking with other pets in a big field. Although I am willing to bet we have all lost a Goldfish. Equally as tragic, much harder for the parent to explain where they "went", as their lifeless body swirls down the toilet bowl.

However, as a child, our recently passed Grammy or Grampy's stuff doesn't end up in our room. We aren't stuffing their silverware in our little child size bureau.

It is learned. It is created. Not taught but learned. Maybe it brings us joy, or peace, or just a really good feeling. Somewhere inside, the "stuff" is realized to bring us a feeling that negates the pain, or loss.

We lose someone, it creates space. Some folks eventually fill the space with another human if they lost a spouse or partner. But you can't fill the parent spot. The surviving parent may find a partner, but you as the child, cannot fill that empty space.

That is when the attempts at feeling good begin. Siblings fighting over this ring or that casserole dish because it is the thing that reminds them the most of their parent who is now gone. I have worked with clients who have experienced a complete breakdown in the family structure when the deceased person's belongings are divided. Often it is over the financial part of the estate, but not always.

Sometimes the breakdown happens when one sibling feels they deserve this or that. They had no control over losing their parent. They want to control what they "get". It is part of the grieving process.

119

My whole life I had felt ripped off! I got a raw deal. My mom was gone when I was just five years old. There was something that this furniture was protecting me from. Being sad? Feeling feelings? Or feeling guilty about getting "rid" of it?

But I did it! Just a couple months ago. A yard sale, Craigslist, and Facebook Market place. Within 3 days, the 'feel good furniture' I had been lugging around throughout all my marriages and homes, was gone. And I was okay. No guilt. No shame. But most importantly, no pain. None. Had I never taken that step, I would never have known that I would be okay without it.

Not only was I okay, but I was also better than okay. I felt free! Wait a minute, free? It is the best way to describe it. Something lifted when the furniture went away. I thought it would hurt. It felt good!

I don't have much experience with hoarding other than 'made for TV' shows that depict those who struggle with the issue of hoarding. Most often it is a void they have tried to fill. Loss of a parent, child, spouse. That's how it starts. But I am here to tell you, there is freedom in letting go of "stuff". Although, I am so far from being a hoarder. But I do struggle with obsessive compulsive disorder. Please don't get all excited thinking, "I knew she had to have issues somewhere." Oh, I sure do have issues, lots of them!!

I don't know if I could clinically be diagnosed with this but can't leave a fork in my sink. I must straighten the magazines, so they line up with each other and the coffee table edge. Is that a thread on the floor? Grab it quick. Someone might come to the door! That's the extent of my OCD. My point is that I don't hoard. I'd be setting myself up for failure with the OCD. Oh, there are more issues, trust me, but for now we are talking about easing pain with "stuff".

And after all, I still have an incomprehensible amount of old silverware. No one, I repeat no one grieves the same. That statement doesn't come from my personal struggles, or friends or family. I work with loss every day. As a Medium I have seen and heard it all. And so, I say again, "no two people grieve the same." There are no rules. No time frame to just "get over it".

# JOHN OF GOD -

I had only heard of the spiritual healer in Brazil known as João de Deus, or John of God, perhaps 10 years before he received his first prison sentence in 2019, following a deluge of sex abuse allegations. He was given a sentence of 19 years and four months for four rapes of different women, according to the court. João Teixeira de Faria drew people from all over the world to his small city two hours west of the capital, Brasilia. He would treat everything from depression to cancer and attended to as many as 10,000 patients per week, performing "Spiritual surgeries".

Hundreds of women, including his own daughter, alleged he regularly engaged in abuse ranging from groping to rape.

Even Oprah visited João de Deus in 2012 to interview him for her talk show and called him "inspiring." After the accusations surfaced, Winfrey issued a statement saying she sympathized with the alleged victims and hoped they receive justice.

João de Deus is facing additional cases related to 10 sex crimes, according to news outlets. He is 79 years old, as of this edit in 2021.

I am including this story in the book for several reasons.

First, Joao had hundreds of thousands of followers or believers. They worshiped him. He was portrayed as a right arm of God. My father didn't have hundreds of thousands of followers, but he had a lot, and they worshiped him as if he was the right arm of God.

Even Joao's own daughter validated his abuse, which was told to be anywhere from groping to rape. You see, it's easy for us to believe someone famous is capable of this type of fall from grace, but why do some folks have a hard time believing this happens right in our small hometown churches, right under their noses. More than one would think. But once, once is too much!

Second, John of God was arrested less than six weeks after my memories began to surface. Only six weeks.

Third, because as you know, I don't believe in coincidences.

I don't need to continue to reference other religious wrongdoings in churches, however, just last year in 2020 a 60 year old Faith Leader of a church in Birmingham was convicted of 24 counts of sexual abuse and rapes. Five of the victims are siblings, abused in their home where church was held, under the guise of religious practice.

And the list goes on. I'm not the judge and jury, by any means. I know only my own story for certain. But I also know, I will shout from the rooftops until the hammer comes down on these men (and women) hiding beneath a religious cloak, in the "House of the Lord."

# FALL FROM GRACE -

Jerry Falwell, Jr has fallen from "grace" finally, as of 3 days prior to this chapter.

Let me start by saying 8/8 was a powerful Lionsgate opening for me and something happened that day that sent me running right back to my laptop. I have so much to say and I'm holding back. Why? Fear? Persecution? Being shunned? This feels hauntingly familiar, as I remember "coming out" of the Psychic Closet as it were.

The Twitter picture that Jerry, Jr. posted himself, shows him and a woman, later claimed to be his wife's assistant, with both of their pants unzipped, with his underwear showing, she appears to have none. Both their shirts hiked up, he has clearly alcohol in his clear cup and later claims it to be a prop for the picture! He didn't take the time to zip up, but he took the time to have a prop? Why a prop? It's not a show.... or is it? He's on his yacht, it said in the caption.

This picture made me nauseous for several reasons. One the underwear, two the "prop", which now makes him a liar as well, and three he had his arm around this woman and his thumb was tucked under her right breast. The girl, she looked a bit uncomfortable.

Their story later claims she is pregnant. Ewww, just ewww. Now, I am all for having a good time, a drink or two and belly showing. BUT not with someone else's spouse, with their pants unzipped. When the reason you have a yacht is because you run a religious school. Someone in this highly revered position is expected to uphold a certain persona. This statement is far from judging, it is fact. I personally don't care what or who he has done. What I care about, is the portrayal some folks have out there in the public, often in the religious sector, which is so far from reality.

Some get "caught", Jimmy Baker. Some "out" themselves, Jerry Falwell, Jr. Some take it to their grave and leave behind them a trail of destruction.

As of this writing, Jerry Falwell, Jr has stepped down from his position as president of the Liberty University, a private evangelical Christian University in Virginia. Formerly known as Liberty Baptist College.

When I saw this picture on 8/8 it screamed to me, "finish the book". People have no idea what goes on under the guise of religion, or church, and no one wants to talk about it. But I sure do!

# MORE –

August 12, 2020 the "technical ending date of the Lionsgate energy", but it continues. Although I think the kaboom part has passed.

"Mary" -not her real name- is a friend of mine. She is also a gifted Medium. I have watched her evolve and expand her gift times 1000, since I have known her. I had asked her to do a Mediumship session for me, in hopes to get information about my mom, dead or alive, here or there, what is the story once and for all.

This wouldn't be the first time we talked about my mom. When I lived in NH, we would have our "witches" together for drinks, snacks and always cards at Mary's home. We often spoke of my mom. No one at circle ever thought mom passed when I was 5, but we didn't know where she was / is. We did have some great laughs though! Her husband, who makes a mean Cosmo by the way, always kept our glasses full! Often, we didn't get much "work" done but it was a great release and we all needed it. They all work at what I refer to as a "secular job" aside from their spiritual work, I don't. Mediumship is my life, my work, my job.

She has been a huge support through all of this. When I had my discovery of abuse on that day in Hawaii, 10/6/18, she was the first person I shared it with. We have since deduced that many light workers have had similar experiences as we had.

Way back, well over a year ago, she asked a friend, also a Medium, what she "got" when she heard the name Grace. The woman, without taking a breath said, "she is alive". But being that our brains couldn't comprehend what she was saying, we figured she meant my mom did NOT die when I was just 5 years old. She went on to say she saw a man with her in the back seat taking her somewhere. Several other Mediums also describe this same action.

And most recently on a whim, Mary showed a picture of my mom and brother to a Medium friend of hers, and the Medium said the same thing, "she is ALIVE, right now she is alive". "Her brother is dead, (my brother) but the mother is alive. Like now. Alive." These words just blew my mind. But I believed. If I didn't believe then I have no business doing this work.

To describe this limbo that I am in, words escape me. To describe the sometimes urgency I feel, would be impossible. To describe the newly discovered grief I have, leaves me breathless, sleepless, and a bit numb.

Just as I need my "helpers" along this bumpy road in my journey, I have those who still need me.

"BUT STILL, LIKE DUST I RISE" *Maya Angelou*

No truer words spoken. As I typed those words "but still like dust I rise", on Friday August 14, 2020, I received the "dreaded call", from an EMT in an ambulance, a mom's worst nightmare. My son had been in a car accident on his way to work. He'd been gone less than 30 minutes, after leaving the house under my pleading for him not to go. "Don't go to work today, please, you are going to get in an accident!" I knew he would, and he did.

Folks in some circles would say I projected that on him, I would counter with, "no, I just knew something was going to happen."

With a swollen and cut up nose, my youngest son lay in that Emergency Room, helpless, bumped and bruised. He showed me where it hurt, I mean isn't that what we always ask our children, "where does it hurt?" He didn't look good. That is the only way I can describe it. Mumbling something about the accident, I realized he had no clue what was going on. The situation had gone from scary to terrifying.

It's Monday today, and I am just getting back to my computer. Primarily because the confusion did not end there in the hospital on Friday. "Are the kids in the car?", he asked with sincere concern. "In this car? No son, they are not with us. You were on your way to work."

"Wait did I work today?" "What day is it?" "Is Mandy with us?" "I have to call Jimmy!" "Did I miss Jason's birthday? No, it's tomorrow, right?"

The accident was, in fact, on his son's birthday. My grandson turned 6 that day, completely unaware of his daddy lying on a stretcher in an emergency room, less than a mile from his workplace. The place he never made it to that day. Although bruised and confused, he did get out of the car and start looking for his kids at the scene. He is always a dad first.

The tow yard smelled like dirty car oil and metal. The hot August sun was beating off of the smashed cars. Whispering "thank you" to his dad in heaven, I approached the car. He walked unsteady as though he had smashed his head on concrete, although that poor head of his has taken a beating since the time he could ride his bike at age 2.

The rearview mirror, hanging from its perch, had been hit SO hard with such force from his head, that it shattered the windshield. Not just cracked. Shattered.

The axle that once held the wheel on the car, lay on the ground with the wheel on an angle, as if confused about direction. The smell of fluids mixed with the junkyard air and the afternoon heat causing my stomach to turn. "Is it totaled?" "Yes, hunny, it's totaled."

Although he had been told at least 20 times, he still had no idea that our amazing neighbor had loaned me her car to get to the hospital. Side note *I never buy a car till I find the exact right one. Even if it has been 5 months!!*

It wasn't just once, I told him the same story several times Friday, Saturday and even a few times on Sunday.

Enter the insurance company.

As we currently wait on many things...... the big one is the police report. Typically, the police report is boring and just something that needs to be handed from one person to another and another and so on. Everything we don't know should be in that report. It was and is my assumption that he hit more than a car, based on the extensive damage to the car. Damage to the car, and damage to him.

The pain increases by the day. Knees, ribs, face.......... Swelling, bruising and confusion. That sums it up. The police report holds the answers, unless his memory comes back before then. I pray that someone saw brake lights. As it stands now, it looks like he was blacked out before the accident.

My mind will always go to his heart. It's been mentioned several times over the past 72 hours, that in a year and a half he will be the same age as his dad was when he passed. We would be 100% oblivious to not think of that in situations like this.

It's 10 pm, 3 days after the accident. I just got the same old text.... "I don't remember".

"And still, I rise."*

# A DAY IN THE LIFE ~

A message received: "So I have to tell you, I got goosebumps!! My aunt came here from New Jersey. We were talking about how we both went to a medium. At different times in different states.

We both got emotional talking about our experience and how great we thought our Medium was.

Well as were comparing our stories, we came to find out .......... YOU were the Medium for both of us!!

I seriously am shocked!! We both got goosebumps and we just couldn't believe the odds that would happen!! I just had to share!

*UPDATE 8/18/20* from client: "I never updated you, but it gets better. My best friend who lives in New Hampshire also had you as her Medium! And when I was telling her the story, she said 'get out of here! She was my Medium too!!'"

New Hampshire, New Jersey and Florida. Ahhh the reach Spirit has!!! I am so blessed!

# HE'S GONE –

April 21, 2008 – It was a chilly spring morning, as I sat with my ever so young, 47 year old brother, the same one who I was forever bandaging up in his younger days. This would be our last conversation, our last hug, the end of our human-to-human interaction. I wouldn't be bandaging him up ever again. I wouldn't be pulling glass from his body again. I wouldn't be covering for him again.

I wiped a tear from his eye as he began his transition home. He asked to be turned around on the couch, so he was facing the window. That would be his exit point. His broken shoulder unphased by the move on the couch.

"I see Grammie, she is waiting for me. Brayden is here too." He turned and looked at me. "Sis, you are special." Assuming he meant I was his favorite, I said "no you are special. You have fought and fought, and now it is okay to go home."

"I can see right through you", he said. Although that sounds like a questionable phrase, he went on to explain "no I can see the TV right through you". Whatever experience my brother was sharing with me at that time, would end up being the beginning of awakening to my gifts and to the fact that it was time to use them.

When he was ready, his heart slowly stopped beating and his soul left through that very window that he had asked to face. I wouldn't trade a minute of this time. Not one. I was alone with him when he passed. There's no surprise there.

Our father had been there earlier that morning, but always true to form, he had left for his own chemo treatment, while knowing these were his son's final hours. Thanks to his chemo, he got a year and 6 days more than Tim did. Diabetes released its grip on my brother Tim that day. Adult onset, insulin dependent, juvenile diabetes is hereditary. This was discovered in his 30's after a close call with a diabetic coma, and near death. How did we not know he had it??

# HE'S BACK –

"Tim was the first to come through in Spirit last week. Mary described him to have a "bowl cut", a term used for his particular hair cut during the 70's and to this day. Later on, a photograph would validate that was the bowl cut she was referring to. Being on the other side "was like sky diving", he shared. A daring fete he had absolutely experienced in life.

Tim was afraid of nothing. Climbing cliffs on the highest of the White Mountains, was a favorite. He jumped out of planes. He hitchhiked across country. I don't know anything he didn't dare to do.

"He will be your guide", Mary said. "All things are possible." He told her about the woman who sits on a bench here in life. He showed Mary the Rte 111 sign as well as NEWfields. Highlighting the NEW. He is giving me important information. I feel it in my gut. (The Route 111 sign ended up being VERY important)

"Secret secret secrets", he blurted out in spirit. Secret seems to be the word of the day, the week, the month. He definitely emphasized the word secret. "Who has the paperwork?" He asked. I asked Mary the burning question; "who was his parents?" To which he responded, "who has the paperwork? Someone knows more than they are saying.

The story of my life.

# WAIT, WHAT??

As I think of Tim, I just remember it being dark, I feel like it was a cold night. My brother Tim waving an old, wrinkled newspaper article around like it was a white flag. But when you've been lied to by your father and the rest of the adults around you for 16 years, for him it was probably more of a red flag! I know it was for me, even back then. "Where did you get that?" My father asked. "Auntie gave it to me. She thought I knew!" he yelled back at him, the pain and confusion, now a white mask, covering his teenage face.

Now I'm not one to judge about adoption, I'm not one to judge about the appropriate time to tell a child that they are adopted, if there ever is a perfect time. But the deception involved with many adoptions can often be perceived as a lie. Especially to a sister such as me, who has had many questions. I took nothing any adult said to me to be true. There is a lot to support that distrust I had. To me, as an 11-year-old, this seemed like one of the worst things that ever happened. One of them.

As a child I learned that lying was a sin. It was drilled into my head many, many, many times. Just one of the many things that I could potentially do wrong and be threatened with hell as my final resting place. Years later, I would receive a letter from the man who "lied' to my brother for 16 years, informing me that I will go to hell if I were to get a divorce. My father. A letter. Mailed from 8 miles away.

Watching my brother's horror that night, it felt like he'd been lied to his whole life. But hadn't he? Not by my mother, she had been "gone" 6 years at this point. But by my father.

Who was his mother? Who was his father? Why didn't they tell him? I didn't have the answers then, I don't have the answers now. I've always said, "not telling someone the truth or avoiding the truth is a lie. As is deception."

My poor ex-husbands wondered why I had trust issues. Tim's discovery of the truth was just the beginning.

Was that article even the truth?

On this warm August day, "in spirit" Tim was very eager and happy to share. You see he had learned a lot of things on the other side. He learned who his mother is, he learned who his father was. He also showed me that there was a lie about the lie. How deep does this go? He went on to show Mary that he and I MAY have the same father, but he has a different mother. Learning that information several times over the past few weeks repeated to me the same way, every time, by several different Mediums, just adds to the confusion, adds to the questions and adds to the lies. I intend to get to the bottom... I intend to get to the truth. My brother said he will guide me.

Enter my father in spirit. Showing Mary clocks, a symbol with a dual message. He and I went to many an antique store and auction to purchase antique clocks to add to his collection. He especially loved the ones with moving eyes. His collection was extensive. It was sold soon after his death. We spent SO MUCH time together those days. He had more than ample opportunity to have a "come to Jesus" moment with me during that time. I also took him to many chemo and doctors' appointments. But not a word of the truth, no apology, nothing .......
until his death bed. And now again in Spirit.

Through her own tears, Mary continues, "about the clocks, he is also showing me it's time to find her, that is the other meaning of him showing me clocks. Time is running out! You were so close. She doesn't have much time."

He went on, in an attempt to right his wrongs, including admitting what he had done to me and what the other men had done to me. "Did you know there were others, Karen?" Mary asked. Yes, I did. I figured it out a bit before this, and then one of them was validated in a reading a couple months ago. Two of the men had the same first name. It clarifies and validates so much, so, so much.

He then asked for forgiveness. "There are things I am not proud of."

He "stepped back" a bit, only to have my grammie, Maggie "step in". I couldn't help but laugh when she stepped up, as I remembered the lunch I had with Mary, when she was talking about something and used a reference point of "like a grandmother named Maggie" in her example. I busted into laughter over my ice cold and much needed margarita, Mary not understanding the laughter, as she had never known my grammie's name prior to that moment.

# GRANDPARENTS –

My grandfather who passed before my birth, had 4 sons and a daughter with his first wife who had died fairly young. Then he married my grammie. They had my mother, as the story goes. However, and this is a BIG "however", my mom had a Massachusetts Social Security number! Seems like a semi-important piece of information. Although, with all the other fabricated stories in my childhood, I'm truly not sure where my mom came from. I'm guessing Massachusetts and not Exeter NH.

You can find almost anything on the world wide web these days. Including the census' from the early 1900's where this oddity is pointed out in the notes. Seems a bit important to me.

Grammie passed when I was 10. She has been described to me as knowing about, and even having something to do with my mother's disappearance. Today, in spirit, she used the phrase "gag order". It makes sense. She tells me through my Medium that my mom sits on a bench. Outside of a building. with nurses in scrubs. She has longer hair. Someone visits her. She showed some numbers. She spoke of a visitor that sees my mom. It is also not the first time I am hearing about this "visitor". The tunnel where she is or was, has come up in readings before.

In New England, a tunnel connecting a medical facility's buildings is not such an anomaly, but it is important.

My grandparents both went on to share some fragmented details and before I knew it, my hour was complete.

But that wouldn't be the ending of amazing messages that day.

I offer Mediumship Mentorship programs a couple times a year. I have had some amazing students go through the program and do some awesome readings. A former client, now a student and also a friend, was due for a little test. Through her trepidation she would deliver a great message for me. I am so proud of all of my students. This day I was super proud of her. We did a Zoom test reading and I got to watch her work.

A tunnel was the first thing she spoke of, using her psychic senses to play out the scene. The old building, the "bench". As she described the building, "no longer used for the same purposes", armed with information discussed with Mary about it earlier, I realized she spoke of the old Portsmouth Hospital in New Hampshire.

# DISASTER –

Nearly 30 years ago, in a longing to fulfill an overwhelming urge to help people, I became a volunteer for the Disaster Services program at the American Red Cross. Eventually it morphed into the paid position of Director of Disaster Services. I traveled all over the country providing relief for victims of disasters. Obviously helping people is what I was here to do, its just the manner of the help that has changed. My disaster assignments were three weeks at a time. I have helped hundreds, if not thousands. I have seen it all. Earthquake, hurricane, tornado, flood, severe winter storm, forest fire, every natural disaster imaginable.

I've also seen manmade disaster. The worst imaginable. Specifically, almost twenty years ago.

We all got calls that day. If I remember correctly, I had a "go bag" always packed. Within hours I would be covered in dust, soot and sobbing nightly, as I sat in my hotel room in New York City. It was 2001 and the Twin Towers had been attacked.

'Not going' wasn't even in my realm of thought. Not for a minute. When I arrived, there was still so much confusion. It would be quite some time before we even had to have any type of ID or clearance. During that time, I put myself in the middle of the commotion. The photos I took that day are forever imbedded in my memory. It's a story I don't tell often. It's a story that I still cannot wrap my head around. I don't need to share the details, we all know. We all have the emotions around it, some of us have different emotions than others. We all felt it.

# RED CROSS –

Home base for the Seacoast Area Red Cross was in Portsmouth. Conveniently located in none other than the old Portsmouth Hospital. I know that building like it's my childhood home. In the hallway by our offices was a dumbwaiter. We loved to hate that thing. Some days it worked, other days you didn't know if you'd spend hours stuck in there. But we needed it. Our supplies, office and disaster, as well as "Resusci Annies" for CPR training, were stored "underground" in what we referred to as the dungeon. The large storage rooms had formerly been used as the morgue for the hospital. It freaked people out but didn't bother me.

Our offices were located on the first floor. The two floors above us housed various community resources offices. Many offices were empty. I absolutely loved my work with the Red Cross. Part of working in the Disaster Services Dept, was the Mass Care service we would provide to emergency workers, feeding, water, and support.

In 1997 the whole world had eyes on Portsmouth Police Department as they searched for a 10 year old child's body from Massachusetts to later be found in Maine. During the search, emergency services and law enforcement from 1000's of miles away, converged on the Portsmouth Police Department. One whole wing of the former hospital housed the Police Department with its various offices for their staff. We were charged with feeding those who were helping during this horrific search. It was then that I learned about the tunnel. There was a large meeting room where Emergency Operations Center would have their briefings. The tunnel joined our side of the former hospital building with the City Offices and Police Department. The tunnel was the easiest and fastest way to get food from our side to theirs. We made great use of it during this horrific incident.

While my student so aptly described the building, the tunnel, the room where "people weren't aware she was there", in my mind I walked through the tunnel I knew so well, "almost all the way down the hall, turn left a little". She had given me directions on how to get from the Red Cross to the PD when I worked in that very building. She "spoke" of shock wave treatments, medication and visits from 'him'. Several visits to be exact, and mentioned payments that were involved. She tried to converse; she was always looking for us. Brushing hair like she used to brush mine when I sat on the floor in front of the couch. A memory that I actually retained from my childhood. Brushing and singing. Brushing and singing.

"This Little Light of Mine, a song that I hear in my head so often, is just one of the 'ditties' she sang to help her survive when she was in the dungeon", said my student. My ears must be deceiving me!! I swear she just said "DUNGEON"! The exact name that I, and all the other workers called the downstairs of the old hospital that housed the Red Cross as well as many other City offices.

Somewhere between there and wherever she is now, she tried to call me. Four kids she had, and it was me she called. Tears streamed down my face! "The call", from 20 years ago, the call when she spoke my name and said she was my mom, and that her name was Grace. She 'told' my student that it was okay that I didn't know it was her on the phone that day. "It was okay."

How would it have turned out if I had done more than look in a couple nursing homes at that time? I wondered often about that. But when you have been convinced that your mother was dead for 30 years prior to "the call", why would anyone believe it was truly their mom on the phone that day? I have played out many different scenarios in my head since then, and even more so over the past year.

141

She again referenced sitting in the chairs outside and that she isn't "hidden" now. The records were ruined. I guess that part went without saying. I've been told more than a dozen times "there must be records" "records" "records" ~ I knew in my heart of hearts there was no records. There never has been. I never even knew her fabricated "cause of death" until the 90's.

The sheep was something I know my student was hesitant to mention that night. Why? Well, if I were the reader, I'd be asking my guides what sheep had to do with anything. Not far from the old hospital, on a rural residential road, daily I'd pass the house set not far back from the road, on my way to the office, the one house in the city that was home to sheep. Joy referencing "sheep" made total sense to me. Relief came over my student's face.

"She brushes hair. Is it a styling head from days gone by? Is it a toy horse's mane? If I see her, I will know. When I find her, when I see her, I will know." She said that I can ask "PA". Everything is something. I tell all my students and clients that… "everything is something". "Please don't spend too much time trying to convince them", she went on. "Everybody has their story. Other family members don't have the capacity. But you are not content, until she is found."

> Two roads diverged in a yellow wood,
> And sorry I could not travel both
> And be one traveler, long I stood
> And looked down one as far as I could
> To where it bent in the undergrowth.
> Then took the other, as just as fair,
> And having perhaps the better claim,
> Because it was grassy and wanted wear;
> Though as for that the passing there
> Had worn them really about the same,
> And both that morning equally lay
> In leaves no step had trodden black.
> Oh, I kept the first for another day!

Yet knowing how way leads on to way,
I doubted if I should ever come back.
I shall be telling this with a sigh
Somewhere ages and ages hence:
Two roads diverged in a wood, And I -
I took the one less traveled by,
and that has made all the difference.
~Robert Frost~

This poem hung in my mother's bedroom. It now hangs in my bedroom and many other places as well. I have always made it a point to take the road less traveled by. I have always been the one to question and doubt everything that has been said to me, no matter who has said it.

"Your brother Tim, in spirit, has visited her." I'm excited to hear this for the second time today, that he will help me connect the dots.

Still in my 'test' session, which my student definitely passed with flying colors, the room gets cold as it did earlier when my father 'came in'. "He really isn't happy about the truth coming out, but he does have some remorse. He goes on to show me that there is so much that is going to be revealed. It is going to be uncovered. "I am going to be exposed!" "He is still working on these things on the other side. He still has a lot to do. He is working thru a lot. He lived a life of deceit. A lot of wrongs on a lot of levels. His soul is tainted still." This coincides so much with what my Hawaiian healer had shared.

Throughout this last year and a half journey of sorting through the last 50+ years of my life, answers have brought questions, almost as much as questions have brough answers. It doesn't stop here. It doesn't stop till I uncover the truth. All of it. With every ounce of my being here at 10pm on August 19, 2020, I 'pray' for clear understanding and awareness to find my mother. I just need to see her, even if from a distance. She will know. She's like me. She knows things. I leave for New Hampshire in 3 days.

# THANKSGIVING DAY 2020

It has been a wild ride since I last wrote, 3 months ago. Today I have so, so, so much to be grateful for. But I also have 3 months to account for. I went to New Hampshire back in August, right after the last time I wrote in this book. I drove to the facility in Hampton, that I was so drawn to. I came in the back way. The way in that I knew as a young person in Hampton. After seeing rainbow signs steadily for 2 weeks prior to my trip, it was no surprise that there were rainbows in almost every window in the place. There were so many signs there that day, even I was blown away.

*note – I will not be sharing exact locations I visited, due to the fact that as of the writing of this book, my family knows nothing of this search. Yet. *

I feel as though I spent most of the day there. I had packed all the notes from the readings that I had prior to leaving. One of the things that stood out the most, was stopping my search to have some lunch at Lamie's Inn and Tavern, a Hampton landmark for my entire life. My favorite room at the Inn is the Goody Cole room.

I later traveled to Portsmouth, remembering of course, my way to the police station, as it sits in the building I had worked in for many years. The same building that MANY Mediums have described as the place my mom was put when she was first taken from me.

Over the past few months, I have had a few readings. More than one Medium has described a place where folks were taken when they suffered any type if mental health differences. I refer to it that way, as it wasn't like it is today, with thousands of forms, permissions, tests, etc. to get someone "committed". Back in 'the day' many were put into institutions based on any type of 'different' behavior, that may have made a spouse or other family member uncomfortable.

Historically, until the mid-1960s in most jurisdictions in the United States, all committals to public psychiatric facilities and most committals to private ones were involuntary. Since then, there have been alternating trends towards the abolition or substantial reduction of involuntary commitment,[5] a trend known as "deinstitutionalization" *Wikipedia*

As I pulled into the Safety Complex in Portsmouth, many memories of my tenure with the American Red Cross rushed through my mind. There were local disasters, national disasters that I had been dispatched to all over the country, and day to day office work, and disaster relief planning.

Pushing all of that from my mind, I retraced the layout of that building, including the "dungeon", the basement where we stored supplies, once housed the Portsmouth Hospital Morgue.

"The Portsmouth Cottage Hospital was the first hospital built in the city of Portsmouth, New Hampshire. Opened in 1884, it was one of the first hospitals in New Hampshire, and it served as the city's primary hospital facility until 1986, when Portsmouth Regional Hospital opened. Its 1895 campus has been repurposed to house city offices and the police station, and a senior living facility. A portion of that facility, representing its oldest buildings, was listed on the National Register of Historic Places in 1996.[1]

# HISTORY

The Portsmouth Cottage Hospital was founded in 1884 and was an outgrowth of charitable impulses that included the operation of almshouses for the poor and needy, and the provision of care for wounded veterans of the American Civil War. The driving force in its founding was Harriet Kimball, the daughter of a local pharmacist. The hospital was originally located at 51 Court Street, in a large house now located in the Strawberry Banke museum complex. That building quickly proved inadequate as a hospital facility, and fundraising began in 1889 for construction of a proper dedicated facility.[2]

Land for the new facility was purchased on the south side of the South Mill Pond, and the core of the hospital complex, a 2-1/2 story brick building designed by Boston architect Harry Ball, was opened in 1895. *The hospital was run as a secular charity, providing a significant number of patient stays at no or reduced cost. It received a small amount of funding from the city until 1903. The main building was enlarged several times before 1962, when a more modern facility was built directly adjacent. At that time, the old building was converted to house an outpatient mental health clinic as well as hospital administrative offices. The entire complex was acquired in 1983 by the for-profit Hospital Corporation of America (HCA). HCA opened the Portsmouth Regional Hospital in 1986, closing the old campus.[2]*

The city purchased the campus in 1986. The 1962 building and a former nurses' housing building were adapted to house city offices and its main police station.[2]"

146

Based on what other mediums have said and the synchronicity that I actually worked in that building for several years, I am 99% sure she has been there.

On to several other facilities in Rye and Portsmouth NH. All of them to be exact. I drove to each and every facility that my mother could potentially be at, throughout the New Hampshire Seacoast. He wouldn't have made the effort to take her any further. I ruled out most of them. My mind fixated on one in Hampton and one in Exeter.

I would leave unsuccessful, this trip. Lots of signs, more than I had imagined, but nothing concrete. I look back and laugh at myself for actually going to the door of one of the facilities, thinking maybe just maybe, I'd get in and just have a "look see" around the facility. I was turned away. Covid felt as though it would put a choke hold on what I was aiming to accomplish. HOW would I ever get in one of these places? Family members of the residents have had to do window visits for months. Now what?

I thought about her every day. There was something about feeling like I was getting closer. Like it was really going to happen. Would I find my mother? What if I did find her? Would she know me? How would I get into the nursing home or memory care? What would I say? What would she say? How would she know it was me? Would she ask for my siblings? Does she know Tim died? Does she know my father died? Does she have her memory? Had she been subjected to the medical procedures done back in the 60's to people who were deemed mentally different? Would I ask so many questions or would I freeze? Would she ask so many questions? Would she freeze?

During two months prior to my next visit up to New Hampshire, I needed to work real hard. I had done a lot of work on forgiveness. A lot. My focus had been primarily on forgiving what had been done to me by those I trusted. By those "men of God", my father - the pastor and the "deacons". What had I ever done to deserve this vulgar treatment? The answer is nothing. Try telling a child who has been assaulted that. Or a woman who has recently brought forth these horrific memories.

"Forgive them for they know not what they do." Luke 23:24

As part of my journey and soul searching, I spent a lot of time wondering WHY?? I felt I needed answers to the lies and crimes committed when I was a child. Maybe I do. But those involved, those who committed the crimes and told the lies are dead. Well, the majority are. It's up to me to find answers. Although I am well aware, it changes nothing.

Today, as in when I saw the Jerry Falwell, Jr news, I felt like more and more pastors are being exposed. The news is saying, Carl Lentz, formerly of Hillsong Church in NY, has been fired from the church and accused of having an affair. No one is too sacred. No one is a saint.

While searching for answers, the main question I am left with is "how could this man, upheld so high by his church, do the things I remember him doing, as well as the things I believe he did to my mom?"

*"Most of the perpetrators of child abuse (neglect, physical abuse, and sexual abuse) were family members. For example, 80.8% of (instance-based count, rather than person-based) perpetrators were parents, 5.9 percent were relatives other than parents, and 4.4 percent were unmarried partners of parents. In addition, the perpetrators included sibling, victim's boyfriend or girlfriend, babysitter, other caretakers, and strangers. There is no indication that the pattern of offenders of sexual abuse, which accounted for 9.1% of the cases, differed from the general one. The data is also consistent with the practitioners' observation about sex abuse perpetrators. As reported in American Psychological Association website, the majority of sexual offenders are family members or are otherwise known to the child." *Psychology Today*

*A study of victims of father–daughter incest in the 1970s showed that there were "common features" within families before the occurrence of incest: estrangement between the mother and the daughter, extreme paternal dominance, and reassignment of some of the mother's traditional major family responsibility to the daughter. Oldest and only daughters were more likely to be the victims* *of incest. It was also stated that the incest experience was psychologically harmful to the woman in later life, frequently leading to feelings of low self-esteem, very unhealthy sexual activity, contempt for other women, and other emotional problems.[98]" \*Wikipedia*

# "PROCESS OF SEXUAL ABUSE

## FATHER

*Before the sexual abuse starts the father is nurturing, caring and supportive of his daughter. Over time this nurturing turns into sexuality. Often the sexual abuse starts as incidental touching. This can be things like he becomes aroused when his daughter sits on his knee, "accidentally" rubbing up against her or brushing against her bottom or breasts. The most common form of incidental touching is through wrestling. The father "accidentally" puts his hand between his daughter's legs or brushes against her breasts etc. The daughter may be aware of this but often the child isn't even aware, but the offender is sexually aroused and aware of what is happening. During times of wrestling if there is incidental touching and the mother is in the room, the daughter may wonder why the mother isn't saying anything, why she is letting him do this to her daughter. The mother is most likely not aware it is happening. This causes more strain between the mother and daughter and reduces the trust the daughter has in the mother to protect her.*

*Generally, something will happen, and the father will become extremely stressed and then there will be a fight with his spouse. He will then be drawn to his daughter, the only one he believes loves him, and he will sexually offend against her. After this first incident, he will be disgusted with what he has done and swear to himself he will never do it again. Sexually offending is a way he releases the stress he was under but then when he realizes what he has done his stress level increases again because he has to deal with what he has done. The stress continues to build and build and then he ends up offending*

150

*again. This cycle continues. The father has maladaptive ways of coping with stress and his boundaries are blurred......*

*Once the father has offended against his daughter, he will work very hard a creating a relationship with the victim to try to ensure she doesn't tell. He will work at continuing to distance the relationship between the daughter and everyone else in the family......."* \*adapted from Families of Sexual Abuse: The Roles Each Member Plays. by Sabrina Trobak M.A.C.P., B.Ed -August 11, 2011

There are many things that fall into place for me in regard to abusers, and my abuse. My personal reference points are many, although most not suitable to discuss precise details here.

In addition, I have another deceased family member, convicted of molesting two or more young family members. So, to me, nothing is farfetched. To some those who knew my father, and the church, it may be too scary to believe what they were capable of. To others, they know all too well. Those are the ones that I want this book to reach.

Over the past two years since my original discovery of my sexual abuse, I have had so many questions that will go unanswered. Why did my father apologize right before he left this earth? Was another family member and abuser? Were they abused at home as well?

*"Researchers have found incestuous fathers to be quite diverse. Characteristics which appear repeatedly in descriptions of these fathers include poor impulse control, overdependency and desertion anxiety, low self-esteem, insensitivity to the needs of others, an endogamous family orientation, and a **history of having witnessed abuse or having been physically and/or sexually abused as well as emotionally deprived and rejected in their families.** A bipolar personality pattern has been observed: at one extreme, fathers who are passive, meek, and rather ineffectual; at the other, fathers who are dominant, tyrannical, and controlling. **Some of these fathers have stable employment** histories yet others are chronically unemployed. **Some are professional men—"pillars of the community"— who lead private lives far different from their public personae.** Others have public and private lives*

*that are less at odds—they may be known for explosive tempers and aggressive behavior. Gross psychopathology has been found in only a small percentage of these fathers. By and large, since they do not seem to differ significantly from the profile of the average man who is generally in good psychological health, their pathology has been termed "restricted" (Wells, 1981). However, as is the case in incest research in general, the research on abusers is seriously flawed both conceptually and methodologically (Finkelhor, 1986), making this information preliminary".* *http://www.survivorshandbook.com/the-incestuous-family/*

# HIS PARENTS –

I remember his parents. My paternal grandparents. We saw them at Thanksgiving and MAYBE once or twice a year. I'm not even sure that it was that often, I remember only Thanksgiving. Per GPS today, they lived 50 miles away, less than an hour trip. I also remember the drama around that trip, not so sure that my father even wanted to go. I don't remember it being that exciting, but I know my brother loved it. It was, however, one of the few times we went anywhere as a family. I don't remember my grandfather ever speaking or smiling. The family dynamics were extremely strange, looking back now. My grandmother made the meal, I don't think I ever saw her smile, either.

The house was filled with "boarders". Typically, men, that had nowhere else to go. Some were allowed to be around us, most weren't. We weren't allowed upstairs; I feel now it's because that is where the boarders were. I try hard to recollect those few visits but there is EXTRAORDINARILY little there to pull up. Much like most of my memory, there seems to be nothing there.

I have attempted to try really hard to remember my grandparents. I remember sights, sounds, smells, but not interaction, not emotion, and definitely no affection. I don't know that hugs were freely given or given at all. I remember wanting to stay out of Nannie's way, so always being in another room. I have no idea when or how my grandfather died, but I know Nannie died when I was a teenager, which meant all my grandparents were gone before I was 20. As was my mother.

153

Feeling unwanted or in the way, was the extent of emotional connection to most adults in my young life. Well …. aside from the abusers. But that made it even more twisted. I know Tim didn't feel that way, but if I try to analyze it now, it seems to be in response to the secret adoption and making sure he was not feeling less than. Secrets = Lies.

In my adult life, I have said to more than one person, specifically my husband(s) and children, keeping secrets is the same as lying. Then when it comes out, it will feel like a lie.

My father always referred to his brother Carl and his sister Julie, as adopted brother and adopted sister. Yet he never referred to his oldest son as his adopted son. Intentional? Maybe. Deceptive? Absolutely!

An adopted sibling is a sibling in my world. I have never thought any less than about my late brother, nor would I have, if I had known. I don't know who July and Carl's biological parents are, but I know my Nannie got them when they were 3 or 4. I often wonder if that is another missing piece of the puzzle. Were they Pop's kids, yet not Nannie's? I think at this point anything is possible. I think I will leave that stone unturned.

I think of Tim's death, how was it so easy for the rest of the family to just leave him that morning when he was dying? Did they connect to him less? Because he was adopted? Let me put some stats out there. Tim was 6' 4" tall, thin with hazel eyes. My father, his supposed "adoptive father", was 6'4" tall, thin, with hazel eyes. Any deductions from that statement are logical.

Today is the first day of the year 2021 ~ I found out over the holidays that my "adopted Uncle died maybe two or so years ago"?? I address this topic again. Why is he and his sister different? Why are they referred to as adopted? My brother was never referred to as any less than. And although my interpretation may be skewed, why is it any different? I was told it was an age thing, that they were originally foster kids to my grandmother and then she adopted them. A fact that I also find quite interesting, since I feel she didn't care much for us……. Was it financial?

Which is not meant to be derogatory, however, I still beg the question. My grandmother took in "everybody"! I knew this already, but it was confirmed recently.

I remember not being allowed upstairs because of the less than honorable men upstairs. While I utterly understand her stance in needing money but as a grandmother who currently has grandchildren living in her house, I cannot imagine allowing "less than favorable" men or any men, for that matter, to live in my home. I remember some of the men. In all states of disrepair. I do remember going up those stairs. We snuck up. The smell was enough to send us right back down. I often can't help but wonder, and I do often wonder, were the males (and/or females) in my family molested? Were they molested by one of the "boarders"? Or was it a family member who molested his children, and that's how they turned out that way. It doesn't just start in a family line out of nowhere. That is my belief anyway.

As I study more and more about ancestry, I am painfully aware that men who abuse, have been abused. Their whole life is a lie. They kept secrets but acted out later on in life on their own children, nieces, nephews and the list is endless. I don't blame, I wonder why. I don't hate, I actually feel bad for them.

I live in a time where not only is it okay to tell, but it is encouraged. Coming out of 2020 and its recently publicized molestation cases, with more coming to light daily, I don't want to "jump on that bandwagon."

What I do want most of all, is to encourage others to speak their truth. Men and women alike. I don't pretend to know all the details, but what I do remember of my childhood, and what I am aware of that my now deceased uncle did, (yes, he was prosecuted and found guilty), I know that secrets can be nails in a coffin.

My secrets could have ended me. I had pre cervical cancer cells. I know why. My first encounter with a male, was apparently not my "first", I learned as a teen. Without being graphic, you know. But I never "knew "until I woke up that day, 10/6/2018. The day I began to remember. The day my eyes opened (literally) in Hawaii. The day that would forever change my life. The day, that "the book" ended up telling the story, ALL OF IT! There are so many components to my story. But the most important one is that I truly feel like I have forgiven. I don't know what my siblings know. I don't know what they remember. What I do know, is that learning last week that my little brother wants nothing to do with me, has released me in a way, to be even more free.

# HURT –

I have not set out to hurt anyone with this book. I have set out to free others, those who may not even be aware of their own abuse prior to reading this book. Those who know but haven't told a soul. I set out to tell the truth as it has never been told in my family. The truth about my sexual abuse, the truth about the church that to me felt like a cult, the truth about my mother, and the truth that will be healed. Not just for myself, but for those who walked before me, male and female, and those who come after me. My children, my grandchildren, and their children. The lies, the secrets, the pain stops here.

I know there will be family members who accuse me of lying. Of making things up. And that I am going to hell (won't be the first time I've heard that!). Accuse me of trying to hurt the family. To that, I am here to say, THE HURT WAS ALREADY DONE!!! I AM HERE FOR THE HEALING.

I am resigned to the fact that by writing this book, I will potentially lose the only living sibling that I have a relationship with. The last time I met them for lunch in 2020, as I hugged them goodbye, I knew it would be the last time. For the one sibling who does care about me, they will be okay. For the thousands of girls, women, boys and men who have secrets, family secrets, church related secrets, I do this for you. For stopping the cycle. For my kids, my descendants. Also, for my ancestors, to release them from any shame and trauma that they have endured.

It is not my job to make my story okay for people. To sugar coat it. To pretend it didn't happen, as the rest of them have. It's my job to expose the wrongdoings, so that others can remember, just as I did, and start their healing. That is what brings me peace, facilitating healing.

People expect me to be mad. Angry at the abusers. I feel sorry for them. They are sick, not me. They will be held accountable for this in the afterlife, not me. They have had rough lives, not me. Because when all is said and done, I know the truth. And as a famous book says, "the truth shall set you free!"

I have all the information I need to move ahead. I have found the strength somewhere to not only write this book, but to know it will be public. I don't have to worry about what others think. How it affects them. My only concern is myself and my family, comprised of my children and grandchildren.

My heart rips out with every word that I type. The healing, for me, and I hope for you as well, is in the pain. We learn to restructure that pain and do something with it. This book is what I have done, for me and also for you.

# DICK –

Social media has been all the buzz with stories of abuse. I wholeheartedly believe the stories. I believe someone with childhood trauma can live in complete denial and totally unaware of the abhorrent things that happened to them. Not intentionally, but because our minds protect us. I believe this because it's true. It is MY truth. Based on my life. That's why we are here together. I'm writing, you are reading. Not for the gory details, or to place blame, but to draw awareness to the fact that I am not the only little girl that survived this. We are here to heal together.

What exactly does a life of lies create for adulthood? The inability to trust. Quite often the inability to trust the person of the opposite sex, or depending on personal relationship preference, the same sex, as the abuser(s). There are many reasons I don't trust. Abuse and believing my mother was dead, are just a few of them.

As I unpack these things, and feel the pain so deep, I realize that there are many life choices that I made that are a textbook response to childhood abuse.

As I mentioned, my first real boyfriend, was my first and only abuser in my adult life. He hit me on many occasions, hand, fist, baseball bat, and whatever he could find. I wanted so badly to be loved, so badly to receive attention from him, that I truly did not know better. He was on the football team. Girls were so envious of me. Envious of what they could see on the outside.

People ask why didn't you leave? Abuse is abuse. Physical, sexual, emotional, mind control, financial control.......it is all abuse. After experiencing all of this as a child, and being conditioned to believe this was actually love, in some weird, twisted way, why leave? To some that statement would make no sense. But it's reality.

The very last time he laid hands on me, I will never forget. I was the only one who worked and made money during the entire relationship. Short of a couple months when he worked for the town, but had no license, so I drove him there and picked him up, while still holding down a full-time job. I don't even know what set him off this day in particular, it could have been anything, it could have been nothing. But as my protection angels would have it, my best friend in elementary school had moved into the apartment next door. Prior to this day, she had told me that she hears everything and will call the cops one day. She wasn't kidding.

When he was bad, it wasn't a one-day thing. It could go on for a couple days at a time. The day prior I had locked him out of my apartment. I call it mine because he never gave me a dime towards anything. I came home from work to find him standing in my kitchen. In the dark.

When you live with an abuser, and you try a "stunt" like locking them out, they find the strength and ability to get in. It is, as he claims, a "blackout" when they supposedly don't remember their actions. As strange as it sounds, I would never advise this if you were in a similar situation, as it is a trigger. If you do try this, be sure you don't come home alone, and make sure you have a cell phone in hand. We didn't have cell phones back in the 80's and after I spotted him, that was the first thing he did. Rip the phone cord from the wall. I assumed this was it. I was going to die.

It's hard to describe someone's face when they are in that state. I compare it to coming face to face with a bear. Only a bear I would probably try to outsmart.

After taking me to my knees with his then "best friend's" cane, his football player frame, with "blackout abuser' force pushed my 120-pound body to my bed. Where he then attacked me. I was quiet. I'd been here before. Better to be quiet, so you don't get in trouble for being bad. Does it make sense to you? Maybe not. But at that point in time, survival is the only thing that is reeling through your mind. That is, if your mind is even present still. Victims often speak of blacking out during sexual assaults. This is their mode of protection, especially as a child. However, it also attributes to the blank spaces in their memory, of which I seem to have many.

He wouldn't leave. I begged him to just leave. He never saw the "wrong" in his actions. Even to this day he doesn't (I'll explain more later).

The following morning was a Saturday. I know that because I didn't get up to go to work, while he did nothing all day. I still had no house phone. He didn't unplug it, he destroyed it, the night before. He was not done. It is so interesting, there are places that I have lived that I cannot remember the exact layout, yet this apartment, I remember every square inch. I remember the bathroom was not a safe place. That is clear. Have you ever walked into your home, what is supposed to be your safe place, and wondered if you would live to see tomorrow? I have.

Again, another recollection of "I don't know what set him off", but he was loud. I remember hearing glass shattering. At this point, I didn't have many breakables left. The one attack that morning that I do remember, was his hands wrapped tightly around my neck. I only remember that, because it would be the topic of discussion, many times after that. My neighbor yelled, "the cops are coming" and he was gone. Had I known that was his exit invitation, I would have had her yell it every day prior.

I opened the door to the loud banging, only after seeing the 2 cruisers parked below my second-floor window in the center of the little town I grew up in. The sub shop below would not be open at this time, and I was deeply concerned about who knew, who heard............. more concerned than that of my own survival. "How did you get those handprints on your neck ma'am?" "I don't know, I responded."

I know, I know, armchair critics and analysts reading this right this moment are yelling in their heads, or even out loud, "tell them! Why didn't you tell them? This is your opportunity! They will keep you safe!" No, they won't. They can't. A restraining order is a piece of paper, not an arsenal of armed guards. I would learn this more than once in my adult life.

What is his name? What did he do? There were broken things on the floor, it was obvious that an attack had taken place, and I was the recipient. A throbbing black eye was developing at that point as well. You know............. that weird color that starts when you can't determine if it's from crying or being hit? "Ma'am if you don't tell us everything, there isn't a thing we can do for you." "I understand that sir, but if I do, he will kill me".

Understanding the mind of a survivor of physical and sexual abuse is not something in our DNA. Our literal mind says, "well its really easy. Tell someone. Lock the door. Do this. Do that."

If you are not playing in the Super Bowl, you don't know what the best play would have been. If you haven't been in a dangerous, abusive situation, you also don't know what the best play would have been. It's all a gamble. A survivor can't get into the abuser's mind, a fan cannot be on the football field. Those are facts. Yes, there are variables in each play, there are variables in each abuse situation. Keep in mind, I had seen this man pull a knife on his brother. I had seen bloody brawls in his family's home. This was not new to him. Conflict and fighting were his norm.

Some variables that played into my abuse situation, began with family. My father hardly spoke to me because I was "living in sin". His wife never spoke to me. I was the "black sheep". The one who spoke up. The one who knew there were other ways to look at issues, religion, and life in general. I wasn't quiet about those things. I am not quiet still, and here we are.

Often survivors of abuse, aren't able to turn to family for many reasons. Abusers, whether physical, emotional, or sexual, use control as a tactic for having a constant upper hand. They often move or attempt to separate their target (typically a spouse or partner) from their family. They tell their target person that their family doesn't care.

He didn't have to do that. I knew. My siblings had their own lives. My father "didn't want to hear this stuff" a phrase that my brother used so many times in his adult life. Afterall, if you don't know, it's not happening, right?? Wrong. But what if you know? What if you know and still allow your child to live like this?

Please know that if my father had attempted to intervene, that I may not have accepted his help. I did walk out of his house on my 18$^{th}$ birthday, vowing to never return. It had been my plan since he got married a couple years prior. I won't talk here about his marriage, but I will say this, it was NOT a home I cared to live in for a minute longer than I had to.

# FAMILY –

Those who do have a loving caring family to turn to, often don't. They are embarrassed, ashamed, and fearful of rejection. I didn't have that. So that never entered the equation. "Oh, but you're a minister's daughter." My point, exactly.

Additionally, with all that took place when I was a little girl, why would I walk back into that house? Yes, a different physical house, but the dynamic was still there.

The police took a report. They made their own assumptions. They knew that he would be on foot, whoever he was. I didn't want him caught. The fallout from that would have probably ended my life. I was only 19.

I used the neighbor's phone. I chuckle as I write this, that one call would forever change my life. That seems overly dramatic to some, but to me, had I made that call to anyone else, I wouldn't be sitting where I am this moment, listening to our grandchildren do "distance learning" upstairs in the little 'offices' our son made for them.

I couldn't even speak through the sobs. I had held it together for the police, but as I asked his mom if I could speak to him, I lost it. Suddenly I had emotions. Up until that point, I hadn't shed a tear in the previous 72 hours. She sounded so caring, so motherly. No one had sounded caring to me in my life.

She put him on the phone. "I'm coming to get you; you'll stay here tonight." I will never forget the words of my abuser's BEST friend that day. He did pick me up that day. I did stay at his parent's house with him that night, on the couch. Safe. With people who cared. That warm spring day changed my life.

We would be engaged by November. My "knight in shining armor", as I called him, and I, would be married June of the following year. Welcoming our first-born son, the following January, and our daughter, in June just two short years after our wedding day. He had a baby when we met, so we had an instant family. We now have 6 amazing grandchildren and I know he smiles down on all of them from Heaven.

I would later have another daughter, to bring my current stats to 4 children, 3 birthed, 1 blessed. Six grandchildren. Five birthed, one blessed.

Unfortunately, that wasn't the end of the trauma. My "knight" lovingly convinced me to move to my father's house while we were courting and later engaged. To start out right, and to save money. So I would be safe. So he didn't have to worry. Afterall, I had a beeper. He could beep 143 to me day and night. I'd know he was just on the other side of our little town. If you had a beeper, you knew the "code". Again, I chuckle.

I hadn't been staying at my father's house for long, when I was awoken in the middle of the night. The banging on my bedroom window put me in such a state of horror that I would remember this night as one of my most frightening. "If I don't let him in, he will break the window and get me," is all that was running through my mind. I will never forget his words that night, nor the words of my father. Were my abuser's words scarier, or the fact that my father wanted to know what I thought 'he was supposed to do about it', while I was screaming for him to wake up and help me!

"Oh, I don't know, PROTECT me! For once in my goddamn life, protect me!" A genetic trait that he seems to have handed to his son as well, ignorance. If you don't look or listen, it's not happening.

My father's house was a typical New England cape. We hadn't grown up here, we had moved here shortly after his marriage, as my childhood home was apparently then not "good enough". Three bedrooms upstairs. A bathroom across from the top of the stairs. His bedroom to the left of that, and my room and my brothers' room, to the right. Almost the exact footprint of my "knight's" house.

My abuser, we will call him Dick, as I am quite honestly sick and tired of calling him "MY" anything, as I have no attachment to him.

The back of the garage was low enough to the ground that a tall guy like my big brother, could boost himself up to climb on it, as he had done before. Someone like Dick would need something to stand on. Which he managed to find that night in the dark. He set the remainder of his 6 pack down near to the roof and made his stealthy climb up. The boys' window faced the backyard. Mine faced the driveway. Although drunk, a typical condition for him to be in, he was successful climbing the roof of the back of the garage, onto the steeper front of the garage roof, and up to my window. I'd be lying if I said, "good thing he didn't fall".

He failed me again. My father would not call the police. Afterall, what would the neighbors think? What would the church folks think? What if someone found out? His thought process for every situation in my life.

I grabbed the 1980's handheld phone and did it myself. I quickly let Dick know that I was on the phone with the cops. He so stealthily disappeared again, this time into the night. The half spent 6 pack left behind for the police. This time, I spilled it. I vomited out all the details, whatever they wanted to know. His name, age, parent's address, and a lot of the rest of the story, leading up to that night. It made no difference. Not to me and at this point, not to him. I wouldn't see him again, or so I thought.

# THE KNIGHT –

I pause here because the next years of my life are a big part of my life. If my knight were still alive, I would absolutely gain his permission to speak about the next 14 years of our lives, both good and bad. But because he passed when our kids were young and because he can't agree or disagree to some things I would say about him, me, us, I have opted not to. His siblings and I don't speak, and his parents passed over the last few years. I have our children and grandchildren and that is what is important now. Not rehashing our life. This book is about lies, and trauma and healing that trauma. None of that applies to our lives. To his death, absolutely, and I will speak to that, but not his life.

I don't consider him 'gone' most days, as we have children and grandchildren that remind me of him daily. In appearance and action, and even some of the phrases they come out with. I hate the hole it left in their lives, as well as our grandchildren never meeting him, but it was all part of the plan. It was his journey, our journey.

Unfortunately, there would be three more encounters with Dick, one being just 2 years ago.

It was 1983. I was working at a local insurance company. Just one short mile from Dick's family home, where I assume he was living. Just ½ mile from my then fiancé's house. Dick must have heard about the engagement. I don't remember much about that day, other than being ready to leave work for the day, looking out the window of my office, and there, just off the driveway in the field by my building, was my soon to be husband, beating the air out of Dick.

We had purposely stayed away from Dick. However, this day, my fiancé must have had an inkling that there would be trouble and came to meet me after work, only to find Dick near my car. I truly don't know what caused the altercation, but I would assume it was Dick's short stature and big mouth!

I also don't know what would have happened if my fiancé hadn't shown up that day. I don't know what would have happened if he hadn't picked me up at my apartment when I was all tattered and torn. I don't know. But what I do know, is everything is meant to be. When someone shows up, on a white horse or not, it is meant to be. We don't need to know why. We just need to trust.

# AGAIN?? –

I worked for many years at a family business. Nothing about that time will I share here, as it serves no purpose. Well, other than this story. Dick worked for the local utilities 10 years ago. It had been a good 25+ years since I had seen him last, at which time he was being pummeled outside my work, by my then fiancé.

We had received notice from the utility company that some work needed to be done and a certain employee, yes it was Dick, would be out to do so. I begged my boss to call and have them send someone else. I was nauseous. We would be in the same tiny office. We would be as close as we were the day I wore his handprints around my neck.

I remember dressing down that day. I remember wanting to be invisible. It's all I knew. Years of practice. Since a child. Years! I remember thinking, "after all this time, you can do this, Karen. You've got this." But I didn't. I didn't have it. I was so far from having it, that he walked in and I walked out. I couldn't do it.

There was only one entrance through the front of my office, so when he walked in, I went out of the office into the shop and went out that door. I begged my boss to make him come back sometime when I wasn't there. That was a big NO. For once in my goddamn life, protect me! See the theme here?

I don't know if I became ravaged with anger while I sat in the other building wishing he would go away. I don't know if it was hate, or just the fact that there were other humans around and maybe I had a sense of security, be it a false sense of security or not. Maybe, just maybe I had had enough!

I will never forget the moments following the urge to just "not sit there while Dick acts like there is no problem." I got up and waited by the window. This would be my day to say my piece and for once, just this one moment, he couldn't get me, or even get to me. I would stand my ground. By myself. I, and only I, would protect me. Mind body and soul. Something NO ONE had ever done for me. I would finally do it myself. Although, I don't recommend the following for others who are a survivor of domestic violence.

Walking briskly, and on a mission, I came out of the other building, the one he wasn't in, as I saw him nearing his company truck. I was on a mission. No one and no thing would stop me. Or even try.

He looked up, not surprised at all, yet with a blank face. A confused face. But not an angry face. I didn't know this face. Aged from years of living in hate. Of himself, and most likely others near to him.

I had a plan. I knew what I was going to say. As I got closer, I went blank. Dizzy and nauseous I remember thinking, "don't fuck this up Karen. This is your one chance. You may never get this chance again. Do not fuck it up!"

"HI!" Did he just seriously say "hi" to me as if we were colleagues that hadn't been for coffee in a decade? That did it. I don't know what would have happened if he hadn't spoken. Nor does it matter. He spoke. One word. Two letters. His voice. I hadn't heard it in so many years. There was NO turning back at that point. He had struck a chord.

Abused women, and men too, often say the hardest moment is facing their abusers. Seeing their face. Hearing their voice. Looking in their eyes. I don't have words to describe it. Maybe I went black. Maybe I have no feeling or emotion around it. Maybe that was all I knew.

"HI??????" I found my voice! For the first time ever with him, I FOUND MY VOICE!!!

"What?" He asked. "What????" I snapped back. "You could have KILLED ME! Do you understand that? You would be in jail right now, not working here!"

Now you, the reader, may not have noticed, but sitting here 10 years later, after years of healing work, and self-discovery, I realize that even though I stood up for myself and talked back to him, I had still made that comment be about him and not me. It looks as though I am stating facts, but analyzing what I said, there was a tinge of pity that he would be in jail. I've worked through that. He doesn't get any power or pity.

"I don't know what you are talking about." He said, staring at me with his blank, emotionless face.

"You do and I know you do, stop with the excuses of blacking out, or alcohol or whatever the fuck. Own it!" And I continued walking.

For another 7 or 8 years I would do the work. I would learn forgiveness for the men, for the people, who let me down. Disappointed me. Lied to me. Stole many years of my life from me. Patterns repeated. History repeated.

What had happened to me back when I was young was not a secret in my family. Although most, if not all, members of my family chose to handle it the way they handle everything. If we don't discuss it, it didn't happen. A reminder of the way we had to behave when my mom was gone, when I was only five years old.

I wasn't going to share the last encounter until later on in this book. However, I have been working a lot on forgiveness and release, and if I want to truly forgive Dick, I need to wrap up this chapter and clear the energy. I have now forgiven him, but just recently.

# AND AGAIN?? –

Fast forward to 2018. I remember the call. A family member extremely shook up because Dick had shown up at his place of business. The audacity! "It will be okay, just hear what he has to say," I said.

I was able to watch the encounter on the security camera app on my phone, and just couldn't believe my eyes or ears. How dare he say it was my children's now deceased dad who had done all those things to me? When that didn't work, he claimed not to remember. His MO, his modus operandi.

Do I believe him? I don't know and it quite frankly doesn't really matter, does it? I am not his judge. He will have to be held accountable for it later, or maybe even now. You see, he has cancer. "Lower extremity" cancer. There is something to be said for all that, but I'll leave all that up to you, the reader. Again, I'm not the one he will answer to. I've done my work that I need to do around it.

That should have been the end of it. He said what he had to say that night and didn't get an ass whooping from my family member. After all, at this point it had been more than 35 years!

I don't pretend to know why this all happened. I surely didn't line my life up this way. Not consciously, anyway.

We come to this earth on a journey. Every journey is different. But each journey has meaning. A purpose. Without being abused as a child, and then as a teen, would I have some of the experience to help others? Much of my work is intuitive. But who am I to assist others in their struggles, if I have no earthly clue of what they are dealing with?

"History repeats itself" they say. I don't know for a fact, if anyone in my family has been abused. But I do know there were two abusers. One got caught and had his reckoning on earth, one didn't get caught and had his reckoning when he got to the other side. I'm not the judge. Neither are you. This is MY story. Not my siblings', not those who thought they knew my family behind closed doors. Mine. Which makes me free to tell it.

Our logical minds would think that would be the end of it. Why would Dick ever show his face again?

No logic can be found when thinking of the day, not long after encounter with my family member, the day when I was sitting in the family member's business, when he walked in. He walked right past me. Didn't see me. I knew he didn't. I could tell. He went down a couple stairs into another part of the building, but thanks to strategically placed mirrors, I was able to keep an eye on him. A "one up", for me for a change. It was a weird sense of power having that view of him when he didn't know I was watching. Again, this is my situation, and I don't recommend encounters or interactions with abusers, let me make that 100% clear.

I continued to do whatever it was that I was doing, checking the mirror intermittently for an update. I could handle his presence if I knew where he was. After all, there were 20 other people there, AND he had no idea I was even nearby.

Until.........duty called. I assumed he had a colostomy bag, so imagine my alarm as he stumbled up the couple of stairs. The bathroom wasn't far from where I was sitting, but as he neared the bathroom, he wouldn't have looked at me straight on. He would have only been able to see me out of his peripheral vision. Ahhhh, did he or didn't he see me? Time moved slowly, although I didn't have a plan.

The bathroom door opened. Would he wave? Would he acknowledge the fact that he is in MY space? I continued to look down, not out of fear or anxiety, but I had no desire to engage in ANY exchange that he may have had the possibility of ensuing.

"Hi Karen." There he stood smack dab in front of me. "Do you remember me?" His voice trembled and trailed. But mine would NOT tremble or trail. Not this time. He was going to hear what I had to say. After 35 years, I was the one who was going to do the talking. I may never have this opportunity again. Not in this lifetime.

I don't know what it is like to be in an abuser's mind. Are there holes? Or just sheer darkness? Do they lose their memory like their survivors do? I'm assuming the answer is no, considering the very last words my father uttered to me was, "I'm sorry."

How the hell would I not remember him? But this was it. Probably the last time I'd have my chance to speak up for myself. "For once in your goddamn life Karen, protect you!", I screamed inside.

After this, I would only be able to speak up for others. Loudly. Being a survivor of physical and sexual abuse, can alter your life. But watching someone living that life daily, will bring out a fire in you that will burn until you speak up and stand up for change!

I didn't look around for someone to protect me. I did not wish it wasn't happening. It just was.

"Of course I remember you." I said in a casual tone, a blank stare on my face. I flinched as he reached to shake my hand. The last time his hands were this close to me, they were around my neck. Was it his appearance? Aged. Calm. Well, not a peaceful calm, but not angry. Perhaps a bit fearful. Cancer ridden. However, I was not the least bit fearful. His presence would not affect me. Not this time. I returned a firm, strong handshake.

The power in that handshake to this day, symbolizes to me the power to survive. The strength I now have, that he nor anyone else could ever take away from me.

"Karen, I don't remember things. A lot of things. But I do know I need to apologize to you." "Yes, you do." I exclaimed firmly with a stare that could have burned holes in his face. I looked him straight in the eye. In two years of his violence and control, I don't remember every looking into his tattered, bloodshot eyes.

Many survivors don't ever get the opportunity to face their abusers. Moreover, most don't ever receive an apology. To me, this apology represented a mutual understanding that he, those broken memories of violence, and his name, no longer have control of me.

I still get extremely nauseous or even vomit, if a scene in a movie brings up similarities of my life prior to age 21, but that reaction isn't all on him and the two years we spent together. That reaction goes way back. Back to my younger days.

"I'm sorry."

Incredible. Almost 10 years after the first apology from one abuser, I heard another one.

I had already forgiven Dick. He had way too much power over me all those years when I had not seen him or heard from him. The mere sound of his name would make me cringe. But I worked through it. I was healing.

Typically, a spontaneous response to "I'm sorry" is "it's okay". Not this time though. I was not about to utter those words, I was internally clear about that, while also searching for something, anything, to fill the dead air.

"Thank you for saying that" was just about all I could manage to muster up at that awkward moment.

"Ok, well take care, Karen. "Yup, you too." Chapter closed. I am FREE.

Or so I thought. Until 6 months later on the Island of Molokai, when my worst fears, my memory, would be revealed to me.

Like driving to a destination, maybe even a vacation destination. And you arrive. Bags and baggage, you arrive. Set those damn bags down and enjoy your release!

# HASTE MAKES WASTE –

I want to explain an issue I have. I wonder if others have it as well. In the last year, I feel as if I am in a car or plane more than I am home. Last night when driving home from my daughter's house in Greenville, a four-hour drive from her door to mine, I was doing a lot of thinking. Its typically an audiobook or thinking, never radio. This time it was both. Audiobook on, listening to Robert Kiyosaki's, 'Rich Dad Poor Dad' for the second time, I was thinking about the pickup truck in front of me in the "passing lane" … "MOVE!" I yelled, as I looked at my speedometer. I was already doing 81 in a 70MPH zone. "What is my issue?", I wondered.

I consider myself a cautious driver, but not one who likes to fiddlefuck on the road. His speed was not offensive, so why was I having such an issue with it? I paused my book, just as Robert was reminding me that a house is not an asset. I needed to think about that.

Although I was sure the grandchildren were waiting for me to get home as a bedtime deterrent, there was really no rush. And pickup truck guy was already going way over the speed limit.

After a few miles of leapfrog, which I was originally going to refer to as Frogger, but leapfrog seemed much more fitting for this story, I thought, "Karen you've got a problem". Leapfrog in traffic to me is when you get aggravated with someone in front of you, and ever so subtly let them know, they pull over into the granny lane and you proceed to

177

zoom on past them. Like "finally, you got out of my way". But you've then conquered them. It's soon safe to hop over in the slow lane, granny lane, and go maybe 10 miles over the speed limit. A speed that is much slower than you were going when you were all up in the pickup guy's business. So, guess who then comes out of the slow lane, making his way past you. That repetitive game of leapfrog can go on for miles, even though neither driver is consciously aware of it, until one concedes or reaches their exit. What is the logic here? I see none. But I needed to reflect on this for a bit.

Here is what I concluded as a highway life lesson, that I can see magnified in my whole life:

I don't really need him to get out of the way. We are both already way over the speed limit. You see, I WANT him to get out of my way. Because if he stays in front of me, he controls my speed. HE CONTROLS MY SPEED! What a metaphor! I have no desire in life OR on the highway for anyone to determine how fast or slow I go! It is my life. I decide whether to speed or not.

The same goes for someone on your ass, tailgating, or even worse, flashing their high beams at you! Clearly, they want you to get out of the way. Only to later find that the Leap Frog game has ensued yet again. Fast or slow. We get to determine our speed. On highways, (short of speed limits) and in life.

I decide my outcome. I decide whether fast or slow. I get to decide when I will get to my destination. If someone or something is in my way, I go around. You should too.

*disclaimer ~ always follow posted legal speed limits, as a speeding ticket can often be the result of not letting someone get in your way*

My grammie used to say, "haste makes waste." Not in my book, I have one speed, fast.

# FORENSIC MEDIUMSHIP –

Forensic Mediumship is the Metaphysical work more commonly known as a Psychic Detective.

A **psychic detective** is a person who investigates crimes by using purported <u>paranormal</u> <u>psychic</u> abilities. Examples have included <u>postcognition</u> (the <u>paranormal</u> perception of the past), <u>psychometry</u> (information psychically gained from objects), <u>telepathy</u>, <u>dowsing</u>, <u>clairvoyance</u>, and <u>remote viewing</u>. In murder cases, psychic detectives may purport to be in communication with the spirits of the murder victims.

Although there are documented cases where individuals claiming psychic abilities have assisted police in solving crimes, there is considerable skepticism in regard to the general use of psychics under these circumstances.[1][2] Many police departments around the world have released official statements saying that they do not regard psychics as credible or useful on cases. (Wikipedia)

Throughout the years, I have unintentionally been called to work on many forensic mediumship cases.

One specific Florida case was dropped in my lap in 2008, when a little girl with a name that starts with "C", woke me in the night to say "HI!". I had no idea when I turned on the TV a couple days later, that the vision I saw of her would match a picture of a missing 2 year old child, whom I knew was deceased. Afterall, she had come to me a few nights earlier. She and I "worked together" for the weeks following, and all the information collected was then turned over to the Sheriff's Department. There is a lot more to this story, however since her mother keeps popping up in the media, this is all I wish to discuss currently, but the whole story will be in my next book, that I have already begun writing.

In my years and in many cases, the information I have been able to provide by either tapping into the deceased, if that is the case, via mediumship, or psychically tapping in to the missing person or animal (a gift referred to as animal communication), has been pivotal in helping the case, whether it was a missing human or pet.

# MISSING TEEN GIRL –

Most recently I was guiding a local mom and the police to her teenaged daughter, who had allegedly been assaulted, and was missing. That case, where I guided the authorities to where she was hiding due to her fear after the alleged assault, ended up in the reunion of the teen with her family. They don't all end up that way. I may be working on a case such as that one, and as happened that night, feel an energy shift in the "victim". Sometimes the shift means death, or they are headed in that direction.

In this specific case, I was in Florida in my hotel room and had FIVE missing persons cases going at once, as well as being asked to assist with a missing horse up in New Hampshire. I focused quite a bit of energy on the missing teen, because at that moment, I knew without a doubt she was alive. I knew that if they listened to me and my messages, although I was in Florida and they were in Myrtle Beach, SC, that we would find her, alive.

It was 10pm on a warm September night. I don't know where mom had heard about me. I don't advertise that I do this work for many reasons. It can be dangerous. It can put my family in danger. I do this service pro bono, no matter how many hours / days / months or years it takes. I don't want a bunch of national missing persons cases landing in my mailbox.

I require three things: first, the family, spouse or very close friend must be the one who asks for the help. Second, I have the family's permission. And third, that it is kept confidential, if possible, that I am working on the case. I need to protect myself and my family from anyone with malicious intent in these cases.

This was a particularly memorable case for me, for many reasons. The first being of course, because we found her, and she is alive today. The second being, I was able to use all my senses. I could see her, it was dark, but I could see her at the beach. I could feel her, she was so cold. Trembling from fear and from being in the ocean earlier, her fear ran right through me. But I also felt a strong young lady and a scared to death momma all working together. The energy was inexplicable.

I typed quickly into my phone with fake nails that were screwing up the whole process of speed in this case, "she is so afraid, which means she isn't going to trust anyone." "She doesn't know her friend is safe" "They either walked past her or they are close" "Have them turn on the blue lights, if she sees them, she MAY feel safe" "Her heart is ready to explode from fear!" "She is shivering, her head is fuzzy. She may also have a bump on her head". They are going to have to physically see her and go up to her." "Make sure they let her know who they are." "They are close. I can feel it." "I don't know what they did or where they police are, but if they aren't there, they are definitely close." These are just some of the messages I sent to the mom.

One would imagine that a child who had been assaulted would be happy to see the reflection of the blue lights flashing off the sand, or the sound of sirens in the distance. But that isn't always the case. When someone has been victimized by someone that they thought they could trust, their sense of fear is heightened, and their reality is shaken to the point where even an officer in uniform isn't a welcomed sight. Not until something clicks. A familiar voice, a warm blanket, or even a particular phrase spoken to them.

Most locals did not hear of this case and will not hear of it. It involves a minor and analleged assault. It doesn't need to make the news to be real. It doesn't need validation. The victims know what happened. Their lives and their families lives, forever altered. I know. I have walked this path, or a remarkably similar one.

As I sat in my room on my temporary bed for the week, juggling 5 missing persons cases, this case shocked even me. I was particularly blown away by the man in spirit that popped in as I put my energy solely into this case for a couple of hours.

"This is so weird. Do you know a minister? Living or passed?" I asked. "Yes, my best friend's dad was and her grandfather", the mom texted back. "Wow! Because I just kept hearing, 'the minister is helping.' So this is your friend's dad in spirit."

"OMG she is here with me now and has been praying to them. Just as she started praying, more drones went up to look for my daughter"

A peace came over me and after about 4 hours of helping folks with missing persons from my hotel room in Florida, and then shifting all my energy to help find this little girl, I soon realized my bladder was screaming and I needed a bathroom break.

There is a lot to be said for shows like the First 48. Even in my work, if I am contacted immediately, we have a much better chance of finding the missing person (or animal) alive. This case was no different. I made my way to my fancy hotel room bathroom, leaving my cell phone plugged in and lying on my bed. I was rushing and hoping the mom wouldn't even realize I had stepped away. Then, out of nowhere, a calm, a peace like a warm hug, came over me. I took a huge breath in. I exhaled and ran back to my phone.

"I suddenly feel like she is getting warmer" I quickly typed as fast as my fingers would take me. "Or something is wrapped around her. If they don't have her, someone is helping her! Or they are almost there! I feel a sudden peace!"

NO RESPONSE. It seemed like forever and a day until I would see those three little dots letting me know she is typing. "Thanks" was all it said. Trying to get more information on whether they were actually close to her, I waited a minute or so and typed again, in an effort to keep the mom engaged. Hoping it was empowering her while she waited, hands tied, for someone else to do something that would find her child.

"How many people are searching?" I typed. I don't know … it was all I could come up with at the time to keep mom engaged. "Probably 50. It looks like they are coming back ", she typed finally. "I think she is at peace. The minister is watching over her. She is suddenly so relaxed. It's hard to explain the difference in her energy" I replied. And waited for what felt like an hour. When I couldn't take it anymore, I asked "what's happening?"

"This is her friend," it read. I thought, "ahah, that was the difference in the conversation." Mom had given her friend her phone to connect with me while she checked on her husband." OHHHH you are the friend with the ministers in spirit that came thru to me and are helping?" I asked. "Yes", was all she said. "blah, blah, blah", I rambled on in a 3 sentence message. And I waited….

FINALLY, after waiting for what felt like forever, a message came through, "THEY FOUND HER!!! Thanks for everything!"

I JUST KNEW IT! Her energy had totally shifted, and I had felt it to my core. They had taken her to the hospital and come back to the station with the news!

I shut down my phone and laptop and cried myself to sleep. THIS is why I am here!

A short month later I received a message from the missing teen's mom, "I wanted to thank you from the bottom of my heart for helping me with my daughter when she was missing. She is starting to heal after everything."

Thank you's are never needed in this work. Knowing that a child in danger was found, that right there is all the thanks needed.

It ended there. Well at least that case did.

# SHE'S MISSING TOO?

At the same time the teen was missing and later found, I had a gotten a gut punch when I learned that one of my clients was missing.

When working these cases, although I am sure first responders deal with this, I feel what the victim is feeling. I hear, I see. All the senses are being used on a heightened level of awareness. It is extremely exhausting ordinarily. But in this specific time frame, I had 5 cases going, one being a client.

"I feel her being choked", I wrote to her family member. "Not sure he killed her though" "Hang in there", I pleaded to the victim and then to the family member. "There still may be a chance." "He's had his hands on her neck before, I feel. Let's not give up".

Over the following days I would have my Medium mentorship students and myself working on this. Not being able to connect with my client's spirit was giving us a 1% chance of hope.

"Campground, old shack, hands may be tied, suffocating, tarp or covering of some sort". Just some of the information we came up with while intuitively working on my client's case. I had never "searched" for someone I knew so well, prior to this. This was getting deep into my soul as the hours had turn to days, and the days were turning into a week. But I was in Florida. I had to keep it together, as I was down there to see clients.

One night I said to the family member, "it's weird but I don't think he is near her right now. Does he think he's killed her? Or he has her drugged up." I did find out just this past week that all of the above were true. I've had unconscious people "feel" to me like they are dead. There isn't much difference energetically.

This past Sunday night I did a Facebook Live. I've done many of these before. People love them because they get to ask random quick questions and I answer them.

As I am going along on the Live, Spirit tries to come in. "It wasn't part of my plan, but whoever they are here for must really need it!" I thought. After buttoning up a few other details on the live, I shared a name I was getting. "It might be my mom" one watcher would say. "Oh, that sounds like my gramma, but she didn't pass from that though"

When giving these types of messages, especially online where there is 60+ people, there can be a delay between what I am saying and the comments from the viewers. I can feel the disappointment as I say, "no I am definitely with Jane", she can take all of it." The name I am giving is her mom's name, but her mom's mom (her grandma) is recently passed. "It all fits, the numbers, the way she passed, all of it. "

Connecting with spirit takes focus and energy. No distractions. So, connecting over a laptop with 60 other people watching and commenting, and waiting for Jane to comment, my heart was racing as I read Jane's name over and over.

Finally, I discreetly clicked on the profile picture to confirm it was HER! My missing person / client, whom I had been recently notified was alive, but still in a bad situation, was on my Facebook Live, in her mom's living room. She was now safe and well. Thanks to her Nana, connecting with me that night, we have all reconnected and my client was able to tell her story on my Facebook Live the following night.

There is no greater reward than hearing of the missing teen found alive, or the missing client who had survived over a week of being assaulted, drugged, choked, and sleep deprived, and yet made it home to her two babies, ALIVE.

Now she will assist me in helping abuse survivors by telling her story of abuse, like I am telling mine.

# A DOG NAMED SADIE ~

My brother was a strong willed, extremely gifted finish carpenter. He worked on some of the most elite homes in Rye Beach, New Hampshire. He was a husband and a dad, but also an alcoholic in recovery for many years, before discovering he had insulin dependent juvenile diabetes. He'd make this discovery as an adult after a few near death incidents, a couple of them at his own hand.

Diabetes is such a tricky illness. I saw it mess with his brain and I truly feel due to it being undiagnosed as a child, had led him to alcoholism, due to lack of insulin in his body. I don't know his family history, well not really, a story told in another part of this book

On the list for a liver and kidney transplant, his days were numbered, due to many physical afflictions associated with his diabetes. In the early morning hours of April 21, 2008, at the young age of 48, his life which he had enjoyed to the fullest, would come to a peaceful end. He would transition home. Alone in that living room, we would say our goodbyes, he and I. I cherish that day, as it now warms my heart as I write, in the wee hours of a chilly January morning. Yet, I know he is by my side.

My then husband and I would be randomly driving down Route 16 in Rochester, New Hampshire just 10 days following my brother Tim's death. A pure white dog, that we both know we saw, although at this very moment and throughout the years, I wonder was he real, darted in front of our car, in and out of traffic, with nothing but a purple harness on its body. Was he even real? Or had my brother come back as a white dog?

We never caught the dog but having heard about this lost pet thing on Craigslist, I figured someone would be missing their furry friend. So, the next day, Monday morning, I decided to post what we had seen and where the pup was as soon as I got to work.

No responses, of course. Was nobody missing their pure white dog with the purple harness? Or was there even a running dog that day?

After posting and checking that the post was there, (this was back in the day – before I had any experience with Craigslist) I was drawn to the next ad down from mine, with a thumbnail picture.

"Roxy" was a terrier who had left her elderly parents in Raymond NH, several days prior. A post and a picture placed on Craigslist by their son, a Tennessee resident, formed a vision in my mind's eye, of this dog. I could see her! She was under a green patio set at this home that I later described; "Epping – Raymond line, white house, green shutters, chain link fence," it was all there in my vision.

"Okay, now what to do with this information?", I wondered. As I set at my desk at work, I thought ......

"Okay, I know I am different than other people. I know that I see things, hear things, and know things that maybe I 'shouldn't know'. But this is so different."

I had been seeing Mediums for ten or so years since Brayden's death. Connecting with the afterlife, brought me peace. Well, as much peace as possible, when raising children after their daddy died.

I knew what was happening here with this vision, and I knew I had to do something.

Sheepishly I reached out to the son of the dog owners. He didn't think I was a kook! He contacted his mom who knew right where the house was that I had been seeing in my mind's eye. Trusting none other than a stranger who was seeing pictures in her mind, she went to the house I described, exactly where I said it was, but disappointed to find Roxy was not there.

Now Tuesday, turning on my computer at work (I didn't have one at home), straight to Craigslist I went. As I envision that process now, it seems so antiquated.

"*UPDATE FOUND*" was how the post now read! Although I can see this Craigslist post in my head to this day, uncoincidentally I came across my copy of it yesterday while preparing a workshop for my Jacksonville, Florida office.

I could hardly see through the tears, grateful that I was the only one currently in the office, yet I read it repeatedly. FOUND it said, it really did. "Roxy is skinny, dirty and now at the vets, and by the way Karen, you are not a KOOK, she was found right where you said she was, this morning." I would later find out that when his mom had gone to the house that I described, she left her phone number there, in case Roxy showed up. As the homeowner did her morning dishes, she looked out and there was Roxy under the green patio set, as if she and I had made a plan together, from worlds apart.

The commotion of the autobody shop went silent. Well, at least to me it did. I heard and saw nothing but that post over and over, I read it until I realized that I also had an email from the original poster thanking me and providing the details of Roxy being found.

This event, the one that started with the mysterious white dog, dashing into highway traffic, would change my life forever. It brings me to where I am today. My brother passed, and while passing told me I was "special". He was not kidding!

Neither I, nor Roxy's human brother, were prepared for what happened next.

His email box filled up with other missing dog owners and searchers who wanted to know, "who is this Karen and HOW did she find your dog?" A legitimate question.

"Can I give these people your information?" he asked in a follow up email. That entire day would be spent in my upstairs office at the body shop, fielding calls and emails. They were coming in from all over the country, but I would be comfortable with only the ones in New Hampshire. I mean a minute ago, I was the former Disaster Director of the American Red Cross, now trying to save my little brother's business, while mourning the loss of my older brother, just days prior.

Bailey was a black lab in Wilton NH. While on the phone with an extremely distressed momma, I described a house. "Yellow" I said, "there is a trellis in the yard, a pickup truck in the driveway, fresh pavement on the street, with the gravel that would take down a bicycle, between the new pavement and the grass. Some flowers, perhaps a small garden. A cape with white shutters. This is where he is or was last," I told her. "That's my house" Bailey's human mom exclaimed. "Well, that's the last place he was or is, or that is where he passed, ma'am." I'd later learn that he'd indeed left in that pickup truck in the driveway, never to be seen or heard from again.

Jane, a sweet New England senior, with a wide array of rescues in her home, has felt drawn to help missing pets. Like hundreds of other pet lovers, Jane had seen the part where I 'wasn't a KOOK' when Roxy was found and like many others had gotten her hands on my information. Just yesterday she popped up on my social media. She will always hold a dear place in my heart.

"My friend needs your help!" the email began. "His dog Sadie is missing, and he's afraid she may have been shot by the neighbor."

George was a nurse in Concord, NH. He and Jane had previously worked together at a New England hospital and formed a bond. No one knew what that bond would lead to, especially me. George and his partner Ross, lived way up in New Hampshire, in a remote area, famous only for the well-known case of Maura Murray, a college girl who had gone missing after a car crash during the winter, less than 4 years prior.

George's bond with Sadie was so intense and beautiful, that as I made my way up north New Hampshire, a two and a half hour drive from my home, I could literally feel his pain for his girl, as he feared the worst.

"Please relax and go inside. I know you think you know where Sadie would have gone, or may be hiding, but I need you to breathe and let me do this." A stranger telling him what to do, may have been something he wasn't used to, but George hesitantly complied.

"Let me do this??" What was I thinking? I had never "done this" before! Seeing pictures in my head while sitting at my desk in my office, was one thing, definitely a safe thing. If I mess up or look like a fool, I can just hide behind my computer monitor and that would be the end of it. This here, was some real life stuff.

I began to breathe, not that I was holding my breath, but because it made my 'connection' stronger. After all, I had at this point been experienced at finding animals for a whole week! A week! But I had a belief, a confidence that came from somewhere deep in my soul. A confidence and belief that my five hour round trip to a stranger's home in a town where a young woman had gone missing just a few years prior and still to this day, has not been found, a town that was so remote, that I had no cell service, would soon bring peace to a distraught young man.

A 'tingling' in my calves is the best way to describe the feeling I get when I am on site finding a missing pet. "Okay Sadie, I know you are here" I whispered, as I crept off in the opposite direction from where George had directed my search. "As I get closer" I said in my mind's eye, "please make the feeling stronger, Sadie".

Writing this, 13 years later, I think of this day in my logical mind and the only word I can use to describe that day, that moment, is trust. I had to be in full trust that no matter the fact that I had been a working Animal Communicator for 10 minutes, (that's an exaggeration, but seriously less than a week), I was going to find Miss Sadie and bring her home to her daddy, no matter what.

I remember looking at my watch, the one I actually just stumbled upon yesterday for the first time in a decade, and thinking, "this isn't going to take long."

Sadie's sweet lifeless body laid just a couple feet into the brush beyond the tree line near the driveway of George and Ross' driveway. Her soul now over the rainbow bridge. Five minutes after sending George inside, I would be finding the strength to go back into their home to break the news.

Emotionally wrought from the pain of the loss of his girl, George wanted to stay home, while a stranger, turned friend, and I took sweet Sadie's lifeless body to the vet to begin the process of closure for those two men. I honestly believe to this day, unable to get away from a larger wild animal, Sadie had passed not long after she had escaped out of the door, earlier that week. If I were to ask George today though, I think we still lovingly disagree on this point, and that is okay with me.

Email being our favorite form of communication, although we'd not see each other again in New Hampshire, George and I stayed in touch.

# MELISSA –

It was a warm spring day at my home on the water in Lennox, New Hampshire. I would often walk around outside while on my cell phone, due to lack of cell service in my home. "I just really need you to help me with my dog. But I live in Jacksonville, Florida, and I believe in all this. My brother George speaks so highly of you. And his friend Jane, who you have helped with so many missing pets, said you are amazing. "

A phone conversation 13 years ago, brought to us by Sadie, who was brought to me indirectly via Roxy, that all began with a beautiful white pup, playing Frogger on the highway in New Hampshire, just 10 short days after my older brother passed in my arms, not long after telling me I was "special", has brought me to where I am today.

An animal communicator, morphed into Psychic Medium, as well as many other things since that summer 13 years ago, I'm now working beside my dear friend, at an amazing center built by George's sister, also known as Sadie's 'Aunt Melissa' and her husband Doug, in Jacksonville, Florida. Everything for a reason. We may not understand today, but it's all part of the Divine plan.

It all began with a pup, either the mysterious white dog, Roxy, or Sadie, but any way you slice it, it all began with a pup. I am forever grateful to the animal kingdom for lining up this life. Melissa and I share a passion for healing others, at the Mind, Body and Beyond Center in Jacksonville, Florida.

One of Melissa's pups, Dilly, who I met that year on my first of many visits to Jacksonville, passed peacefully just over a week ago, while I was in Jacksonville seeing clients at the Center. No coincidences.

This alignment, the story that was created long ago, to the mind makes no sense. To the literal brain it gets excused as coincidences. Making things up. Imagination. You name it, the brain can find a way to excuse the phenomena I like to refer to as Divine. Divine intervention. Divine timing. Divine creation. Divine alignment. Divine guidance.

# MOTHERLESS DAUGHTER –

In preparation to tell my story, I have consulted with many Mediums, Psychics, Intuitives, and Healers. These are my people. Many I don't know, or I didn't know. But my story is unique. The thing that has never wavered with any of the Intuitives, is the fact that my mom is alive. No one has argued that fact. The other piece they all came up with is that I suffered abuse as a child. Now, none of these women know each other. I think back to many other readings prior to my awareness of her being alive. Brayden comes thru, my grammie comes thru, and then other odds and ends from the other side.

However, in researching my journals and notes of these readings, no one, not one person said the name Grace OR referenced my mother being on the other side. I wondered often, "how that could be?" But I am also aware, that some spirits on the other side just choose not to "come thru". Fine by me. I didn't think it was anything to question. When you are conditioned for 50 years to think something is one way, especially when it involves something so precious as a parent, there is no room in your mind to question that.

Every time I have ever misstepped, and there have been many times, I always have fallen back on, "well, my mother died when I was 5." Or (although very few knew) "I have been emotionally, physically and sexually abused as a teen by my own boyfriend."

"There ya have it," I thought. Those two things, even one, in and of itself explains it all! Boom! "Don't question my actions, imagine if your mother died when you were just five years old!"

But it worked. Has my mom been gone since I was 5? Absolutely! But the dynamic changes when she was only gone, she was not dead. I guess in my mind, nothing changes. Not as I look back over those years. Did I dream of having a mom when I got my first period? Or my first boyfriend? Or my wedding(S)? Or delivering my first baby, second or third? Absolutely! But I was, as others are, a Motherless Daughter.

After my first child, my son was born, I called the only parent I had left. I had given birth to his first grandchild. To my first child. My mom wouldn't have ever left my side. I begged him to come to the hospital, to meet his first grandchild! I BEGGED! Finally, he showed up on day 2, maybe? I don't remember, but there is a picture somewhere.

I had hoped that just once, maybe this time, creating and pushing out a 9 ½ pound butterball, would warrant SOME acknowledgement. Nah   I think he fit in his visit somewhere between Men's Gospel Breakfast and preparing his Sunday sermon. The same begging I did that cold day in January on the birth of his grandson, would be the same begging I would do just 13 short years later, when this same baby's (and our other children too) dad died.

Some would question me wanting his attention like that, after the abuse I suffered, I can't explain it. Abuse, recovery, survival from a traumatic childhood is like a snowflake. There are no two "cases" that are the same. The dynamics, the abuse, the disempowerment is all different. The people are different. The survivors are different. The recovery is different.

# I'M OKAY –

I think I am okay. I chuckled as I wrote this. I do though. I help hundreds, if not thousands of people every year. All over the country. I have over 500 clients in both New Jersey and Florida, to give an example. I am okay? Right? Wrong. See I can't fix myself. Yes, I've had "counseling" off and on throughout the years. Mostly during one of my marriages. Interestingly enough, I had trust issues. They were destroying my marriage. I owned them. I knew I needed to work through them. Afterall, "my mom died when I was just five years old!" Here we go again. This pattern has reared its ugly head over and over and over for 50 years.

It's January 8, 2021. Many think the world has gone to hell in a handbasket after the random events of the week. I'm just sitting here chatting with myself, "where do I want to buy my house?" "What month will I go to Hawaii?" "When will I put my new business plans into action?"

In the past, prior to October 6, 2018, I had sailed along, living this life that I am so grateful for, but feeling like a damaged warrior. On the outside I was fixing people daily. (Although, I prefer to say guiding them to fix themselves) I still am. On the inside I still have so many questions. Most are superficial. "Where has my mom been living this whole time?" "Were others abused?" "Who exactly is my oldest brother's parents?" Technical stuff. But once I woke up and remembered it all, or at least what my subconscious has let me discover, the insides are broken. I am broken.

That doesn't mean I suck. That doesn't mean I can't do my work daily. That doesn't have any reflection on my gift, my calling, or my business. I think it all kind of runs parallel. But what do I know? So many questions.

# HEALING –

Let the healing begin.

For the two years since my memory began to come back, and the shorter time since I've discovered my mother is alive, I had a couple cries. Real good cries in Hawaii, and more when I shared with a very select few. But it's been a bit. "Am I not sad?" "Have I created a new wall?" "Am I scared to feel?" So many questions.

Answers, healing and self-discovery about the abuse, lies and deception start today. Time to unpack it.

When we don't want to feel, when we are afraid, we distract. We avoid. And we most certainly procrastinate. I'm okay. Right? Wrong.

Today I meet with a real therapist for the first time, EVER! I'm excited but know that the hour will go by faster than my sessions go when I have an intense client. I will open Pandora's box today... Life begins again today.

I am very curious and maybe a little concerned about what is in there? What will we uncover? What do I need to work on?

I am committed to sharing it with you. I cannot lead, or help others heal when I am ashamed of the process. Not that I am ashamed, but sharing it in this book, as much as I am able to before it goes to the publisher, is therapeutic. It also doesn't leave those of you who are reading this and just now realizing that you have a story to tell, hanging in the dark. I cannot present to you the multiple traumas and tell you to go "have a nice day." I am telling my story to help others. That includes the healing process.

Understand though, I have done a lot of healing with meditation and journaling, which I highly recommend. But this is the real deal. The professional stuff. It needs to happen. I will share it. Why not? I've already borne my broken soul. Let's all see how we mend those wounds. Or can we?

# THERAPY ~

I don't know what exactly I had expected. I don't think I was imagining a 'one and done' scenario, but I see now that it is a process not an event. Therapy started by learning that I am not broken and whether you have experienced any abuse or not, neither are you.

Trust is something that will be an ongoing, evolving lesson. Lesson isn't the right word. It means I must learn something I don't know. I know trust. We all know trust. When we are born into this world, we have no choice but to trust. We trust a parental figure to feed us, nurture us, take care of us and keep us alive.

We trust until we don't. Why don't we? Because someone stripped that away from us. Very often in childhood. We learned that the humans we trusted to do the right thing, to behave in a certain way, to protect us, oh yes, especially to protect us, have not only failed in that department, but.......... have violated us in a way that strips us of trust. In addition to adding doubt and fear onto our plate. Yes, even in childhood. Lies, abuse, neglect, failure to protect, they all lend to trust issues. I was exposed to all of that. Not a victim statement. Just a statement. Awareness, acknowledgement.

Some people do come up into adulthood very trusting, and they stay that way. I've always envied that kind of person. Others come up into adulthood very trusting, only to have a partner cheat on them. As an adult, their ability to trust is stripped away, often in minutes.

Children, like pets, are so trusting that it takes a lot more for them to realize who and what they can't trust. I do think though, both children and pets, can sense energy, and may pull away from or behave badly towards someone with faulty intentions. Unless that person is a parent or sibling. I would add grandparents into that mix, as well as aunts and uncles. I want to be incredibly careful here to bring awareness to the fact that although my memories are of my own father, as well as men from the church, abusers of the 'secret' kind, are often family members, older siblings or step siblings, grandparents, and even aunts or uncles. Typically, they are a person in power.

We have seen in the recent years, priests being charged with sex crimes, and more recently sports coaches, doctors, teachers and therapists. Why the sudden "movement"? Our collective tolerance has become almost nonexistent. We are hearing daily about "persons of power" being involved in sex crimes, and it has now permeated a space in our minds, and hearts, where we have no choice but to believe. The #metoo (me too) movement among celebrities, actors, film makers, producers, agents, has opened the public's eyes to the fact that not only do "Superstars" have vulnerability, but as we have seen recently, they have the unwavering courage to stand up and say, "no more!"

As I research for this book, I realize that attention is so often brought to the diocese and the catholic church as a place where sex crimes have been going on for years. Just recently we have become aware of indiscretions by several "public servants of God", as I referenced with the Jerry Falwell, Jr case. Which has become very eerily quiet.

What's my goal with this book? It's twofold.

I have already spent time working on forgiveness, understanding and comprehension of the effects that my childhood had on my adult life. So firstly, this book is for you, the reader. Perhaps you haven't had any of the experience I have spoken of thus far. But maybe you know someone who has.

Secondly, to expose the trauma that has taken place in my home as a Preacher's kid, as well as the lies that I endured all thru childhood about a mother who was never dead. Secrets, lies, deceptions. To talk about how there is so much that happens in a church, in the preacher's home that no one wants to talk about. Well, I do! I want to open this conversation. I want to draw awareness. I am here for you, as I stand up for me. I will hold your hand.

No one's story is better or worse than another. Not when it comes to the violation of trust. Do people have more disgusting acts of abuse against them than another? Absolutely. But when it comes to trust that is stripped from a child, the results typically show up in similar form.

# ANSWERS –

The following is an interview with my therapist, and friend, Melissa. After years of working with clients, I highly value all she shared with me. These questions were Spirit driven, they just rolled off my tongue.

*Interview with Melissa Fenton, PhD, LMHC, Founder & President –Mind, Body and Beyond Center*

1. *Although this is a difficult question to factually answer, in your opinion, is it possible for a victim of childhood sexual abuse to go through their entire life unaware?*

   Yes, if there are no triggers. Suppression and more so, repression of memories can be permanently away from conscious awareness

2. *Do victims (or survivors) of sexual abuse ever base their awareness of abuse entirely on memories? If so, is it more of a struggle to work through, than if someone had say, evidence; whether physical, someone else having knowledge, or some sort of tangible proof?*

   So, oftentimes the person that was the abuser is deceased, or no one was alive to corroborate or was there at the time. So most definitely entirely on memories. Now I know in a court of law they need proof beyond a reasonable doubt. Trauma that happens certainly is considered real in memory form and equally as traumatizing.

So, the trauma itself isn't really about if we can confirm it, then you can experience or feel the trauma. It has nothing to do with if its real or not. It is the interpretation of the stored experiences or memories that caused the trauma.

Some people can say "well this might not be true because I don't have facts to support it. I don't have evidence to support it." But that doesn't have anything to do with the trauma itself. *So in your experience is it harder for the patient to work through it without physical proof or someone else having knowledge that can corroborate?* I think the part that makes it more difficult is the patient or the client or the victim of the trauma is always second guessing the reality of it. So, it's almost like a double injury because "I feel this, I'm experiencing this, but I don't have absolute proof, so there must be something wrong with me." "Am I crazy? Am I messed up? Or are these just feelings or memories that aren't real?" So that is like a secondary injury that can happen with self-judgment.

3. *Which IS the correct phrase to use, victim or survivor?*

You know I hate to use the word 'victim' because that identity makes the person feel helpless. There's such a sense of helplessness. In essence you know we have the two terms the victim and the abuser, but I prefer to say that they experienced trauma. Helpless has a negative connotation, not as empowering. So, I would say that it really depends on the individual. They are not a victim at that time when it happened. They were helpless and they were victimized as children because they couldn't protect themselves. But now as adults, they are no longer victims unless they perceive themselves to be that way. I would prefer it to be more empowering.

With one, the brain hears the negative and perceives themselves to be always in a victim state, one that can't overcome their past. The survivor says, "I'm strong, that happened in the past, it's no longer happening to me now, I've survived that past event and I'm good.

*Me: That's a really good answer to a really short question. I've been using "survivor", as I've been writing the book. So ya, I get that 100% minding our words*

4.  *Is there a typical or more common age when someone with repressed memories, such as myself, becomes aware of childhood sexual trauma?*

I've had clients tell me when they've had become mothers themselves when they've been sexually active and they're trying to have normal sexual relations with people, not necessarily when they are in their dating years, but more so when they are in the years of marriage and family. The time when their connections with another person are really deep. When it matters so much, and then the fear of pain, abandonment, loss, and rejection shows up.

This is when oftentimes a lot of my clients have experienced memories from childhood trauma that they were not aware of prior to that. I've also had clients who something has happened to their children where their children were molested, and it triggered something from their own memory.

Or again, a family member dies, and after that person dies, it's almost like the subconscious says it's safe now.

*Me: Oh, that's remarkably interesting.* (for my own situation)

Then, I've had other clients as well, that when they've had children and thought of leaving their children with the grandparents, but they just have a sense that it's not safe, and they don't know why. So, a lot of times it's when it has to do with becoming a parent themselves. Other times, it could memories brought back from so many things. For instance, the smell of a perfume, or after shave, or a song on the radio. There are so many different ways it can come to the conscious awareness through triggers, or different life events that that bring those memories on.

5. *In your opinion, based on your work, are females more often abused then men?*

*Which of the two is most likely to come forward?*

I don't think there's more abuse of females than males. I think that the females come forward more because the males are not socialized to believe that there's molestation that goes on. If it's an older babysitter or if it's someone that is seven or eight years older in the neighborhood, they don't see that as molestation, as we do with a male molesting a female.

Even if it's a stepmother or where you know it to technically be considered molestation. According to the law in this scenario, if there is a five year age difference between the abuser and the victim, it denotes a sexual crime. For instance, the babysitter is 18 and the child is 13.

If you think about it, how many people have had babysitters sleep over that are older than that?

What I have found is that nothing's always absolute. But over the years of working with clients with sexual issues or concerns, I find that males often have been molested as children. So as men there may be hypersexuality. They might be seeing prostitutes or have a strong porn addiction. Often infidelity or have multiple partners. Or they have some bordering on what I would say, deviant sexual interest. With the individual in counseling, after we do a sexual history, going back to when they were first sexualized way back, we find many of them have had issues with sexual molestation.

So, you see it showing up differently in females who are more sexually averse. They have issues with low sexual libido or an aversion to sex. Not necessarily when they are of the dating years, but it shows up more when there is a real love, mature love, marriage and children.

The hypersexuality oftentimes shows up for males in adulthood, where the hypersexuality shows up for females sooner. Usually, it's when they start dating and thinking this is what love is.

Also, you see a lot of addiction, not only sex addiction, but we're talking about alcohol and drug addiction right away, as a way of distracting early memories of abuse. You see that in both males and females.

*Me: So, you are saying probably both males and females have been equally subjected to molestation, but males tend to call it sexual initiation, females call it sexual molestation, which is what it is.*

Yes, men tend to be socialized to believe it's cool and not abusive, so they don't see it as a disempowering. I mean if you think about it males may brag to their friends at school. Then later on have a hard time feeling angry at the abuser, because they didn't really feel anger toward them initially. The anger, the sadness and the feeling of victimization is so covered up by the earlier emotions.

*Me: I don't know if you're familiar with the Pamela Smart case in New Hampshire, which I wasn't going to bring up. At my high school, she had been carrying on with one of the 17 year old or 16 year old students and he ended up actually murdering her husband, allegedly at her command. That was at my high school. I mean I was out by then, but when you were just talking about that about the teacher or mentor, she's doing time for the murder of her husband. But I often wonder if the boy who actually pulled the trigger, if he is had to in his later life, had to deal with these issues. It was his teacher or student aid or something like that, but she was twice his age. I think he was 16 she was 32 or something. This was back when Brayden was alive because he was on the jury.*

Yes, it was abuse of power, that child is still a child, and he still doesn't understand. He is under a spell, so yes, it takes a long time for those feelings to come out, and then it's traumatic as can be.

6. *Do victims or subjects of childhood sexual abuse often have a tendency to find a partner in adulthood or even in their teenage years that repeats the behaviors they were subjected to as a child?*

Yes and no. It certainly can happen. You know how they say that an abuser can become the abuser? The abused can also become the abuser. Are you asking if it's subconscious or it's conscious?

*ME: I'm actually speaking of myself. My first real teenage boyfriend pretty much repeated a lot of what happened in my childhood. Although I was consciously aware of what the teenage boyfriend was doing, but I was not aware of my childhood abuse at the time it took place. Does that make sense?*

I would say there's familiarity, so it's secure for people. Even if what's familiar is what we considered unhealthy and dysfunctional and toxic it's something that we know. The brain is wired to go to what we know versus the unknown, even if the conscious mind doesn't realize. Like the person who marries an alcoholic, is often a child of an alcoholic. Oftentimes they will consciously say, "but I didn't know. They didn't show the signs." Or, "they were not actually drinking or using." So, there's something in the subconscious so subtle that the conscious mind is not aware of it. What things are similar that drew you to that person? So, to answer your question, yes, oftentimes but again, not always.

*ME: When I think about this guy from when I'm 17 or 18 and I'm like," that's what it was!" I was so passive. Again, I remember that relationship, but I didn't remember anything from my childhood. I always question myself like how did I get involved with this guy (Dick)? I should have known better. Why didn't I know better?*

That's where the female has so much shame and self-blame. Like, "I should have known, so therefore I am at fault." So, it's a constant battering or judging themselves for the abuse of power that the person finds themselves in.

211

It's been modeled to us, if someone else is not going to abuse us, we're going to abuse ourselves. The extreme self judgment and shame that we experience is taking on the personality of the abuser. Sometimes it's a double whammy. It's in the partner, but it's also in ourselves.

**7.  *And again, who is more likely to come forward?***

Females.

**8.  *Do abusers typically choose one family member and not another?***

Yes, it's quite common for that to happen. Yet there's so many factors; personality, birth order, opportunity or availability. All of that factors into which one or ones will be abused and those that will not. It doesn't necessarily have to do with the sex, either. It can be male and male, or male and female. Sometimes it's the youngest, sometimes it's not.

There's a lot of grooming that goes into the process. Sometimes the person reminds them of a deceased loved one and the other one doesn't. Sometimes it's an age. If they get to a certain age, they are not attracted to them anymore. Or they're afraid they are going to tell.

Then the abuser may go to the younger one. Sometimes it's sexual with one and physical with another. Sometimes it's sexual, physical, emotional and verbal. Then all siblings get a different variation of those forms of abuse.

***ME: Just to just to go off that question a little bit and I didn't have this on my list but is it, and I guess you'd have to be an abuser's head, but is the abuser CONSCIOUSLY choosing one or the other?***

Not always. Sometimes, yes, but not always. Sometimes they have no idea what it is. "I'm just attracted to that one" Or "I just don't have control around that one, but I do the others." Or sometimes it's kind of like the injured one in the animal in the wild. Like, "they are the easiest target, so I choose that one."

9. ***Talk about some of the fallout that comes with a middle aged person remembering their abuse. How does that memory just come up? How long before they tell? WHO do they tell? If anybody. How does one who has been abused make a decision to tell someone? Be it their counselor, their sister, their mother. I'm sure it's different with everybody. But is it an empowering thing? Is it a fear thing?***

It could definitely be both, depending on the circumstances. Depending on when it's coming out. If they are really young and someone notices that there's some strange behavior or bruises or something, or some adult is keen to it and then brings it to the child's attention. Then other times, a child may speak up if they feel close to a school teacher or school nurse or an aunt or someone where they feel safe enough to reveal it to them.

Other times they don't know. Perhaps they get to adulthood and they have trigger and then they go into counseling and they talk about it. There are so many different variations of how it can play out.

The bottom line is that oftentimes the person, child or adult, has to feel that it's safe enough to do it. They have to feel safe with the person that they are disclosing it to. Otherwise, if asked they will deny it. Because remember, children are always, always faithful and loyal to their parents, even in times of abuse. It's all that they know. So, the fear of losing the parent, for whatever reason, can supersede the need to tell. Often times they will not reveal something when the abuser lives in the house because it's not safe in their mind. Or they are afraid they will get in trouble or get their parents in trouble, or make their parent be taken from their family, so they don't say anything. They will hide it at all costs.

10. ***Name some of the coping mechanisms. Addictions, etc.. You had mentioned some of the, for lack of a better term, coping mechanisms,***

*such as addictions and things like that, earlier in the questions. I don't
know if you remember which ones you brought up, but are there any
other ones? I mean addictions or anything else that we're missing?*

Addiction, as you know, is highly prevalent with childhood abuse.
Childhood abuse is also through negligence, and not only sexual
abuse. The coping mechanism of *using*, whether it's through drugs,
alcohol, sex, or gambling is not uncommon. There are also coping
mechanisms of a higher incidence such as borderline personality
disorders and eating disorders. And then obviously depression
and anxiety are underlying conditions that show up in childhood
trauma. Also, a lot of the personality disorders you can see as a result
of using coping mechanisms.

We can say that there's a high correlation when there's a lot of abuse
or dysfunction in the childhood home. As the brain is developed and
things are modeled to them, and as certain behaviors are learned,
we see these disorders show up. Often at a higher rate in adults and
adolescents and adults.

*ME: When you speak of adolescence, would self harming fit into that
category, or is it something completely different?*

Self harm is a way as well. Also, there is a higher suicide rate.
Suicide and self harm are not the same thing. You can self harm and
not be suicidal. Self harm is just a way of trying to deal with pain
or numb the pain. "If I can cause physical pain, then my emotional
pain kind of goes on the back burner, it distracts me from it." Some
have learned to dissociate from their childhood traumas when they
create pain through cutting or burning or something they can feel.
They are able to realize they *can* feel something.

**11.** *When someone has suffered childhood sexual trauma, what potential
struggles could that bring to their adult relationships?*

Struggles in interpersonal relationships with a lot of mistrust of
people, a lot of pushing people away. You're going to see a lot

of interpersonal issues and also a lot of control issues. They are controlling for their safety, or for their children's safety. Often overprotectiveness of children.

Also, basic mistrust in others. When there's basic mistrust it creates difficulties with really knowing what love is. I don't want this to be a grim outlook because we have choices, we when we have awareness.

We can heal through these things; we can't undo them; they are in the past. But we can see how the old ways of thinking or believing as someone who was powerless, helpless, or was taken advantage of, now isn't that way anymore. Reminding ourselves that's not who we are. We have to learn techniques to be mindful of the old ways of thinking, and create newer healthier ways of seeing the world, not through the eyes of the abused.

### 12. When does one know that they need help from a professional?

When you start to feel breakdowns in your life. When you hit a wall and you ask, "Why am I not happy? Why am I continually having difficulties in relationships? Why am I angry at the world? Why am I mistrusting?" Or you are using defense mechanism or old coping mechanisms.

Sometimes there's an illness that happens, or a loss that makes us realize this. Or the way we're living or thinking or seeing the world or acting toward our children, our family members, or friends or colleagues. "I can't hold a job. I keep leaving, it's not for me anymore. I don't know how to change it; I don't know if it's possible. I'm just realizing this old way is not the way I want to continue living."

When someone else tells us. A parent or a friend or a colleague says, "you know you really need to get counseling; you've got a problem." But that's not as effective as when we just feel ourselves hitting a wall, and we can't move forward. We are frustrated with ourselves or we feel hopeless. Maybe hopeless to the point being suicidal. Or we have a run in with the law because we got caught with a DUI.

We feel like we can't live like this anymore. Or a partner says, "I'm going to leave you if you don't do this." Or we're just realizing, "this is too much. I'm going to seek some kind of help." Seek help, whether through a counselor, whether through the church with the clergy, or some group work such as AA. It is all there to help you. There are so many different outlets.

**13. *Why don't we just "tell" when we are young? Is that where the guilt comes in? If not, why DO we blame ourselves? I think we have covered most of this already, though.***

We don't tell when we're young, because it's not safe and / or we don't know any differently. We don't know that this is not going on in other households Think about it, until you leave home, and you see the world differently, that's all you know. So, part of it is not being aware. Part of it is safety. Part of it is loyalty to parents. Part of it is fear of the unknown. All of those things factor into why we don't tell.

***Is that where the guilt comes from that we didn't tell?***

Yes, that is the guilt we carry on into our adult life. There can be guilt wondering if there were other siblings that were victims of the abuse. The guilt and the shame that says, "I must have been culpable. I must have had some responsibility in this, if I didn't tell or if I didn't run away." Or "maybe I gave some sort of signal to my parent, or to that person, because didn't I run away." "There must have been something I did that I liked it." Which, none of that is real, but this is how we try and make sense of it. We can't understand the mentality of being victimized and the control we were under. We don't see it fully, so we fill in the blanks with things like, "if I didn't leave, then I must have been okay with it at some level." Which is just not true.

**14. *If someone discovers through memory, or being told, or another or form of awareness that they too suffered childhood sexual trauma, what is the best course of action they should take? I just added this***

*question because this book is twofold. It's part one to tell my story, and part two, to help somebody who is unaware of what the heck to do next.*

Memories can come up in any of the five senses. It doesn't have to come up crystal clear in visions. If you just have a feeling of there's something that just feels wrong, trust those feelings. It doesn't matter if it's not real to the point where you have facts to corroborate it or to back it up. Which means you don't have to have someone say, "yes that happened." Or "yes I remember that happened to you." Or even to have person you believe abused you come forward and admit it, because likely that's never going to happen. Oftentimes if it comes up to the surface as an adult if the abuser is now deceased. Or they don't have contact with them or something.

But the first thing I say is just to be kind with yourself when the thoughts, the feelings, and the memories of any kind come to the surface. Treat yourself as if you are treating your own child, with kindness, kid gloves and compassion. If this feeling is a memory or it is a dream that you had but you don't know if it's real or not, but it feels real to you, that is all that matters.

Then the person has so many choices. They can journal about it or they can get a book on abuse, to start. I think "The Courage to Heal" by Ellen Bass and Laura Davis, is a great book. It's an old one, and it's never been updated. It's one of those books that came out in the 80's, but it's a good one. I know there are so many that have come out since then, as well. So even just taking that book and doing the exercises and journaling, is a start. Then I'd suggest doing some healing work, whether it's going to a counselor, or talking to someone that you trust. Then really doing some self care and asking yourself, "how do I want to handle this?" "Maybe I don't want to handle it all."

"Maybe I'll just write about it." "Maybe I'll just show compassion to myself and do some visualizations and meditation." "Maybe I need to go to a counselor." "Maybe I need to confront the person." "Maybe I need to write a letter to that person, but I'm not going to send it, either because they're gone, or I because I choose not to." "But I do need to get it out." "Maybe I need to write a letter to myself as a child, with love and compassion and forgiveness"

There is no right or wrong way to take action. There are so many things one could do, but at the end of the day, the ultimate goal is forgiveness of self. The child is never at fault, I don't care what the circumstances are.

Again, there is no right way or wrong way to take action, once the thoughts and the memories come. You may be reading something that jogs a memory, or maybe you've always known, and you decide you want to get help. There is not one specific way to do begin to heal. Except to recognize that you, the person that was once the child victim of molestation or abuse, was not at fault. Then to start working toward kindness, compassion and forgiveness toward that child. That in itself creates so much healing. So much of the trauma is the interpretation the child holds about themselves, as a result of the abuse.

*ME: Okay so you said, if I'm hearing correctly, that someone can access their own guidance without seeking out a counselor or therapist?*

Yes, maybe they just don't ever, ever want to tell anybody. So, there are self empowering things they could do for themselves, absolutely. There is so much, today especially, at our fingertips that we can read, as well as podcasts, visualizations, meditations, to access that little girl. Then let the feelings and sensations come to the surface and let it flow. Let the emotions come out and then really work on forgiveness of the child, and compassion, and then forgiveness of the abuser. The hardest forgiveness is self forgiveness. Sometimes it's easier to forgive the abuser before forgiving self, but not always. It really depends on the circumstances.

The interview I did for the childhood trauma part of this book, as well as what the reader may need in regard to their own struggles or healing journey was amazing, and Melissa was clear and on point, as always.

As the reader can see from the interview, Melissa hit some really strong points, ones that I was not expecting. Although I had reached out to Melissa last year for therapy, something I never saw myself doing, my questions now seem to have had an intuitive connotation to them. What I mean is, my questions felt like information that any trauma survivor may benefit from, but her responses, took me to my knees. We got through the one hour long 14 question interview, and I was great, so I thought.

I slowly began to edit the interview. I had used the "dictate" feature on my laptop, which wrote Melissa's answers for me. The dictate feature does not include punctuation and also adds words or deletes them. I quickly found myself saying, "ya, nope. Let's just save this part for another time." "Okay, its break time, time for lunch," I convinced myself, as I needed to get away and absorb all that I had just heard.

Lifeless on the couch, my favorite writing spot, I ordered Uber Eats. That would take no effort on my part. "Okay" I bargained with myself "I will have some lunch and get right back to the book in an hour". And that I did. Well, till my son texted, and a friend reached out. They were welcome distractions.

Two hours after the interview with Melissa, after lunch, after welcome distractions, I could hardly stay awake. Now I am a person who has been, for the past few months, up at 5 am, without using an alarm, and I function daily on 5 to 6 hours sleep. That's just my norm. But today my mind and body were screaming for a nap. It makes sense though. As the interviewer I was fine. But rereading all I had written was really hitting me with my own trauma survival. After my first therapy session with Melissa, I remember her asking me how I slept, and I had slept like a baby, 8 hours I believe.

Music wasn't helping. Walking around wasn't helping. An hour later I woke up, after having a vivid dream of cardinals all over this particular field. Dozens of them. It was really a blessing. I imagine those cardinals represent my ancestors. I need their support, so for that I am extremely grateful. However, I also dreamed of my sister sitting in an alley way, arms crossed with her back turned towards me. Not sure the relevance, but it's okay.

I reached out to my "Healing Group" on Facebook for some positive energy. This is becoming a lot. I came here to write my story of childhood trauma in the minister's home, for many reasons. One, it needs to be told. People are not always who you think they are. Especially people in "power". And two, I am not alone. There are many people who need healing. Some who don't even know it yet. I pray this book falls into their hands. So today, I took one for the team. I took one for us. Trauma survivors. Those of us put here to heal the ancestors before them and the generations after. This journey is for us.

# PIGGY –

When a child is called names that sting, for reasons they surely do not understand, they stick. I don't care who you are, they stick.

Piggy was my father's name for me. Brat was one of the Deacon of the Church's name for me.

Hmmm where do I start to unpack this? Well, I promised a chapter on addictions, or self-harming behaviors, etc. This was also touched on in my interview with Dr Fenton.

So, we may as well open up a dialogue. After all, this book is for you.

I was an underweight child, tall, fairly lanky, but not sure where the petty name of Piggy came from. I liked food for sure. Maybe that was it. I was very active, as well. We didn't have junk in the house. We often had homemade cookies that I would always try to trade at school for Hostess snacks, because it was embarrassing to bring cookies in a sandwich baggy, or even worse would be the wax paper wrapped around them. The less I was "allowed" to have store bought snacks, the more I wanted them.

Cumberland Farms downtown had a flavor of the month. It was like 99 cents for the ½ gallon. There would be Blueberry Swirl, Peppermint Patty, Butter Brickle, Black Cherry, Coffee, you name it, they had it. It was my father's favorite, and he would get how much he wanted, whenever he wanted. Often, he'd be found eating out of the container in front of the refrigerator, hardly coming up for air.

We had a bread item at every meal. There was a homemade bread, muffin, biscuit, something of the like with every single dinner. It took me a couple marriages to realize this is not normal. But I can assure you, this is how I got into that habit. I honestly didn't know as an adult, that everyone didn't have a meat, a potato, a veggie (grossed me out as a kid) and bread, with their dinners. I did it that way as an adult for many years. I still to this day, feel that something's missing if a bread item is not there. I am also that way when eating out. Even with all the hullabaloo about gluten. Note* I know it's a real thing, gluten intolerance, etc. I am just stating it was a habit formed before I understood.

After dinner, you stayed in your seat for dessert. It was served immediately following the finishing of the meal. Typically, something sweet with a fancy ice cream or whip cream on it or on the side. My father had a sweet tooth and lived on desserts. Although I'm the Piggy.

We had Kool Aid to drink with our meal. Not water or milk. A Tupperware jug of that ice cold red or purple goodness sat on the table with all meals. I still need sweet with dinner; water seems like deprivation. I would later become addicted to soda, eventually Pepsi, became my sugary drug of choice.

These are facts, they are not blame. I am setting the stage for understanding. Maybe you can even relate to some of this.

After school, we were allowed 2 cookies. Oh, and Kool-Aid again. By the way, it is rumored we had Kool Aid in our bottles. I have nothing to substantiate that, although I can picture purple Kool-Ad in my little brother's yellow plastic bottle.

Sneaking cookies became a control thing for me. Eating as much as I wanted became a control thing. I remember going to my friend's house because her mom made cream cheese brownies and we could have real chips and Coke. Food was definitely fun. Food equaled pleasure.

Yet I was called Piggy. What harm was it, if I wasn't "fat" (HIS word, not mine) like the ladies he made fun of at church?

I think my addiction evolved or changed over the years.

My relationship with food has always been love / hate. I don't think it is my specific addiction, I could take it or leave it. Although I could be wrong, thank goodness for therapy so we can figure it out.

I do have severe Hashimoto's Thyroiditis, a fact, not an excuse. I also had a hysterectomy at age 36. Something that had been scheduled before Brian died, but I postponed, so I could still care for my children and not be laid up. Having serious dis-ease in that part of my body, is not only telling, according to Louise Hay, it is a fact. More on dis-ease later.

I have a twisted sense of self-worth or lack thereof. Twisted or no self-worth, are analogies that aren't really too far apart from each other.

I hate mirrors. Always have. Always. Since I was a kid, I hated to look at myself. I hated to draw attention to myself. Although I jokingly say these days, "oh I am just trying to be the center of attention."

I have been known to cover up mirrors. I don't own them unless it is a bathroom mirror. I mean, it's hard to apply makeup without one.

I've worn make up since I was able to put it on. I don't leave home without it. Habit? Maybe. Or covering up? Probably.

I have worn the swankiest, slinkiest clothes, for attention. I've worn sweatshirts to deflect attention.

This "self-image thing" is a nightmare.

I have gained and lost weight over and over. I have basically starved myself, and I have not cared and eaten whatever. BUT I can also sit down for a meal with anyone, and I eat less. Hands down. Often half of what they eat. People always say, you didn't hardly eat! We could have the same exact meal and while they finish, and clear their plate, I take ½ home in a doggy bag.

I don't call this an addiction. I would put it under self harm, and I will explain why. Shit, now that I think about it, "self harm" seems a bit strong. So instead of striking it from the page, I am going to just change it to self protection. I am doing it this way, so you all can see the tricks we unknowingly play on our minds.

It is protection. When I was a child, no one protected me. The person I wanted and trusted to do that, my father, did not. Even without the abuse, he never protected me. I was on my own. Protecting myself, from bullies, from boys, from the world. I had no mom and a father who was "too busy" to attend any extracurricular activities that I did. I was left to fend for myself. Afterall, there was some church lady, or two or three, that needed his attention. "His work", as he called it, "free counseling", as I called it.

This was not a job, just a free service, that kept him from us, and kept him from reality. A diversion. And most likely and addiction to having women need him. Whether the women were married or single, didn't matter. They were always at our house, or on the phone with my father for two or three hours per day. If I were a spouse of one of those women, I would not have tolerated it for one minute. But they did.

Aside from that, I protected him. Twisted, oh I know that now. I never told. I always made sure he had his meals, I was even doing the grocery shopping as a teen before he took his second wife. As well as all the times she had a breakdown, threw things around the house, and moved out for periods of time, for the first few years of their marriage. I had to fill in when she bailed. He was incapable of doing it himself.

224

*Side note, I have no idea what those melt downs were about, in all fairness to her, I'd guess all the women callers.*

I was allowed to take the car when I didn't have a license. Probably one reason I hate grocery stores so much now! I became the wife / mother figure in *every* sense of the word. And I took care of him as he was dying. I didn't know. I had no memory. I don't know what would have been different during his last few months of life if I had remembered.

Often death helps the abused realize it is safe to "tell". It took me a few years. Therapy has helped me understand how common this really is in childhood trauma.

I was not the oldest. Not even close, I was second to the youngest. I had an older brother who wasn't required to do anything (by no fault of his own) after the lie about his adoption surfaced. *note – some might say avoiding the truth is *not* lying, I say it is. This is a belief that I carried on to adulthood because of that lie, and it has horribly messed up some relationships. Well, that and I don't trust a soul.*

Tim was held in a place of sanctity so as not to upset him any more than he already had been crushed by our father keeping that secret from him. What was my father thinking, the adoption announcement had been in the newspaper!! Which also means that everyone in the church knew he wasn't their child and they all kept it secret. Well, obviously he wasn't my mom's biological child, as she played the church piano and didn't have a pregnant belly prior to baby Timmy showing up. I will leave that there.

Not that it was the congregation's job to tell, but do you see how secrets start, grow, and gain momentum?

"Whoever is careless with the truth in small matters, cannot be trusted with important matters." ~Albert Einstein~

Yes, there is much debate whether 'to tell' or 'not to tell' in an adoption situation. There are open and closed adoptions. These days folks are finding family members they never knew they had, thanks to the popular DNA tests and subsequent "family tree" websites. Sometimes it's a great thing, sometimes it destroys relationships.

But when a whole congregation knows, and the adoption is announced in the newspaper, wouldn't it be best to tell the child, before he finds out himself? Especially when he already doesn't have the mother who adopted him anymore? Maybe they had a plan to tell him, maybe they didn't, no one knows. Maybe my father didn't have the courage. But Tim was 16 years old. It was time.

Because Tim and my younger brother were male, housekeeping and meals was not their "job". I think they may have mowed the lawn, but other than that, tasks inside the house were "girl's jobs". No matter my school schedule, sports schedule, chorus, etc…. Taking care of the "men" was to be priority.

Let me clarify, I was only on the volleyball team, and bowling team. Today cheerleading is considered a sport. So yes, I guess I was in three sports total, at one time or another. I don't think he was even aware.

Tim was a track star. Class L in track, he held the New Hampshire title for pole vault for a long time. I loved watching him make that jump. I was so proud. I can see him in my mind now. Dad did go to Tim's track meets though if his schedule allowed.

I will forever brag on my older brother, and to clarify, he had absolutely protected me when I was older. He didn't know that he needed to when I was young. But I definitely protected him.

Then there was my younger brother. He broke both wrists as a tween, painting the house. I took care of him. Fed him, did everything for him. I continued to do everything for years.

I have an older sister. I love her to death. She and I have nothing in common. Not that it's a bad thing, we just don't. She has battled her own demons and I don't think I want to share much more. I respect

226

her privacy and although this is "BASED on a true story", I protect her as well and don't want harm to come to her. I will say though, the household responsibilities never landed on her. Just me.

I understand so much more now on how the abused is often the one who has all the responsibilities. I read a book recently that really opened my eyes. As well as, of course, therapy with Dr. Melissa Fenton.

When a child is abused by a parent, but their siblings are not, often the abuser is filling the place of an absent spouse. Typically, the child is having to do "wife" things in the house as well. That was me. Again, I am only assuming my siblings weren't violated, I have no facts on that. Nor does it matter for this book, as it is my book, based on a true story.

I will never forget one of the most horrifying nights in my adolescence. Well, I remember some of them, but this next one sticks out.

# RACETRACK –

For some reason, I didn't get included in a lot of social teenage invites. I think it was because my father was so strict, (controlling) and such. Not to place blame here, but I was super nice to everyone. I wasn't ugly. I was a cheerleader. But the kids, my friends, would make plans and I wasn't included.

I found my niche in this one friend, who was really my best friend, and we would hang out with the motor heads from Seacook. I don't remember being coupled up with any of them, but then again, I don't remember much from that time in my life, other than this night.

I was finally included on plans to go to Star Speedway. My friend had her license, I didn't. We were there with the "Brookahs", as they were so lovingly called at my high school. I was finally out of the house and allowed to do something fun!!

Just into the first race, it wasn't even dark yet, but the smoke from the rubber hitting the track was thick and the noise was defining. We always sat in the "pit" because we were "connected." The race cars had slowed down for a flag, we could finally hear each other talk, and were planning a strategic bathroom run, when an announcement came over the speaker. "If there is a Karen Kendall in the stands, please come to concession for a phone call."

Now I'm not sure about you, but when someone calls you at a massive venue, you'd typically fear the call to be informing you of a death in the family. I screamed to my friends, "oh my God, I am so glad I told my father where I was going. Whatever this is, it cannot be good, if I am getting a call here!!"

"Karen, it's your father." He always said it the exact same way, throughout my life. I had noticed though, that he didn't seem sad or anything. Out of breath and unable to ask him what's wrong, before I could take a breath, **"you didn't vacuum the dining room before you left. You are to come home now and do it,"** he shouted.

I have no words at the horror I felt at that moment and still feel, 40 years later.

I hadn't driven there, so that meant that my friend had to leave too! I would never forgive him for this.

"Vacuum the dining room"?????? *That* is why he called me at a major New Hampshire venue?

This was beyond discipline. This was control. I was not allowed to have fun or be away from the house. I was to go to Sunday church twice, morning and night, as well as Sunday School prior to morning church, Wednesday night prayer meeting, Friday night Bible study. And then in between all that, deal with church parishioners showing up at our house at all hours of the day and night, primarily women.

My childhood was stolen from me when my mother was taken. Then stolen again at the hands of my father, as the child housewife. Then again, when even as a teen I was not allowed to have fun. No school dances. No movies, other than Herbie the Love Bug and the like. So, reflecting back, I guess I do see why no one included me. The answer from my father was always "no". I had to make his life easier. After all he was the "widower". I was there to serve.

I was never protected. I was pretty convinced he didn't even like me. I had to protect myself.

# PROTECTION –

When I first woke up to my horrific memories, although not all of them foreign to me, in 2018 in Hawaii, I was walking and swimming every day. Especially after that day. I could not get enough water, whether it was the ocean or the pool. I was sick for a while yet kept up a good front. The third week of my visit, my friend Anna joined me. Also from New Hampshire, it had become tradition now for her to come to the island one week while I was there. I never uttered a word to her about the memories that had surfaced. Not one. She never knew. I never told. I hadn't even processed my memories myself, how would I tell her? The only thing she did notice was my lack of appetite but again, I'm not one to eat more than half of my meal, so that wasn't too far off.

I truly don't fear much. I think growing up the way I did, I learned to handle myself. My alert meter is always on. I have been in a couple sticky situations but never physically hurt since being abused by my boyfriend when I was a teen.

Protection comes in many forms. This is going to sting. But if I cannot be vulnerable at this point in the book, then I am not doing what I came here to do.

I had just gotten on the elevator at my hotel in Jacksonville a few weeks ago. Signs everywhere that state, "only one party in the elevator at a time", are often ignored. The man got on the elevator sweaty and smelling like booze. I thought, "shit this is going to be a long ride to the 5th floor."

And then I made a plan. I often make a plan. If he does this, I will do that. It all works out in my head. "And besides," I said in my head, "I can take this guy!"

Cool and confident, I stood in my corner of the elevator, and he in his, with no ill intentions, I'm sure.

But that's not the whole truth.

See, 2 years prior, following the memories surfacing, I had subconsciously found a way that no one would ever assault me again. I began to gain a protective layer on my body. The harder the emotions, the more protection in the layer.

I am not proud, but I am aware.

The protective layer grows and grows. This is not about food or lack of movement, it's as if my mind has told my body, "if you were fat and ugly none of this would have happened." Often the mind is not the best place to live.

Adult women who are assaulted, generally have nothing in common with each other, such as size, body type, age etc. Elderly women have even been raped in their own home, or in a facility. For instance, there certainly are rapists and murderers who target a certain type or appearance. Quite often it may be a close appearance or some other similarity to someone who violated them in childhood, or something else they associate with their target. But generally speaking, a man's target is typically a female that they have stalked and made their prey. I may note here, in all fairness, men are NOT the only assailants.

So, to have the notion that only skinny women get sexually assaulted, is a notion that is concocted in somewhere in my subconscious. I speak only for myself in this theory. I have done no research; I have no evidence. This is my truth, only. I didn't just come up with this theory, I have had to put a lot of time, thought and clarity into what in the world has happened with me in the last two years. That is my conclusion.

Quitting Pepsi has been a challenge. I quit for the first time when I was married. It was probably 2012. Sober for 3 years, all it took was a migraine, and using caffeine to dull the pain, with one can of Pepsi. One can. That was it.

Addicts cannot have just one and walk away. Again, this is my belief and my experience.

How much do we need to delve into why? Is it because I was brought up on Kool-Aid, but not allowed soda? Is having as much soda as I want, some sort of control thing? Rebellion?

I guess I don't know why, it just is. Then there is food. I'd rather not think about it. When I am working on myself, I don't talk about it. I just try to do it. I'm not one who says, "hey friends, let's make a plan to do this or that and lose this or workout this much!"

I'm chuckling as I write this because we are only 4 weeks into the new year and I have seen half the people who started out their "new life" the first of the year and were all about accountability blah, blah blah, and now they have gone silent. I want to see everyone succeed. However, it is one of the reasons I don't ever speak of my physical journey on Social Media. People are waiting for you to fail. That's a fact. I have many consistent friends out there, but I have many who jump on the bandwagon for a couple weeks, never to be seen or heard from again.

I am a leader. Food and weight are not something I would even begin to try and lead on. There are many people who can do that. But I am also not a follower. I cannot be around someone who says, "what did you eat today? Did you move?" It makes me cringe to even write that. I have to figure out something else.

I teach people to love themselves. I teach them how to do the hard work. I teach power. But oh isn't it so different in my "own backyard"?

I know many Mediums or healers who are "statistically" overweight. They are all beautiful. I know many Mediums or healers who are gay. Neither of those things have any bearing whatsoever on their work. Someone's weight or sexual preference has literally nothing to do with their spirituality, or their ability to use their gifts to help others.

I will say though, through my own observation and no science or research, that the healer, lightworker, Medium, whatever you want to call it, has very often been the subject of some sort of trauma. Whether in childhood or as an adult.

I know several healers who have had near death or even death experiences, and others who are survivors of childhood trauma of some sort.

We are a product of our beliefs. In my mind, no one will bother me with this layer of protection. This was never an issue until these memories surfaced, over two years ago. I wasn't thin by any means, but I was not how I am now. Some folks can get on social or talk to their friends about 15 pounds or 50. About the size of their ass. About the "Corona 20" that they gained. I cannot. "If I don't acknowledge it, no one will notice it." I have always thought this way.

Some folks swear by this or that as far as health and weight loss. Some folks see things in a different light. Some swear that Keto is a fix. Veganism is a fix. While those methods, as well as others, are exactly what some folks need, it's not the answer to everyone's situation. Even medical intervention may not be the answer. I will say again, I speak ONLY from my point of view, not science or facts or beliefs. Just simply my point of view.

I've met many women, and a couple men, who have had bariatric surgery of some sort. The medical community is always coming out with something new, and in some instances, medical insurance will cover it. But I have also been aware of many startling health issues following these types of surgeries. I know people who have died at a young age, of stroke, embolisms and the like. Never linked to the actual surgery, but I've made my own connection, through the similarities in their health issues. There are also the folks, men and women, including a few celebrities, who have gained some, if not all. of the original weight back. Some even put on extra!

Then there is the emotional piece. I've seen marriages fall apart following weight loss surgeries. I've seen severe mental health issues arise. Addictions developed. While I am very aware that there is a mental health program that takes place prior to the surgery, I hear very often, "nothing could have prepared me for this!"

I don't have a personal opinion on the weight loss surgeries, although when asked in session, I have gotten a huge "NO" from Spirit on more than one occasion. Personally, I think anytime your body is opened up for any reason, you can subject yourself to other issues. That's just my opinion. Have I personally thought about it? Sure. But here we are.

What I do know is that, in my opinion, more often than not, weight has less to do with food consumption, and more about emotions. Although we all know that eating right and exercising does a body good. That's a fact.

What I want to address is underlying, emotional, and obviously physical issues.

I believe we could actually call weight gain, 'self harm'. I say that because it is proven medical science that weight can hurt the heart. It can cause difficulty breathing, often asthma, and let's not talk about the knees and other joints. The sheer law of gravity shows it must be brutal on hips, ankles and especially knees when extra weight has to be carried around. Quite often it prevents someone from exercising due to joint pain. The vicious cycle begins.

Then what is it that needs to be addressed here? In my belief it is the fact that emotions, trauma, and addictions form a basis for weight gain. Or loss, for that matter. I'm here to address gain.

If you have any struggle at all with weight, can you correlate it to a certain "time" of trauma, pain, loss? By that I mean............well let me look at me. Afterall this is my story.

Back to the part where over the past two years, since I had all the memories flow in, and gradually off and on after 10/6/18. I absolutely do not eat a bite more of food than I did. Not a morsel. That is a fact. I don't exercise any less. I am not depressed or anxious by any means. I am suffering with trauma, in many forms. The realization of sexual abuse, the constant barrage of thoughts, "is this my fault?", the incomprehensible fact that I have been lied to for so many years, and the search for my mother.

Quite often my tummy is in knots. Not due to anxiety or panic, but absolute horror of how my life has really been. People were not who I thought they were. Relationships were not what I thought they were. And most of all, this all unknowingly affected all of my marriages. The common denominators of zero self worth, and if there is a number lower than zero, of trust.

Not one of those three husbands, looking at it now, gave me one thing to be jealous about. They never commented about other women, they never were 'not where they said they were', they were faithful and loyal to a fault. It was me.

I know this now. Too late. Again, a reason or a season. I have apologized to the living ones more than once. I assume I'm forgiven.

# TRUST –

I didn't know. I didn't know there were people who could love me AND be trusted at the same time!

How would I ? The one parent I did have, we found holed up in a cabin with a parishioner that he said he'd never go out with because she was fat, when he had told us he needed a "week to work on sermons." And yes, I can tell you even today, who he called names in the church. Mostly women, though. Nope, name calling is not a sin. The relevance here is most the names, if not all had to do with their bodies or their appearance.

Now, don't get me wrong, I am all for silence and meditation alone in the woods for clarity or for writing, but lying to your children, as their father and the "servant of God", can be extremely harmful to a child, for many reasons. To this day, I don't know what happened in that cabin or how long his lady friend was there, but as I tell my children and grandchildren, it is not what it actually is, it is what it looks like. That is what matters. If you don't want to be accused of anything, don't put yourself in a situation that would cause someone to assume something other than the facts. I know what it looked like from a little girl's view, so in my mind, that is what it was. Bottom line, it was a blatant lie. He broke my trust. I am not concerned with how or if it even affected my siblings. That's not my issue.

Or even better, if you cannot hold up the expectations of a servant of God, who claims to walk in a perfect life, free from sin, then do not hold the position of Minister, Priest, Pastor, etc. Just step down. We are all human. Humans make mistakes. We all make mistakes. I am not without fault, by any means.

He lied. He was with a woman and not writing sermons. (I mean, yes, he has a right to have a social life) We caught him, and it was gross. I don't know why it hurt me so much, or why I remember this so clearly, I mean I surely didn't understand hypocrisy as a child. I sure do now though.

Is that where my trust was shattered? I mean he didn't directly do anything to me at that point. Or did he? He did. At the time, I was so unaware of the abuse earlier on in my life, and actually to this day, I don't know if it was still going on at that time in my life, so that was not the issue.

I assume most children would expect their parents not to lie. Especially the minister parent. Lying was a sin. That amongst many other sins, were drilled into our heads. I feared going to hell if I said a swear. That is no joke. I can say I believed I would go to hell for saying shit. Of course, now swearing is a common part of my conversations.

So, I take that one instance, combine it with not trusting him and the others not to hurt me, and add to it the lie we realized when finding out my brother was adopted, I learned at an early age, men in general and men of the church, and most importantly men who are supposed to love and protect me, cannot be trusted.

If I could not trust my father, I would trust no man. Especially one who says he loves me. My siblings have other trust issues. I don't need to address them here, but they are very evident.

## TRAUMA IS THE GATEWAY –

A friend whose wedding I performed as a Justice of the Peace, actually she grew up with my kids, just posted an amazing piece by comedian actor, now sober for many years, right at the perfect time.

Cannabis isn't a gateway drug.
Alcohol isn't a gateway drug.
Nicotine isn't a gateway drug.
Caffeine isn't a gateway drug.

Trauma IS the gateway. Childhood abuse is the gateway.
Molestation is the gateway. Neglect is the gateway.

Drug abuse, violent behavior, hyper sexuality and self harm are often symptoms (not the cause) of much bigger issues. And it almost always stems from a childhood filled with trauma, absent parents, and an abusive family.

~Russell Brand~

# WERE THERE MORE? –

As I just returned from losing my breakfast in the bathroom, right now, in real time, my 'visceral' reaction, as Melissa has explained, tells all. Until this very moment, on a sunny day in Myrtle Beach, I had not put any thought into this. It took me typing it to hit the panic button that just screamed, "holy shit, this could be a very likely reality!" I mean think about it, why would I be the only target in that whole church?

A couple people who would have been young at the time, instantly come to mind. It's quite clear that although I don't remember my childhood, other than a few gut wrenching events, I remember the names and faces of the church attendees. Some I remember being fond of, others not so much. But we weren't allowed to judge. Judging was, after all, a sin. I definitely know what we are going to talk about in therapy on Monday!

Is it my fault? Have they too written a book? Do they have addictions? Do they suffer from the trauma? Do I help them? Will they see my book? Or watch my film, as Joy says it is going to be?

This suddenly feels bigger than it did this morning. Harsher, it feels harsher, or more harsh, I should say. Afterall, I grew up with an English professor for a father. And on that, so as not to always bash my father, I do have an excellent command of the English language, and I do think that has made it easier to write this book. I give him 100% credit for that.

The origin of this book was to help others. Survivors of childhood trauma. Survivors of "cult like" religious indoctrination, conditioning, brainwashing, and fear mongering. I think that covers it.

While many children, including my siblings, did not take that away from their childhood experience, I was not like them. I knew there was something that did not sit right with all of it. Not in my mind, anyway.

I am now presented with the notion that the childhood sexual abuse part of this story, may not be just mine. That is a tough pill to swallow. I have so many thoughts, so many questions. I have to understand my part in this today. Now, not then. I was a small child. None of it did I play a part in. I was exposed to it. Big difference.

I have been battling with my own emotions and there is now a very real possibility that there are more victims, for lack of a better word. To be clear, I suppose that was always a possibility. But it never entered my mind, till today.

My gut says, there are more. So not only do I believe that this book will fall into the hands of those who need it; other victims of childhood abuse and lies, from their parents or family members, clergy, teachers, or other adults in positions of power, but if there are more that were abused in my father's church, I believe this book will fall into their hands as well. Then, I will have to navigate my way through it. As one of my ex's used to say, "don't borrow trouble". *update – during editing it has come to light that there *are* more victims*

In therapy yesterday, I told Dr Fenton what fear had come up for me. About others being victimized at my church. Was it my thing to fix? Should I help them? All the questions I had come up with on Saturday and written here in the book, prior to this.

My logical brain says none of it's my fault but as she explained, the little girl Karen takes this opportunity to say, "see, you *are* bad!" Just as I thought, my instant physical response to these thoughts was a clear indication that the answer to my question is yes, and that somewhere in my subconscious I may even know about it or have suspected it at the time. "But it's okay." She said, "You were the child, you are not and never will be responsible for an adult's actions. Not to you, not to anyone else. You also are not responsible to help them. The knee jerk reaction to think that you have to help them, is natural, especially since you are in the helping business. Your book will help them. Perhaps they have done some work on it. But either way, you don't need to fix anyone."

Someone might say, "okay that makes total sense, good, let's move on." For me, I was going to have to absorb it and sit with that. But that little girl Karen wasn't finished. She had more to ponder. "So, can you concentrate on you and working on this new fear that has come up? If so, how would you do that?", Dr. Fenton asked.

As if little girl Karen were in the room, without skipping a beat, I asked, "So I would help myself and not them?" "Yes", she said. "What would that look like for you?" "I would meditate and journal with music and write whatever came up.", I replied. "So can you do that and not be concerned with helping others?" "Well", as if a 7 year old had entered the room, "I think that would be selfish". And with that statement, I got homework.

# MEDITATION ~

Mornings before the sun comes up, I sit with meditative music, do a deep meditation and journal, and typically get back at this keyboard and write. This morning would be no different. Well, other than today, I would search for a trauma healing meditation. Ugh, I hate that word trauma. Well at least in reference to myself. It feels overly dramatic, although I know in my logical mind that is so far from the truth. Journal ready, I found a meditation that was about 20 minutes long, about clearing childhood trauma. It had binaural beats, although I have no idea what they are, I have seen them on other meditations.

I was overly underprepared. Since the initial onset of my childhood memories, I haven't cried much at all. I can't even remember the last time I cried. Maybe a year ago or something? I really don't know. How hard can this be? I have worked on plenty of issues through journaling and meditation. This is just another one of those things.

The meditation began with a noise I cannot describe. It gave me a jolt, and I was wondering what the hell it was. As it went on, it must have been those binaural beats, because I was crawling out of my skin. I don't recall this feeling ever, in adulthood, at least not that I can remember.

I quickly threw my hands up over my face and eyes, as if 3 year old me had heard a noise under my bed. My face stung as my cold hands slapped my skin. What the hell is this reaction? I wanted to shut the meditation off. But the healer in me said, "this is it, Karen, you HAVE

TO do the work!" I continued to crawl out of my skin, but I knew this was important stuff. I did it! I finished the whole meditation, and quickly grabbed my journal to write whatever came out. Ten pages later I thought I was complete.

I cursed and I yelled, and I cried. It's been a long time since I cried. I heard the phrase, "but don't you love your daddy". I lost it. I became so angry. I hadn't been this angry in a bit, so I definitely needed to address it. Although yesterday's trauma healing meditation was meant to heal, and it absolutely did, I just took the long way, it brought up more memories. I suddenly felt like I should get rid of his watch. I don't know if that is lack of forgiveness, because I do feel forgiveness and also pity as whatever they were all doing was pathetic. During the meditation I also was able to see my mom's "side" of the bedroom, very clearly. His side, not so much.

"May the road rise up to meet you. May the wind always be at your back. May the good Lord hold you in the palm of his hand." It hung right above her empty dresser. Her clothes, jewelry, anything connected to her – gone.

No reason, no logic, no excuse.

In today's society, it may not be considered abuse, you know, "spare the rod, spoil the child". But the horrific memory that I spoke of earlier in the book, having to take my pants and underwear down, or off for whoever was there to watch me be paddled on the naked bottom, with someone watching, disgusts me as much as the rest of it. Perhaps because of the blatant humiliation of having to have my private areas showing while bending over a knee, and having this wooden thing hit me, over and over and over. Abuse doesn't go on a scale. Abuse is abuse. Some so horrific, some not as horrific to read about, but to the child with her pants down, abuse and humiliation NEVER goes away. I will never forget that part of my childhood. It seemed like it was always me, too. I do not remember doing a thing that warranted being naked and spanked, I am not sure what does. Oh that's right, nothing.

The rest of it all so heinous that my mind has not allowed me to remember and view most of it, I don't know if it will ever will. A lot of what I journaled yesterday I can't even read. I guess I did the work I need to do and some of it won't make it into the book, as it is not legible. I can read in the journal that my heart was racing, and my breathing was fast. What I definitely do know is that major healing happened yesterday. And for that, I am so grateful. Again, you do the work, you get the results.

Then last night, Joy connected with Sandy for me. She had so much to "say". Definitely filled in some blanks. I have added it into the book, well some of it. Unfortunately, the names are changed for my own protection, not for theirs. I don't need any adult trauma because I spoke up. I am far from afraid, but.......I don't have time or energy. I also do not want my family harassed, i.e. my children and grandchildren.

They deserve better. I deserve better. The ancestral karma bullshit stops with this generation. It stops here and now with me. With this book. I am **not** afraid.

It is better to have loved and lost then never loved at all.

But yet when love is so twisted when you are a child, how do you even understand it?

Here is what I know for sure. I didn't experience the love of a mother when I was a child. I don't remember my father saying "I love you" ever. Although I think he may have said it on his death bed. So as not to compare my story with folks who have been through losing both parents, I speak only to my life, and my understanding or lack thereof, of love. I have loved a spouse, and I have been loved by a spouse, that is something I will never question. They could have loved me more than life itself, it never would have been enough for me. As I explained earlier, nothing was enough for me, because I did not trust them. By no fault of their own. Love and trust were two emotions that didn't intertwine.

To have known then what I know now, I can safely say things would have been completely different.

# A CHILD IS BORN –

Enter my first born son.

"Hurry up", I need to get home and watch "V". Today I have no friggin clue what that movie was. My OB doctor was a wise ass, to say the least. Sometimes the things he'd say would put me in hysterics, whether I was in full contractions or feeling at all nervous in his office during an exam.

The look on his daddy's face as he looked at me and back at our son, I saw love. I knew love. I was wrecked after delivering that 9 ½ pound butterball, but I couldn't get enough of this baby. I found out within seconds the love between a parent and a child. What love is "supposed to be".

How does a parent not want to smother their child in love? You could be scared to death of this little breakable being that you are supposed to figure out and keep alive, fed, and bathed, but you figure it out. Every time I hear of someone having a baby and their mom comes to help for 3 months, my heart splits apart.

I wonder if she knew. I wonder if she ever sensed, "oh my gosh, I am a grandma". That was all stolen from her, and me. My gut says she knew. A mother's love. I get it. It truly needs no other explanation.

Just nine short months later, my first daughter would be on her way into this world. I remember crying in my bed at night during the second trimester, "how could I have enough love for another baby?" "Like how do mom's do this?" But as she punched her way out after 45 minutes of labor, I knew just how easy and natural it was to love another baby, even another 9 ½ lb. feisty baby!

Five years later, another girl would follow, at 10 lbs. 14 oz. She was the whole Thanksgiving Butterball Turkey, born just a day late!

Although I am constantly accused of loving one of my four children more than the other, I don't truly think that is possible. When you are a parent, your heart expands so big that you have room for each and every child. And then the grandchildren begin rolling in, for a total of six. They are all amazing in their own way. The heart just expands and there is room for all of them.

The point here is how do you not show and tell these children every single day, if possible, as much love as you humanly have possible to give? It's a rhetorical question. However, I do think I was super cute and loveable as a child, however I never knew the love of a parent.

I say quite often though, "I don't know how I didn't turn out like him. I know certainly not from his example. You don't learn how to love, you just love. There is no reason imaginable to harm a child, and / or to withhold love. It is a parent's job to provide that child with love from the moment it is conceived. It's the easiest job in the world. I will maul my kids and grandkids with love, whether they like it or not, especially at an opportunity to embarrass them.

## A THIEF IN THE NIGHT -

Fear, control, brainwashing.......... A Thief in the Night – The fear of going to hell. The constant threat dangled over my head as a child.

I truly believe this is why I created or designed my first tattoo. I knew on a superficial level that I had been threatened my whole life with God making me suffer in the pits of the fire in hell. But until I wrote this book, I didn't realize the serious negative impact it had on me.

"This is it" I said to the tattoo artist in my favorite shop in downtown Portsmouth, NH, "this devil standing in the flames. This is what I want! But can you put a halo above his head, please?" Everyone hated my tattoo. It was right on my chest above my heart. I didn't know what all this hell fire was about, but I am an angel, and I think it's a bunch of crap. That was 30 years ago. Nothing has changed.

"We are having a movie at church Sunday night." The pit in my stomach would unknowingly form and I could feel my skin crawl. "Please, if it is 'A Thief in the Night', I don't want to go, please!!" I begged, "I don't want to go. I hate that movie! Please, can I sit outside?"

"You are going and sitting inside the church". I'd immediately hear. The church itself sat above the small town's Post Office. A meeting room of sorts, I remember the smell. Wooden floors, huge windows and never warm inside, I had nightmares of that place, I still do. I was literally forced to be in church several times a week until I was 18. This was partially about grooming, conditioning and controlling me, and significantly about his image.

I am reminded now at this moment, I hated to go into that bathroom. Dark wood as well, and old, but I was not allowed to lock the door, even if I was in the stall. I remember 'holding it' because of the fear of someone walking in and seeing me. It was co-ed.

My stomach, currently in knots, is actively responding now to this bathroom as well. You, the reader, are being exposed, raw and uncut, to a memory that I am finding less than pleasant.

When I was looking for my mom in October, I did ride through the neighboring towns just in case I was missing something. I went past the Post Office / church and had a physical reaction. It's becoming clear now, why.

He was always smoking cigarettes behind the church. I always wanted him to protect me. Save me. But they favored him. They always bought him stuff and took him places. The one person who had he known, would have made sure NO ONE touched me. He didn't have to be in church, he was different. Special. The "broken one," my brother Tim.

The movie begins with a woman, waking up to her radio saying, "everyone is gone". The 'rapture' had happened and the sinners, i.e. the bad people, were left behind. Hypocrisy is the word that comes to my mind again. The camera pans to scenes of empty cars running off the road, children's toys abandoned in the yard. This is basically the entire movie.

As an eight year old child, I was repeatedly threatened and scared to death that if I don't do exactly what the Book, with it's many different, often opposing, translations, and demands, that I will be like that woman, left behind. "God" would make us pay! Suffer for our sins. Now keep in mind, I was trained that swearing, drinking, divorce, you name it, it was all a sin.

If I did not do what this movie said, I was going to a fiery place for bad people where I would burn to death. The devil himself would be there too.

Who does this to a child? Today, forcing this fear based crap would be considered emotional abuse. I was forced to watch that movie, and others, many times. Although, I wasn't allowed to watch "Lost in Space" at my friend's house, because it was not real and borderline satanic.

Burned (pun intended) so destructively into my little child brain, that 50 years later I remember the words from the theme song of "A Thief in the Night".

"Life was filled with guns and war, and everyone got trampled to the floor. I wish we'd all been ready. Children died the days grew cold. A piece of bread could buy a bag of gold. I wish we'd all been ready. There's no time to change your mind, the Son has come, and you've been left behind. You've been left behind."

FIFTY fucking years! It is still branded into my head. My little brother was 5 or 6. WHY would any adult think it was okay to brainwash and scare the living shit out of a child enough so they still remember the movie, as well as the theme song, FIFTY years later. Although, I do believe it still happens today.

I understand everyone has their own take on religion. I am not one, and won't ever be one, to stuff my beliefs down another's throat. I only wish they would stop trying to stuff theirs down mine. You believe what you want to believe, I will believe what I want.

"Sounder" a movie also released that year, was a requirement to watch in 3rd grade. As well as to read the book. It was about a dog. We watched it several times in school. It was about a dog. It probably had a theme song. I don't know. I do know it was about a dog. Other than that, I've got nothing.

As I just looked up to see what year Sounder was released, I figured I would look to see exactly when "A Thief in the Night" was released. The same year, 1972, according to Wikipedia. I'm actually surprised that anyone even had a record of this religious horror film.

I went on to read, "The film has been described as traumatic for the children, who made up a significant part of its original audience and criticized for using scare tactics to produce religious conversions."

Side note* My father was deeply involved with Teen Challenge those years. I will leave that there for now.

"According to Hendershot," it continues, "Evangelicals who grew up in the 1970's or early 1980's often cite 'Thief' as a source of childhood terror". Hey, but I'm just glad I was saved from watching 'Lost in Space'. I definitely dodged a life altering bullet there!

"This is partly due to depictions in the film of characters who believe themselves to be 'saved' (this word in my church meant, accepting God as your savior, etc.), but are not, and are instead left behind."

I guess I am not alone in my assessment of this horror film that I was forced to watch over and over and over again. Enough so I know the words of the theme song. "Life was filled with guns and war, and everyone got trampled to the floor...." I was a child. A small innocent child.

The ONLY thing being threatened by a fire filled death in hell as a little girl did, was allow them to use their control over me. I truly believed that if I didn't do this or that, I would go to hell. I firmly believe that if it came out of his mouth to me when I was an adult, it absolutely came out of his mouth and other's mouths when I was a child. It was more of a religious cult than anything else. When you teach with fear, and I use that word "teach" lightly, you aren't teaching. When you guide with love, you are teaching.

# FEAR, CONTROL AND BRAINWASHING -

It may be hard for any of the church goers involved in my father's church to believe any of my story. That is totally fine with me. Unless, of course, they already knew.

However, what they saw, and what my life was truly like, are complete opposite ends of the spectrum. I was scared, confused and suspicious of everyone and everything. The only thing I took into adulthood, was being suspicious of everybody. Not that they are scary or going to rob me, but that I cannot trust them in a relationship or in a business capacity. Being self-employed that does not bode well for me, as I simply cannot do everything myself.

I do however have the fear of flight, and it is very real. Not of flying, I love flying. I believed no one could love my enough not to leave me. If I was not perfect, they would leave. I needed to be perfect for anyone to love me.

I also came into adulthood afraid of nothing. I know that seems the opposite of what I just said, but it isn't. I do not fear flying, I do not fear being in this situation or that situation. I have always felt that I can handle myself, no matter the situation. I have a gun. I have for many years. I don't carry often, but I certainly have, no one even knew. Well there was that *one* time…

Many people have asked me how I travel alone all the time, many times a year. I have no issue with it. I am extremely alert. I had even toyed with the notion of doing a blog post or something to help women do things to protect themselves when traveling or any other time for that matter. I have tons of tricks up my sleeve. No one taught me them. I've always been this way.

Maybe having no one in my life to protect me caused me to develop certain protection methods, or maybe it is just experience.

# SAFETY –

Since we are on the subject of fear, or in my case, lack thereof, those who wonder what I do to protect myself, and many have asked, here is a few safety tidbits that I have developed:

When I am alone in New York City:

When walking I ALWAYS have my phone in my hand. If I feel as though anyone may be any type of threat or anything, although it has never happened in all these years, I get right on my phone on that fake call to hunny.

Have a good grip on your handbag, be sure it is zipped or snapped closed.

I always look up. I look people in the face. I walk boldly, and confidently, even when I am trying to figure out which way to go.

In a Broadway theatre or in a restaurant, I don't do this, but a safety tip would be to order two coffees, or beverages, even though you are sitting alone. Carry two water bottles as if your person is just in the bathroom. Or stay near a group of people.

In a parking garage, if the attendant asks when you will be back, always say earlier than you expect. And say "we" so they know you aren't coming back alone.

I don't feel any of these areas are dangerous, but for those who do, this should help.

Alone in a hotel:

Who knows why you might find yourself alone in a hotel. I always am, so there are a few things I have created to do if anyone or anything feels amiss. I don't even think about these things, they just come naturally.

If I am staying for a bit, I immediately befriend the front desk staff. Call them by name. They may not show it, but they often keep tabs on people. If I know I will be back during their shift, I often tell them when I will return. Typically I say earlier than I planned. Or "be back soon." (hotel shifts are fairly easy to figure out)

When you are at the front desk with a question, and the first thing they ask is, "what's your room number?", grab a piece of paper and write it down. Or show them your key folder. Even when you don't see someone standing in the lobby, there could be someone within earshot.

Always enter an empty elevator. If someone is in it, just pass for the next one. Who cares what they think of you. And honestly, since Covid, it hasn't been weird at all.

If someone enters the elevator with you, don't get off at your floor. Wait for them to leave. Always have your car keys, phone, or room key in hand. You can even say into your phone, "ya I am on the elevator now, be right there hunny." IF someone had ill intentions, which in my opinion would be very random, not only do they now know your person is on the other end of the phone and knows you are in the elevator, but there is someone waiting in your room for you.

If you get off of an elevator and are in the hotel hallway with someone, walk past your room. If for some reason you are unable to do so, unlock your door and as you open it yell, "hey hunny, I'm back!"

Don't use the stairwell, unless it is very well lit. Often it is not used all day. I have found many a creep hanging out in the stairwell, not that they are there to harm, but quite often they are just warming up. The reason being, there is typically an outside entrance at the bottom floor. People will wait for someone with a room key to use it and walk in behind them. Or it often gets propped open a crack. This is ALL hotels, not just sketchy ones.

Wear a wedding ring when traveling. Not that the "bad guys" look, but it immediately implies someone is keeping tabs on you. However, that said, don't wear a bunch of expensive jewelry to look rich. Some costume jewelry is fine.

When ordering food delivery to your room:

Order enough for two and eat the rest later, if you are nervous about the delivery person knowing you are alone. Again with Covid restrictions may delivery apps offer a "drop at the door" delivery, which is another way to do it.

Or even if you order for one person only, ALWAYS look out the peep hole in your door BEFORE opening, then just as you are opening the door yell, "it's just the food delivery, Babe", or whatever term of endearment you prefer to use.

Or again, order two beverages. It's only another $3.00 and can give you piece of mind.

Uber, Lyft or another ride service:

When scheduling the ride on the app, they decide who picks your ride. However, the moment your driver comes up on the screen, check out their "rating". Not just the "number of stars" rating but read the reviews. Quite often someone got pissed at the driver for something the rider themselves did, however it wasn't the driver's fault. So then the rider gives a 1 star rating instead of 5. In that case, the driver may have 4 stars instead of 5. So if you want to give them a fair shake, read the first 3 or 4 reviews really quickly. This of course, goes with any ratings and reviews.

I will not take a ride from 3 stars or less drivers. You can IMMEDIATELY cancel the ride if you don't like their ratings and reviews. The app will most likely ask why, and I believe driver rating is one of the choices. These apps change all the time.

All of that said, also check your own rating. Are you ordering a ride and it is taking forever to find a driver? Sometimes it's just a busy time of day, or you are in an area with not many drivers. But it may be your rating. Drivers see this when they accept a ride. So if you don't have a 5 star rating, find out why. You do not want to be stuck somewhere and have no ride service want to pick you up.

My rating on Lyft is 5.0, 5.0 years, 100+ rides. That is what the driver sees. It is right in your profile on the app.

Once your ride arrives:

ALWAYS check the license plate. I don't care if you feel weird. I have actually had the wrong car show up. He claimed he got a new car. Maybe so. But the app shows the car and the plate, and the driver. None matched. I sent him away and took it up with Uber later.

I am by no means saying that ride services are dangerous. I use them all the time. I have met some great drivers, all over the country.

Next, expect the driver to call you by name. I typically wait until they roll down the passenger's window and call me by name. Or if I have luggage, I expect them to get out of the car and assist. They receive a nice tip for doing so. Especially the drivers that show up in pick-up trucks. I pack my suitcases to the max 50 lbs. so............

To recap:
Check the car to see if it matches the one the app gave you.
Check the license plate. You are not in that much of a rush.

Have the driver call you by name.

They SHOULD know where you are going, and not need to ask. Although some do like to validate. Ask them what it shows.

If the Uber picks you up at home: NEVER tell them how long you will be gone or that your house is empty. I always say my adult son is home and in charge till I get back.

In the car:

Always sit in the back passenger's side of the vehicle. Sitting behind the driver does not allow you to see his GPS, etc.

Always buckle up. If the driver were to get in an accident and you are not buckled, in any state other than New Hampshire, you will have some responsibility if god forbid, you get hurt.

I always click on the app to keep an eye on my "in app gps map", and make sure it matches with his, which you should be able to see on his mounted phone, on the dash.

If he takes a call, you have a right to ask him not to.

If the radio is loud, or AC is too high, ask them to change them. You are hiring them. Yes, it is their car, but you are the paying customer.

Always "share" your ride with someone. Not share the car, please don't take that option to save a buck or two but click on "share your ride" in the app and send it to someone.

There is now also an option to click on the app if you feel in danger.

Lastly, if they begin to take you somewhere that is not following the GPS, ask them if they are going the right way.

I have had this experience twice. Both times I got my money back,(an extremely difficult fete) however the Uber driver hit me with a 1 star rating, because of it, so my Uber rating is only 4.94. To be honest I haven't used them since, as both incidents were not far apart, like less than a month.

I was at the Cape. (Cape Cod, MA, for all my Florida friends) I had taken a bus in to stay in my dear friend's beach house that she had loaned me. I took an Uber to get a few things at a Grocery Store, 9 minutes away in the same town. 15 minutes into the ride, we were on an onramp getting onto 95. I asked him where he was going. He said to the grocery, (same one, different town). Why would you take me 30 minutes away when there is one in town? "This one has a bank" he said.

It was a Sunday. "I don't need a bank!" At this point, 25 minutes after he picked me up, we were 5 minutes away from the one he had chosen, so we went to that one. I was so angry. "Well since we are 30 minutes from where I am staying, you are going to have to wait" I said. I am not paying for another Uber to drive me 30 minutes back to where I am staying." Snarky but apologetic, he agreed to wait.

In the store, I couldn't concentrate on what I needed. I quite frankly didn't trust him to be out there when I came out, and I had no idea where I was. I grabbed 10 or 12 things for the week and checked out, with my 3 or 4 bags, and some gallons of water in the cart. He pulled up with his drivers' side to the Grocery store, which meant I would have to walk around. I opened the driver's side back door, emptied the groceries into the back seat, and returned my cart to the sidewalk a few steps away. I then spun around and walked behind the car to get in on the empty passenger's side of the back seat. As I walked behind the car to the other side, he put it in drive and started to pull the feck away!!!!! I bolted forward and banged on the trunk of the car, probably denting it. He stopped finally, I got in and he says, "Oh I didn't know you weren't in the car. I thought you got in the other side." The steam came out of my ears and I didn't say another word. Not then, not when I got back to the beach house.

The next time, I was in Florida. I had been picked up in Fort Myers and I was off to Punta Gorda to check out a potential retreat venue. The ride began with me watching him on the little in app map, on his way to pick me up, go to the wrong hotel and drive behind it. He finally got to me and headed into downtown Fort Myers and I said, "this isn't the right way." I had watched him go past the exit that the app gps said he was supposed to take. He was rambling on and on about how much he hates Uber. That is how he missed the exit. "I've lived here 40 years, and I know the right way to go. This app is no good. It never works. I am going this way" At this point we were already 30 minutes into a 22 minute ride. "Okay, well I have my gps on and it says we are headed the opposite direction of where I need to go." "Where are you going?" He asked.

"Exactly where I typed into the ride app. Punta Gorda!" I said. "Well that's not what you said when you got in the car." "Really????" "I don't need to say where I am going, and I didn't. Isn't that why I booked the ride in the app??" The ride took over an hour. About as long as it took me to figure out how to call Uber, as they don't have a published number.

Other than a few other weirdos, I have had great luck with Ride apps and I have never been afraid, just angry.

Traveling a distance by car:

Rest areas ~ If you pull into one and no one else is there don't stop, pull right back out.

If you pull into one that looks sketchy at all, don't stop, pull right back out. Stop at ones where people are walking their dogs, or there are families.

Typically, shortly before you approach a rest area, there will be a blue highway sign announcing it, which will also say how many miles until the next one. Pay attention in case you do end up pulling back out.

Look everyone in the eye.

Often there is a volunteer inside the building helping with maps, etc… make eye contact and speak to them. If they have a name tag, call them by name. They are trained to notice things. They know how to spot human trafficking. They will notice if you aren't out of the bathroom in a reasonable amount of time.

Case in point. I had stopped at a rest area in Connecticut to change out of jeans and sweatshirt into full makeup and hair, and ¾ length dress for a wedding. I had left New York City that morning and had to be at a wedding in Northern New Hampshire that afternoon.

I had no other option than to get ready on the way. I had been taking a while in the rest room, so the lady at the desk in the rest area came in and checked on me, only to find me with a curling iron in my hair.

You should always be aware of your surroundings. Know where your car is. Car locked, keys in hand.

If you get back in the car and have to look at your gps, tend to your phone, or eat your meal, push the lock button. Most people get so used to the locks clicking as soon as they put the car in gear, they don't think to lock themselves in the car while they are sitting in a public area.

I honestly prefer a truck stop. They are typically easy off, easy on the highway. You can see the sign from the highway, Pilot, TA, Flying J, are just some. Here is why.

A truck stop will always have, food, gas, and bathrooms. That can limit how many times you have to stop.

If it is dark, park in front of the front doors if possible. If not, park at the gas pump, even if you don't need gas. It will be well lit.

If you need to sleep for a bit, you want to park as close to the trucks as possible.

Truckers get a bad rap. They are dads, grandpas, brothers, and sons. They have someone at home. They are out there making a living. They aren't at the truck stop to hurt people. They are just trying to take a much needed break. But they also have their eyes open and are very aware.

Truckers train themselves to notice when something isn't right. They have been credited with spotting abducted children and adults, as well as thwarting domestic situations. They have found the missing elderly after a silver alert.

If I ever have to sleep in a rest area or truck stop, I always park as close to tractor trailers as possible. I know, if anything were to happen, they would have my back. They don't miss much.

If you are traveling alone and have bags and pillows or anything that shows you are away for a while, make sure those things are in the trunk. An easy target is someone who isn't expected home real soon.

No matter where you are, when getting gas, even if you are a mile from home, NEVER leave your car running. Take the keys out AND lock it. Although you are right beside the driver's side of car, you are typically looking at the gas pump, or not facing your car, and your purse is probably in the passenger's seat. It takes a split second for someone to open that side of the car and grab your purse.

Don't ever tell someone where you are headed. Make something up. No one needs to know your business. You can have a conversation with someone without telling someone where you are headed. Yes, there are people who prey on women and men traveling alone. But if you are smarter than they are, aware and alert, you will stay safe.

Unfortunately, Good Samaritans aren't always good. If someone pulls over to help you in any situation, don't roll your window down or get out of the car. Always call the police. You don't have to be polite to someone who stops to help. This tends to be when many abductions happen. Case in point, college student, Maura Murray. If you aren't aware of the Maura Murray case in New Hampshire, Google it. She went missing in 2004 and is still missing today.

Airports:

Some people think airports are scary. Always be aware and alert, however, pretty much everyone in an airport is doing the same thing you are, traveling. These days no one can get past security without a boarding pass.

However, leaving an airport ~ DO NOT EVER share a ride. I do not care if it saves you a couple bucks. Or the person looks nice. Again, no one is expecting you home, so if someone offers you a ride or ride share, absolutely not. Human trafficking is very common in airport waiting areas, prior to TSA areas, or out on the sidewalk.

There are many other common sense safety tips, but these are the less obvious ones that some folks don't think of.

WHO AM I? –

"Do you know your name?" She asked. "Karen." I replied confidently. I looked at my husband and said, "what the hell is happening?" "I have no fucking idea, Kare!" he said in a panic. For him it would not have been a full sentence without the incorporation of his favorite "F bomb", especially in an emergency.

"Okay Karen, your social security number?" "Oh I've definitely got this one", I chuckled to myself. "010-38-0000!! No, wait! Is that it?" I asked. "I have no fucking idea", he said, from the chair next to me. He was so nervous that *he* needed to sit down more than I did. Again…."010-38-……….". "Hunny don't you have your SS card in your wallet?" He asked. "I don't know!", I cried. Even telling the story now, is causing my heart to race just remembering this day, 15 years ago.

"Here it is" and just like that, that problem was solved. Later, I would realize I had been giving them Brayden's social (my kid's dad who had passed 8 years prior), not mine.

"Okay, next question", I was ready now. Being able to give the Triage Nurse my Social Security number, although I was reading off the card, something I have never had to do, gave me my confidence back. For a minute. I remember mine, and all of my husbands' social security numbers to this day. Not sure that means anything, but hey.

It was cold in there, cold outside, but definitely cold in that emergency room. I have no idea how I ended up at that hospital, I guess it was technically closer to our house. The normal bustling sounds of an emergency room, combined with the smells, was making me want to vomit. There was no shortage of attention on me, as no one could figure out what was wrong with me. But they did know time was of the essence.

My face, now tingly and gradually distorting more than when I arrived, combined with a slight headache, was evidence that something was really wrong. Ah, but the questions, they kept coming. "Do you know your kids' names?" Chuckling, I snapped back, "of course I do." I could carry on a conversation, but now had to remember the names of my children. Tears running down my face, I looked at him, he looked at me. I think I was more upset about making him so afraid, than I was about the fact that I couldn't remember the names of my own flesh and blood.

The word "tumor", although probably tossed around quite a bit in the medical field in my opinion, sliced through my body like a knife dipped in poison. His face said it all. I wasn't scared. I was pissed. "How is this happening? What is this? What did I do wrong?" There it is. "What did I do wrong?" In order for me to be in any type of compromised position, I must have done something wrong. I am being punished. I was sure of it.

Although I had stopped attending church the first day I could say 'no', which is also the same time that I moved out, my 18th birthday, the fear of being physically punished for doing something wrong, was still hauntingly prevalent at age 37." You sin, you go to hell. You do something wrong, including swearing, God will punish you." That conditioning takes a long time to go away, if it ever does at all.

It took me up until recently to understand that I am not perfect, I don't need to be perfect, and I choose my destiny, no one else!

Blood work, hours of testing, compounding symptoms, and an MRI later, it was determined I had either suffered a stroke or had Bell's Palsy. I was released from the hospital later that day.

Per Wikipedia, "........could be triggered by trauma" is listed under 'causes for Bell's Palsy'.

"Please turn off the radio, or don't talk, I can't handle both." I cried. The look he gave me when I said that on the way home.

Finally back at home, "Kare, what do you want for dinner?" he asked. "What?" I replied from the next room.

"Okay Karen, tap the headphone on whatever ear you hear the sound on. They will vary in pitch." Within days, I would find myself at the hearing specialist in Portsmouth.

Tears streaming down my face, I'd tap over and over on my left headphone. "Maybe they aren't doing the right ear. Ya, that's it! I misunderstood the directions. I did it wrong." I reasoned with myself. "Okay Karen, keep going, they will do a sound in the right ear any minute now." the doctor said. Self talk was really all I had at that moment. They couldn't hear me. Leaning on the wall for support, after begging them to dim the lights, I thought it would never end.

"Okay you're done" I finally heard in my left ear after what felt like a lifetime in this soundproof tube room, not much bigger than a tanning bed. Okay I might be exaggerating there, but it was small enough.

There is something about being told you have lost hearing, even if only in one ear. Unless you've experienced it, you may not know the frustration that comes with not being able to have the radio on in the car if someone is talking, or being in a room with more than one conversation at a time.

"It may be temporary. All we can do is wait" the doctor explained. I was escorted to the car, unable to walk alone, due to no balance at all. The next few weeks I'd be bumped and bruised from walking into things when I'd lose my balance. But my hearing returned to 85% and as it returned I got my balance back. I am forever grateful. Without a definite diagnosis, I will never know for sure what happened to me back then, but I am glad it is over.

# TEEN CHALLENGE –

In the 60's at Hampton Beach, my parents were involved with Teen Challenge. David Wilkerson, the founder, had visited several times. This group grew to be a worldwide group to help teens, but with that came a lot of controversy. My father, David Wilkerson, Oral Roberts

Teen Challenge was formed in 1960. Now known as Global Teen Challenge, the group has been accused of running conversion camps. I don't have a personal opinion here, but I do know that it was only a few years after their arrival in Hampton, and my parents' affiliation with them, overseeing lodging at Hampton Beach for their visits, handing out tracts, (information about "being saved") and running meetings, that my mother was gone.

Teen Challenge has been accused of being anti-gay, and not allowing a teen to stay in their program unless they profess to be straight.

By its own definition, Teen Challenge is an "Assemblies of God, USA evangelical Christian recovery program and a network of Christian social and evangelizing work centers. It is a 12-18 month program that serves drug addicts, alcoholics, gang members, prostitutes, and people dealing with the life controlling 'problem' of same sex attraction and addiction."

Although it may help in all those areas, "controlling" someone's sexual preference does not seem to be something that comes from lack of judgement. With that same Bible saying judgement is a sin, their controlling appears to be full of judgement.

I have now read several articles and stories outlining control tactics and fear mongering at these camps. I have no personal reference point here, so I invite you the reader, to do your research and form your own opinion, if you so desire, or have none at all.

My point here is this. There is no one perfect way. There is no one perfect "religion". But I do know, as a child, I had the shit scared out of me with just that one film, "A Thief in the Night." That was in fact, the intent of the movie. It didn't work. It scared the shit out of a little 8 year old girl. Imagine your 8 year old child or grandchild being forced to watch a "scared straight" movie as a control tactic. To be threatened daily with the fear of going to hell, including the letter my father wrote me during my divorce. "Divorce is a sin. When you sin, you will go to hell." He said, "And you will never see your mother again." His implication being that my mother was dead and in Heaven. I guess I got the last word in there.

On a sunny, spring day in Texas, David Wilkerson, the Founder and leader of Teen Challenge / Global Challenge, wrote a blog post entitled, "When All Means Fail". He then drove on US 175 with his wife.

With his seatbelt off, he drove his car into oncoming traffic, specifically a logging big rig, and died instantly. His wife survived. She still had her seatbelt on.

Taking a life is a sin. When you get to the other side, in my belief you are held accountable for your wrong doings, including taking a life, murder. Whether it is someone else's life or your own, taking a life is murder.

David Wilkerson, religious leader, ended his life on earth April 27th. The same exact day my father died. Just two years later.

Teen Challenge, Assemblies of God, Full Gospel Businessmen's Association. All these titles. Billy Graham, Oral Roberts Jerry Falwell,

Sr & Jr, Jimmy Baker. All these names. Who is good, who is bad? Who goes without sin? Who has been involved in a sex scandal? Who left this earth squeaky clean? It is all seriously thought provoking. I truly recommend doing your own research and forming your own opinions. I've walked in this life. I know the truth.

# SANDY -

"Does anyone know a Sandy?" my student asked. As part of my teaching Mediumship, I have an advanced group of Mediums. Once a month we hold a virtual "Zoom Circle". I begin circle with a lesson. This month I was teaching about Physical or Spirit. As I explained to the students, quite often we will feel a sensation throughout our body that has nothing to do with our physical being, but it is a message from Spirit. Often a spirit will come through with an illness or ailment they had prior to their passing, or what caused their passing. It can be challenging to decipher, "is it me or is it them?"

"Don't ignore it. You cannot ignore them." I told the group. As that information was coming out of my mouth, one of the student's screen went black. Stunned, I continued on with the subject.

She appeared back into Zoom after a few minutes and explained that she had someone named Sandy with her in Spirit. "Who knows a Sandy?" She asked. No one else could think of a Sandy, but I had one in mind. Most likely because I had thought of Sandy's mother just the day prior, as I was making a checklist in my mind while writing, of the women in my father's harem. Sandy's mother was definitely googly eyed for him. Even as a child, I could tell, I knew. He didn't know I knew. But I knew.

"I know a Sandy from Church when I was a kid," I said. "Okay, this is her with me in Spirit. Karen, you were saying 'don't ignore them, whatever you do, don't ignore them', and just as you said it and I had been trying to ignore this Spirit, my screen went black, I guess I lost internet. So once it finally came back, I said okay I have to tell them." She continued, "Karen she is here to say thank you. For protecting her or something. For knowing and helping. She 'says' you did something or said something, and then there was something about clothes. She really needed to thank you and she wasn't going to let me ignore her."

Joy happened to be one of the students on my Zoom, and although you really can't tell who someone is looking at on your screen during a Zoom, I noticed her eyes bugging out. "Joy, do you have something to add?"

With a sullen look on her face, "Karen, remember when we were in New Hampshire, driving past your childhood home, and I felt nauseous, but I told you that there were two girls. I psychically saw two, but told you one was not your sister? Well, I am getting that one was Sandy." she shared

"It's all in the book", I said quickly to the rest of the class, as if Joy and I had a big, huge secret that the other student had unknowingly become a part of, "It's in the book."

"Karen? What was Sandy's mother's name? I am getting a 'K'," she said. My memory is quite often foggy, I could remember Sandy, but none of the rest of her family's names.

I spoke to the class. I shared with them that in writing this book, the day prior to the Zoom, I had typed in the book my fears around the release of this book. The last, yet not least important one, was the fact that there may be 'others' in the church. Without getting into too much detail, something I felt would be inappropriate to discuss with my students at the time, I said to the student with the message, "thank you. The message you have delivered is 100% validation of everything I had been writing about the prior day. There were others. Here we are the following day with validation to a question I asked the day prior. That, my friends, is how this all works."

Throughout the writing of the book, other than some specific things; dates and times that I needed to research on the world wide web, most validation of all the important things has come from Spirit. You cannot make this shit up.

My student would never have known what I was writing about. She never would have been able to pull up the name Sandy, and then the K name or the situation around it. Impossible. That is how I know it is real. It came from intuition; it came from Spirit.

Later that evening, I remembered the mom's name, Kate. Definitely a K name, and not real sure how I forgot it. Well, and since Google is a thing, I wanted to snoop to see when Sandy passed, if her mom was passed now, and whatever else I needed to know. I'm sure Sandy was married. I didn't find her obituary, so I searched for her mom. Just one of those little blurbs came up, and said potential addresses, etc… not much of anything until it said education. None other than Northern Essex Community College. The college my father was an English Professor at for several decades. She must have been his student and followed him to our church, 'nuf said.

I then actually turned on the mic on my laptop and recorded the rest of the message from Zoom as my student gave it to me. This is the actual recording. Names changed, of course.

"It says it's recording. Okay here we go. Alright, I am ready when you are."

"I believe I have Sandy with me. I believe she's showing me herself how she would have looked as a child for confirmation or validation. She has like mousy brown hair, I wanna say a little longer than shoulder length and kind of going down her back but not like down to her waist or anything. Do you remember what she looked like?"

"I remember that, yes."

-inaudible- "inside but she's showing me herself at your house. I get the two of you were having a sleepover so she's showing me herself in this nightgown, it's like a long nightgown that goes to almost to the floor, but not quite to the floor, a little ruffle at the bottom maybe flannel."

"You pull up a color and you're going to be the winner of the year!"

"Okay before you asked me it was more like a like a little flowery, like a paler, but then when you said 'color', I saw a red, so maybe there are little red Flowers? Again, I think she's just showing me this just to validate that's who I'm talking to. Yeah, there's a big reason why she's showing that, it makes total sense. It's very important as a matter of fact and then she's showing me inside the house. She's showing me.... I don't see you, but I feel like you're there. But I don't see you in what she's showing me. I see her at the top of the stairs and she's looking down the stairs she's like standing at the top of the stairwell looking down the stairs."

"I think whatever she is willing to share. If she wants to share people, she may not. If......I mean names would be lovely. If not, there's certain things that she could say to describe certain people."

"Jay, he has a bit of a bald spot. He's not like slim and trim he's got this little belly he's on the shorter side, I wanna say that one of the things he did at the church was helped count the offering money. It also feels as if there were times that maybe as a as an elder or whatever of the church, maybe they were called upon to read the scripture. I'm seeing him at the pulpit reading scripture. At times that she felt really dirty. Just talking about how dirty she felt when he would read the scripture, because it was like he was reading scripture about holiness and all of this stuff and then she said he would look at her from the pulpit. She's talking about how him especially, but there may be another one. She's gonna tell me about she was brainwashed with the Bible and when he would stand up in the pulpit and read these verses, he would look at her. Another guy, brother something that F."

"Okay, well maybe it's both. Maybe that's why I'm getting both." *inaudible* "Overcoat and hat and was he a pipe smoker? All of that would have been secret and separate from the church because you weren't like allowed to smoke. Interesting smelling the pipe smoke

I'm fairly certain his father did. I don't know if they're driving, I see a white car outside of the church. I'm just I'm asking her to try to show me a little bit more clearly. I think this is one of the houses I think this is one of the happened but one of the houses down near the beach. I was seeing where the bedrooms were. I was seeing no women in the house, but I was seeing several of these men there. It's almost like you and Sandy both knew what was going on, but you didn't talk to each other about it. I don't think that's actually so random from things that I've read, but I'm saying like that's what I'm feeling like you knew and you gave support to each other without ever talking about it. It was like it was like you had both been scared so much that this had to be secret and quiet and never to be spoken of. *author's note – intuitive messages when typed out can often look funky. But in person, it makes sense*

# THE CLOSET -

It is so dark. The walk-in closet in their bedroom, it still had her clothes in there, although I am not sure if this was a month or year after she was gone. His on the left, mommy's coats in front of me and her clothes to the right. She loved shoes. The boxes, all shapes, sizes and colors on the floor and on the bottom shelves. The top shelf was neatly filled with her wigs, and hats. All placed so carefully in their appropriate hat boxes.

The colorful scarves draped so intentionally over the hangers. Her handbags methodically squished in there as well. She was such a lady. I couldn't reach them, not then, not ever. By the time I would be tall enough, they would be gone. Oh how I would love to have some of her clothes right now, a pair of her shoes, one of her hats. Or just a handbag. I do have however, her hanky. I am sure Auntie snagged it for me. Grammie, Auntie and my mom always had one tucked into the sleeve of their sweater, a year round necessity, as they were always cold. The apple falls not far.

I wonder where her things are now. In a landfill, or a retro shop? It has been 50 years, but there is a chance, that something of hers is still around. Imagine that? In my mind's eye, I can see it. At this point in my journey, nothing at all would surprise me. I wore her wedding dress for my first wedding, but I think Grammy had saved it. I think, although I am not sure, that Auntie, my mom's only half-sister, gave it to me, from grammie's basement. I am grateful for that. I have passed it down to my daughter after having it preserved and packed at the drycleaners.

But this night it was dark. I could hide in there and the door had a lock. But that never lasted long. I loved the smell of her clothes. She was always dressed perfectly. Her wigs were a popular wardrobe essential in those days, although I have been told she wore them only because her hair was falling out. As far as I am concerned, NOTHING I was told as a child, or as an adult, about my childhood is true. I have deleted all of that information out of my brain. It now just sounds to me like the teacher on Charlie Brown. "Wahd, wah, wat, wahd."

For me it has made it easier to stop questioning every single little thing, and to just accept my life was, is one big lie. That is, until I got away from him, them, or so I thought.

It is so strange how such a small area, that closet, although it probably felt pretty big to a six year old, was so comforting. Being alone was so comforting, it still is. I had my own pretend world in the darkness of that closet. In my pretend world, no one could hurt me. And even now, if I am alone, no one can hurt me. But I can adapt anywhere. I can stay in the smallest of hotel rooms and make it a nice comforting space for me. Or I can make a huge home, like a few that I have lived in, feel so serene to me and all who walk into that home. Home is meant to be a safe space. My current home has become a safe space now for my grandchildren. There are no coincidences. Life experiences are cyclical.

## CLOSET IN THE FOREST –

I can smell the pine needles. I had secretly made my way down to my elementary school, basically across the street from my house. I could take the path off of Howes Road (named after my maternal grandfather), behind my friend Samantha's grandmother's house, which was a safe space for me. As life would have it, Samantha ended up being the woman in the apartment next door when Dick was attacking me. She is the one in my adult life who called the police.

Or I could take a short cut through the Episcopal church parking lot. Every Thursday the church would have a Thrift shop upstairs. That store was Fifth Avenue Shopping to me. Some things have not changed in my life.…Thrifty kid, thrifty woman.

I didn't care how much change I had or didn't have in my coin purse, I was up there, touching and feeling everything. Not the toys or books or children's clothes. I was running my hands through the ladies' clothes and shoes, handbags and jewelry, scarves and wigs. I wanted everything. Children wouldn't agree these days, but those smells, absorbed from the rose scented sachets in their cedar dresser drawers, or from the moth balls in the attic, drew me in. I just wanted them all. To this very day, my favorite antiques have a smell to them. The thrift store was a safe, peaceful place for me.

Walking a few feet into the woods, I would search until I found it. "This, this here. This is the spot." I would whisper to little girl Karen. My little homes in the woods, which I understand now, were homes for the Fairies. Back then, I was just creating another safe space where I could be alone and just listen to the whisper of the wind. And did that wind ever whisper back to me in those woods. When some of the pine trees would get to blowing, bending, tipping back and forth, the sound was like music. A tree stump would be my pre-made chair.

No one had been back there cutting trees down, pine doesn't burn well anyway, but every now and again, the New Hampshire Seacoast has a storm, and trees do fall either from the weight of ice on the trees, or from the relentless wind, or because the tree is just old. Due to the fact that we were able to access the woods at recess, they would cut the tree down to a stump, so us little ones wouldn't get hurt.

Branches were carefully made into brooms and I was able to sweep out the little rooms in my forest homes. Twigs outlined the rooms, and there were even some walls, sometimes. Alone was safe. And besides, I could talk to all the forest people. Sprites, as I call them in Hawaii. Fairies and Spirits, they all kept me company. I was never lonely. I was safe and I was happy.

# ADULT CLOSETS IN THE FOREST –

Living off of Route 125 in Lennox, NH had it's advantages, and it's disadvantages. We had bought a house on the lake, our first home. The lake and house on one side of the dirt road, the woods on the other side. I was alone a lot, he was an over the road truck driver. There was birch, pine, and many other trees. I would make little brooms. I would divide the little areas with branches. There was a rock. I would sit there, alone. It was quiet. Peaceful. And all my little beings were with me.

After having my eye on a bigger house with a barn for my horses, just a mile or so away from this house, circumstances fell into place, and we moved there. Side note: In my adult life, I have not once wanted a house that I didn't get, whether renting or buying. It is a skill I have developed and teach people often, the art of manifesting by co-creating your desired home.

Although we had horses behind the house in a cleared area in the woods, I sat there, alone on a stump with my little beings. It was safe, quiet and peaceful. "Whispering Woods" was born, it would eventually be my healing center. Reflecting back, I don't truly think Whispering Woods was born while I was adult living in Lennox, NH. It was born when I was a child, creating safe places for little girl Karen, in the forest behind my elementary school.

# THE AUCTION -

A chilly day in January 2012, Friday the 13th, I sat alone in my living room, in the big house in Lennox. Horses fed early, before dark, he didn't like me down there with them after dark, for many reasons, but 2 broken feet later, (not at the same time) I decided he was right.

Rottweilers would soon be fed, after I checked my email. It wasn't odd to get an email from my landlord about one thing or another. Late rent never being the reason. She was a computer nerd at a big company, drove a Mercedes and owned another home in a town nearby.

"Karen" the email read, "I'm sorry, there is nothing I can do now, the house is foreclosed on and going up for Auction, Tuesday morning at 9am. Please don't contact me further. This will be my last email."

"For ten fucking months, hunny, I have been paying this bitch cash!" I screamed at my then husband as he made his way down some highway thousands of miles away. "I have always gotten a receipt though, well most of the time", I told him. Sometimes she had 'forgotten' to leave a receipt when she picked up the envelope containing $1200 in cash every month.

I was no longer whispering in Whispering Woods. For the past 10 months, I had put my blood, sweat and tears into updating the small in law apartment over the garage. I then carefully created a group meditation space and a space to see clients. The windows looked out over the sparse forest and I could always see me horses from up there. My gorgeous Belgians, Maddie and Julia. We hadn't met Marcus yet.

"Call the lawyer!" he said, "and calm the fuck down, you are no good when you are like this!" Have you ever been told to "calm down"? It never works, it makes it worse.

But he was definitely right about that point. I have two sides, 'love and light', and 'I'm going to rip off your head and stuff it down your throat'. There is really no in middle ground with me. But the second mode is what drives me to get things done, to make a change, and take no shit. Well not as an adult, anyway.

My attorneys at the small downtown law firm went to school with my mom. Many familiar brown and white photos hang in their waiting room. It nostalgic there. Comforting, well as comforting as it can possibly be when there is a situation that requires legal counsel.

"Karen", he said in his unmistakable soft and calming voice, "there is no law in New Hampshire that states that a landlord is required to pay their mortgage, even when they have a tenant in their home. There is nothing you can do. Literally nothing." "Oh no, you don't understand! I have receipts proving I've paid her $13,000!! He is on the road, what the hell am I going to do?" "Typically in these cases, the tenant is given a 48 hour window in which they are allowed to get their belongings out of the house, whereas if the homeowner were living there, the sheriff would lock them out at the end of the auction. But you won't know anything until the auction."

"48 hours?????!!!!!! Impossible! I have two massive horses, two massive dogs, a 3 bedroom house, with a 2 car garage full of my shit and HERS (the landlord) where the hell will I go?? I can't just stay in a hotel room!"

"Karen,"

"Nevermind Paul, I am going to figure out something before close of business today, and I will call you Monday first thing and figure out what to do next". (At this point 'close of business' was less than an hour away, but I still had another weekday coming, Monday) I don't typically hang up on people and I am not sure if I did say 'goodbye' but as my finger went for the "END" button on my Blackberry, a louder voice on the other end said, "Karen, I am not here on Monday, it's a holiday, Martin Luther King Day."

All weekend, numb and quite frankly beginning to get scared, I wracked my brain to come up with a plan. Nothing. My hands were tied, and the landlord kept her word. She never responded to a single email.

I truly believe when you are really in the thick of it, your hand is to the fire, it takes great self-discipline to be able to just say, "Oh it will be fine, there must be a reason, there must be something better." Although I teach this practice often, I surely wasn't using it in this situation. After all, do as I say, not as I do. And yes, there is always room for humor.

Tuesday morning, dressed for a blizzard, although the sun was shining, four men gathered at the end of the driveway. It was 9:01am as I made my way up the semi steep driveway. Not dressed for the weather, I was shivering, but maybe it was fear and trepidation. As I walked up, I felt like I was already missing something. Although they had just pulled up and barely gotten out of their cars, I heard "going, going, gone!" as I approached the road at the end of my driveway.

The auctioneer smacked his clip board with his hand as he said those words, and I lost my shit. In true "Karen" fashion, a current negative connotation, I was gritting my teeth as I spoke, "Sir, you do not understand….." I tried to mutter. "Ma'am it is not in my control. Talk to the bank." He said. I am sure he has said that phrase hundreds of times.

"Well that should be simple", I thought, "what bank, where, what do I say?? Easy Peezy." I am often sarcastic, even with myself.

When you have no plan, no solution in sight, it is really easy to get into the fetal position while sucking your thumb and crying. There I was, on the couch. A Sherriff's department warning, now taped to the sliding glass door, became a constant reminder. Whether I was in the kitchen, or letting the dogs out, it was a reminder that 'Karen had no idea what to do next.' "Whatever, I'm just going to bed."

I don't typically answer my phone when I don't recognize the number, but 'whatever the hell', at this point I was up shit's creek without a paddle. Afterall, I would have to function that day at some point.

Big dogs and big horses don't like to miss their breakfast, so I told the woman on the other end I would call her back, "just let me talk to my husband".

"Cash for keys" something I had never heard of, is a way for a landlord (or a bank, in a foreclosure situation) to convince a tenant to vacate a property in exchange for an agreed upon sum of money.

"We gotta do it, Kare, we have no other choice." As I thought about it, he was right. This program gave us two weeks to clean out the house, lock, stock and barrel, in 'broom swept condition', a realtor's phrase for clean. Ya – we could do it. Afterall, I am the most organized packer and mover, that I have ever met.

There was hope, after 5 days of none, here it was. $3000 once we left and left nothing behind. It had slipped my mind that we had no place to go, but hey, we had $3000 to work with.

Anson is a small town that borders Peterson, an eclectic place in New Hampshire filled with artists and music, and a friendly group of people. With no pictures in the Craigslist ad, the gentleman on the phone said, "you just have to see it for yourself". Sitting on 88 acres, with a three stall barn, heated garage, and studio designed perfectly for "Whispering Woods", he was right, this was the most stunning home I had ever seen. "Rent is $2000, and the security deposit is $1000", he told us. See what that equals??? Yes! $3000 even!

Being mid-month and having paid full rent and utilities two weeks prior, we basically had only the "Cash for keys" check to available to spend. Perfect. Although he understood the urgency, there was still an application process, credit check and employment check, for all of the rental applicants.

Within hours of meeting us, I received an email on that very Sunday evening that read, "I haven't done the credit or employment checks yet", (obviously…. It was Sunday) he went on, "but I just feel like you would be a great fit, the home is yours." We now had 10 days to clean out all of the landlord's crap from the garage, yard, and basement, as well as pack our belongings. The hubs had to go back on the road the following day. Ten days later he returned with his tractor trailer. I had everything done, swept, and off we went.

Being the architect of the home himself, our new landlord had pointed out many exquisite features of his beautiful house that he had designed, with the most scenic outside feature being the view of the popular ski area nearby that would light up like a Christmas tree, every evening but Sunday. With binoculars, I could watch the night skiing. Sunday, they would put all the lights on and make snow. You cannot pay any amount of money for this kind of scenic view. I still remember every square inch of this house. It took my breath away every single time I made my way down the quarter mile dirt road that had one house on it, mine.

Lou had decided to rent out the house after a recent divorce from his wife. He had built them their dream house, but they now had both moved out. Living alone in a small condo he had built that could barely be seen thru the trees on the other side of the dirt road, we really didn't see much of Lou.

At that time I was completely unaware of his intentions, as was my husband. Although he had made a couple unintentionally intuitive (at the time) jokes about Lou.

Whispering Woods quickly settled into it's new home in the studio, a building apart from the house. After some updates, scrubbing and paint, it was open. I had my *real* healing center. Many visitors went thru those doors for sessions, workshops and healings.

Marcus, a severely abused stall bound, underweight and bruised, yet absolutely stunning Belgian draft stallion, would soon join us. Followed shortly thereafter by two calves, Makayla and Mackenzie. The barn was full, my heart was full. "Don't ever be in the stall with him alone. You are a female. He is a big ass stallion. He will be mean and most likely hurt you when I am on the road", my protective husband said. Marcus didn't have a mean bone in his body. He immediately became my best friend. He crossed over the rainbow bridge with my arms wrapped around him, just a few short years later.

Our home was everything we both had wanted. We had everything we needed. We were out in the middle of nowhere and loving every minute of it. Never having had animals during my childhood, I quickly learned the labor of love involved with running a farm, albeit alone most days.

Not long after moving in, on a hike through my acres of woods, I happened upon a grandmother tree. I had never seen a tree that was this intentional. She wanted to be found. On the edge of the clearing for the power lines, my tree stood alone separated from the other trees, as if to say, "hey look at me". A friend took some stunning pictures of that tree that I hope to discover again one day.

I built cairns out there. I hung wind chimes and magickal decorations from the other trees. Over time I moved some fairly big limbs to make two paths to my very special tree. I had a lantern out there. I created a safe little space in the forest for me, my Spirit friends, the faeries, and any other beings that wished to join me, which were quite often Native American ancestors. This was my quiet, peaceful, safe space that I had created it in the forest, again. This life was bliss.

The Universe had a plan on that Friday the 13th of January. We never would have left Lennox, in search for a bigger, better home, if she had paid her mortgage with my rent money, if there was no auction that day, or if I had somehow managed to interfere with the Divine plan. Note to self, don't ever interfere with the Divine plan.

A few years later, I would look back and refer to this house as the divorce house. The home in Anson where *two* marriages had now ended. You can often have everything you ever wanted in life, and it sometimes is still not enough. My heart shattered, then slowly glued back together, he and I are still great friends.

# VALIDATION –

I have included in this chapter, notes from Readings, Channelings and Regressions that I have had done, or I had done myself. The dates are when the entries were made in my journals. Some aren't complete stories, just simply notes that I took. That's why some parts are choppy. It would not serve me to add or subtract words to make it comprehensive to the reader. So I will leave it just as I wrote it.

**Past Life Regression 2001** – *coincidently right around the time my mom called me*

"My father was my father in this life, and my sister was also my sister."

"My father and sister both watched me walk into the ocean and end my life" I committed suicide. Not sure why.

I also received a message from my mother in this Regression, I asked her "why do I always think I am not good enough to make someone happy?" To which she replied, "It's not everyone, it's your dad, and you will never make him happy, so don't bother trying." Wow wasn't that ever true. "Just make yourself happy."

Brayden came in on a white horse as a knight, with shining armor. He took Dick out with a sword. Then said a message to me "Trust your instincts, I will take care of the rest."

## READING THIRTEEN YEARS AGO ~ 3/13/08

"Your mother is still trying to smooth things out." (*Now mind you he's talking as if she's alive. But because I THOUGHT she was dead, I wasn't sure what this all meant, but I still wrote it down thankfully, because now I get it*) Your father backed away from your mother twice before he finally "left her". You didn't want it to be that way. Situations whether it be MOLESTATION or whatever." (*I had no fuckin idea what he was talking about here*). "There is something at the base of your mom's brain. That creates more crap. There is a lot of deep sadness within there. Around the age of 31 was the most difficult time." (*This would be right after my sister was born*) *He then mentions "forbidden" things in my childhood again.*

He goes on to say, "a trip, possibly Hawaii or the islands gets postponed to work on a project. This is bigger", he says. "It can't be put on the back burner. This is more important." (*my book*)

*He references Bell's Palsy.* At the end he says, "your grandmother is right here, your husband is right here." *NO mention of a mom in Spirit.*

### June 2011 ~ Session with one of my favorite Mediums:

"Writing a book, a BIG book. Positives and negatives. You will also be working police cases"

He also spoke of a situation involving two people, and town government *AND A PYRAMID OF POWER*. I believe this is how the details of the fake death were secretly handled.

"Your grammie is here. She is wishing you much success, and happiness and she is showing me RAINBOWS which is the sign for much happiness." *Author's note: RAINBOWS??*

"They are showing me liver or kidneys, which is about anger or hatred with your dad, is he crossed? Do you have issues with your father? He saw things through thick glasses."

Speaking of Brayden, "He saved your ass. You've got to trust. Don't listen to other people. You've got about ¼ of the truth. You know what is going on. He is showing me 37. That's him validating his age when he died, so I would know it was him." "They are telling me you don't need to search. I keep seeing Dorothy on the Yellow Brick Road. You need to just follow the Yellow Brick Road. You don't need to go searching, just open up inside. Don't block the truth". (*Reminder - this was 10 years ago.*)

## READING – OCTOBER 14, 2012 –

"SUNFLOWER is your name. Keep searching. We are here to help you. They show a basket of money."

**JOURNAL ENTRY - SEPTEMBER 4, 2013** ~ FIVE years before I would discover my childhood trauma. I must have subconsciously written things to tell myself that something was going on. This isn't the only one like this. It is extremely prophetic. I may or may not have commentaries throughout.

DECEIT ~

"When we have been lied to, or had things taken from us and we feel there was deceit involved, that is very difficult to get around or get over. It may have happened in our childhood. We may feel we lost something, i.e.: a parent, due to someone else's deceit." (*Oh boy – this totally sounds like I knew somewhere deep down*) "Maybe not lies (*um yes, definitely lies, but little girl Karen was probably still protecting her father at this point, 8 years ago*) just not telling the truth, not telling the whole story. So then we have to learn to trust. But do we just start to trust people, only to have them be deceitful again? I feel that leaving out details or leaving out parts of stories, is very deceitful. In other words, not telling the whole story, in some instances is deceitful. People who are deceitful can never be trusted.

(*I think here, I was alluding to the fact that my father lied about my brother being adopted, so I never should have trusted him with anything else*) But perhaps they are in your life for a reason. It's okay to trust people, but the minute you smell deceit, it is time to run for the hills."

*I guess what I was starting to feel back then, was me questioning everything. Everything I had been told as a child. Everything that I thought was a certain way, was not. And I must have known deep down that he had been lying about other things as well. I was trying to tell myself the truth, EIGHT years ago.*

## JOURNAL ENTRY – SEPTEMBER 11, 2013

SELF PRESERVATION ~

"Reflect love and love will reflect back at us. So when we are trying to "self preserve" is it love that is our first emotion? Typically, it is anger. Someone has hurt us or done us wrong. Whether it was intentionally, or not. We need to strike back. But we get much better results if we step back not strike back, take a second look at the situation, send love their way and forgive. That is not to be confused with allowing someone to use you as a doormat.

But when you send anger their way, it is sure to be met with anger, and the cycle continues. Set loving boundaries. Stand your ground but reflect love back at them. What they do with it will only reflect how others treat them, and the cycle continues."

"When you trust halfway, that is all you wind up with, halfway results. IF you can let go of the controls, miracles happen, all the time." ~unk~

## JOURNAL ENTRY - SEPTEMBER 10, 2019 - CHANNELING

"The movement about ministers will be massive. You will share what you need to, and the rest will piece itself together. Glass ceilings will shatter."

## READING BY BROOKE – SEPTEMBER 2019

"The woman with the skirt." She said. (*The church lady that was at my house when I found out my mother was gone*) "Well I know who that is." I replied. *Then she listed the specific name, Frank.*

289

"Two Franks", she said.

"An aunt helped him. He left with her in the car."

"Blood issue".(*hemochromatosis*)

"She made the call from her room."

"She didn't pass. She left."

"Others besides Frank." She said.

## JOURNAL ENTRY ~ SEPTEMBER 27, 2019 – STORAGE ~

The most amazing thing happened today. A week ago, I found the info about my storage unit in NY. The last payment that was sent was 5 years prior. 9/20 – on a Friday afternoon, I took a chance and left a message after trying so hard to find out where my unit even was. TODAY SHE TEXTED ME! "You are in luck with your storage unit! We have been procrastinating on cleaning out a few abandoned units and yours was one of them. And for $500 I could have the contents of my unit!!!!! I will be going there in October.

## JOURNAL ENTRY ~ OCTOBER 26, 2019 ~ AMAZING GRACE ~

It is amazing on this day, as I did my last Mediumship Gallery before leaving for New York to empty out my storage bin after all these years and retrieving what little I have that pertains to my mother, I realized that there in the home I was in, was a wall hanging that said right on it "Amazing Grace". The synchronicities are unbelievable some days.

## JOURNAL ENTRY ~ NOVEMBER 13, 2019 ~ SOLD ~

In Meditation today, I was suddenly thrown into a space where I wondered how in the world my father bought the house left to us 4 children from us, in 1980 I think, for $40K??? In prestigious Hampton,

NH, on one of the two roads that goes from the town center to the beach. It makes no sense. Although I cannot do anything about it, I really wish he had waited until we were adults to give us the option to sell it to him. Like how did he make that decision? As our guardian? He was able to sell it to himself?? Doesn't sound right.

## JOURNAL ENTRY ~ NOVEMBER 19, 2019 ~ 3RD PERSON ~

Had a great healing with my Hawaiian healer. Although he was unaware verbally of many things, he talked a lot about forgiveness. I remember during this time, I began this thing where I was talking in 3rd person. Wikipedia states "When we are stressed, we may speak in the third person to assert our dominance over the situation. We tend to assume that when a person refers to themselves by name, they are egotistical. Yet sometimes people use this style of speech as a coping mechanism." 'nuf said.

"Sam" also taught me how what I was going through or had gone through was generational. I also studied some ancestry after this and realized the "losing the mother" pattern started many, many generations ago. So crazy!

"I do not know which way the wind will blow, or how the crows will sing. But I do know I am the one who can have everything." ~unknown~

## JOURNAL ENTRY ~ DECEMBER 20, 2019 ~ JOHN OF GOD ~J

John of God, the Brazilian healer known all over the world, for his spiritual surgeries, was sentenced to prison following 300 women accusing him of sexual abuse, including rape. This is one of the many "men of God" who have been brought to light in the last 10 years. Does this compare to what happened in my church? Abuse is abuse. How many isn't the question. It's how. How do we trust these men and women of authority to be above all others? Above sin? We can't. If this man who interacted with 1000's of people per week, is capable of these incomprehensible crimes against women, then a few men in a small church, are not above this same behavior. The general public assumes these authoritative figures are without sin. Quite on the contrary, the sins ie: sex crimes, against women and children are slowly but surely coming to light. NO ONE, I repeat NO ONE is above sex crimes. This would be a different story if my father were alive. He would be convicted, and others would be too. As a survivor there is so much guilt. As the daughter, the guilt is compounded. I thought he was a strong man. People believed he was a strong man. Strong men don't take advantage of women and children.

CLUES ~

I remember when one of the mediums did a reading and said my father came through and said, "there are things I am not proud of." Then went on to reference Psalm 111 – When I looked it up, it said, "The works of the lord in creation, providence and grace." He also told the Medium he was "not happy with the truth coming out" she said he had more than remorse. "There is so much that is going to be revealed. It's going to be uncovered. I am going to be exposed. I lived a life of deceit. There were wrongs on a lot of levels." Also that there were other men who sexually abused. Then he referenced a town secret. He shared with this Medium who didn't know what happened in my childhood.

The Medium went on to describe my grammie, with her name and that she was stylish. And how she had a "gag order". No wonder she passed only 5 years later.

They also mentioned the following in regard to trying to find my mom:

~ Long horizontal windows
~ Green valley with grass
~ The story is incomplete, and I need to uncover the rest
~ Tim will help me connect the dots
~ A CNA with auburn hair and blue uniform
~ She is not hidden
~ Chairs outside
~ Records were ruined
~ Going down the hall to the left, almost all the way to the end.

~ In between where she was then and where she is now, she called me. It's okay that I didn't know it was her
~ Someone helped her make the call
~ Shock wave therapy
~ She was always looking for us
~ "People" didn't know she was there

June 4, 2021 – (*Tomorrow is Tim's birthday*) - Sitting in a hotel room in Florida, as I near the completion of this book, my daughter Tandy sent me this song on You Tube just now. I copied the lyrics. Her timing was impeccable.

## SAVAGE DAUGHTER

Sarah Hester Ross

"I am my mother's savage daughter
The one who runs barefoot
Cursing sharp stones
I am my mother's savage daughter
I will not cut my hair
I will not lower my voice

My mother's child is a savage
She looks for her omens in the colors of stones
In the faces of cats, in the falling of feathers
In the dancing of fire
In the curve of old bones

I am my mother's savage daughter
The one who runs barefoot

Cursing sharp stones
I am my mother's savage daughter
I will not cut my hair
I will not lower my voice

My mother's child dances in darkness
She sings heathen songs
By the light of the moon
And watches the stars and renames the planets
And dreams she can reach them
With a song and a broom

I am my mother's savage daughter
The one who runs barefoot
Cursing sharp stones
I am my mother's savage daughter
I will not cut my hair
I will not lower my voice

We are all brought forth out of darkness
Into this world, through blood and through pain
And deep in our bones, the old songs are waking
So sing them with voices if thunder and rain

We are our mother's savage daughters
The ones who run barefoot
Cursing sharp stones
We are our mother's savage daughters
We will not cut our hair
We will not lower our voice

We are our mother's savage daughters
The ones who run barefoot
Cursing sharp stones
We are our mother's savage daughters
We will not cut our hair
We will not lower our voice

Karen Whisperer

We are our mother's savage daughters
The ones who run barefoot
Cursing sharp stones
We are our mother's savage daughters
We will not cut our hair
We will not lower our voice"

# COINCEDENCE OR SERENDIPITY ~

Back in 2018 I met a brand new client named Jane. I was up in my Concord, NH office and she had decided to have weekly sessions with me. One of the sweetest humans I had met, I connected with her grandmother who she had been very close with, following some childhood trauma. Grandma had passed just a few months earlier and was anxious to let Jane know that she was okay and at peace. We had a great visit, and made plans for her next session, the following week.

My office in Concord was very aptly placed on Loudon Road, and the driveway to our building, when I shot straight out across Loudon Road, took me directly into the driveway of Goodwill. This was sheer bliss. Remember the Thrift Shop story from when I was young? It never goes away. It's in my bloodstream.

It was a Friday, and I was headed out of town for the long Memorial Day weekend. Finally some much needed alone time. I shot out of the driveway and straight across to my favorite Goodwill in the whole country. And believe me when I say, I have been in many throughout the USA.

The shelves in the back was where I always started my trek of treasure hunting. Dishes from someone's wedding, that went out of style 20 years prior can always be found back there. I always take my time, but today I really wanted to get on the road, before the 93 north traffic turned into the holiday parking lot. A couple little treasures in my cart and I was good to go. Books are always a huge score for me, and I had also grabbed a wall hanging that fit my office décor.

"Shoot, if I am going to be on the road for a few hours, probably at a standstill, I better use the bathroom, before I get in the check out line." I thought. And I rounded the corner to do so. As I passed where the bigger toys usually sit against the wall this "thing" was there instead. I truly wasn't sure what it was, but hey at $30, I was fixin' to take a second look, after potty.

Being a fairly avid antique collector, I figured it to be from the 60's. It was a light wood, with two doors on the front that I'm sure were meant to pull down to open, but I was not about to play with it. I took a couple pictures, checked the price tag and thought, "okay well, I don't know what it is, but if it's here when I get back on Monday, it's mine. And besides, I can't move it, it is definitely heavy and bulky. Oh, but there is absolutely room for this piece in my storage unit, until I get a bigger home to put it in."

I walked away and quickly made my way to the check out, as I was now suddenly in a rush to get on the road north now that I had done my thrifting for the day.

If you've met me, you know that I obsessed over whatever that bulky piece of furniture was, all weekend. "Was it an old fashioned entertainment center? It seemed to have speakers. And what was behind those doors in the front? Storage of some sort?" All very valid questions, I asked myself.

Monday couldn't come fast enough, but it eventually did show up and I was back in town and headed straight to Goodwill with my $30. Pulling into the parking lot, I quickly noticed plenty of available parking spaces. Oh Lort, NO!!!!!!!! It's Memorial Day and they are closed.

Pulling into a full parking lot on Tuesday, $30 still ready, I thought "what are the chances it's still there from Friday?" As if I was getting one of my children a Cabbage Patch Kid in the 80's, I plowed my way through the store. The wall that the mystery piece of furniture leaned up against, now covered with Little Tykes toys, very much like what I was used to seeing there. "Oh well, not meant to be.", I thought. Not really, it was more like "mother effer, I should have found a way to grab it on Friday, damn it!"

"Well since I'm here, maybe a treasure awaits me in the dishware section," I told myself, as kind of a bribe. Turning quickly to walk over, the angels broke out in a chorus of "Hallelujah", a golden light blasted my eyes, and through that golden light...........there she was, in all her beauty. "She will be mine. Oh yes she will be mine." The chorus, golden light, etc. never happened, but you get the point.

An experienced Goodwiller, I knew to immediately grab the paper that the price is on, and it is mine.

As I proudly made my way out of the store, entertainment center on a cart in tow, a man stopped me and asked, "do you know what you have there?" he asked. "No, but I'm sure it is complete", I replied. As if I knew what "complete" actually was. The date on the paper was the Friday I had initially seen it. I don't know why no one bought it on Saturday or Sunday, but it was mine now. Their loss. I was now the proud owner of this thingamajig from the 60's.

The Koronette 1960's Stereo Bar / Entertainment Center, Google showed me, has doors that open on the front and reveal a little spot for making and serving drinks, as well as a little gambling table as the door folds down on one side. The other side houses a turntable and radio. It was completely intact, and I already had the little faux fireplace that goes in the bottom in my storage unit. I had bought that at a yard sale for a dollar. Perfect! Such an amazing buy, and a fantastic piece. I get compliments on it all the time.

Of course I needed to immediately post the pictures and the story of how it was there on Friday, and how it waited for me till Tuesday to draw attention to myself on Facebook, as always.

"So here's this 60's Entertainment Center, it has so much cool stuff inside the doors in the front, it has electricity, and I already had the fireplace that fits in the bottom. I went there on Friday and didn't buy it until Tuesday. I cannot believe someone didn't snatch it up." I said in my Facebook post.

I have a team of folks that never let me want for anything, including information. Within minutes someone had researched it and added pictures and told me they sell for $500 to $600. That kind of thing doesn't matter to me. I'm not looking to sell. Maybe someday, but I enjoy buying low and knowing it is worth more.

Last summer I bought a group of fake rings at a yard sale, 4 for $3.00. I happened to have them with me when I was at the Jewelry store up in NH having a repair done. The sweet associate Jenna asked, "what are those rings in your little pouch?" "Ha, ha these things?" I replied, "Just silly yard sale finds that I pretend are real. They make me look rich." Grabbing her little tester, she went straight for the green ring. "So this ring is 14K gold. No one would put fake emeralds and diamond chips in a gold setting." The appraisal recently came back at $1500 for my 75 cent "fake emerald" ring. That is what gets my blood flowing.

"That is the coolest thing", folks commented on my Vintage Entertainment Center Facebook post.

"Wow, what a score!" another comment read

"What are you going to do with it?" someone asked

"Karen, OMG that's my grandmother's entertainment center!!" was the last comment

As I reread the comment from my new client Jane, I picked up my jaw from the floor and typed, "WHAT? Jane, how is it your grandmother's? You mean the one that just 'came thru' last week, that passed recently?"

"Karen YES!" she replied "We have been cleaning out her house and

Finding Grace Through a Lifetime of Lies

brought her things to the Concord Goodwill, Thursday night! That is hers! I can tell you exactly what it looks like inside. Did you open it? Were the records in it still?"

I now have my client's grammy's 60's entertainment center in my dining room in Myrtle Beach. Coincidence? I think not.

301

# STUFF –

Three days before this particular trip up to New Hampshire, I had been determined to get all the rest of the "stuff" from my newly emptied storage unit taken care of and put up in the attic. For days, I had been navigating around boxes in my room, leaning over them to get to my dresser. And of course, stubbing my toe on my trek to my bathroom in the middle of the night. Something inside me knew I needed to finish this task before I left. Well, something other than my OCD. I believe we procrastinate the most around things that make us be up in our feelings. I admittedly have procrastinated around many chapters of this book and now it is all lurking as my deadline approaches, less than one month from now.

My normal behavior is to rummage through as fast as humanly possible, tossing a few things in the trash, but basically just reboxing the "stuff" to take up to the attic. What came over me was unexplainable at the time. The particular boxes that I had not addressed, primarily had photos of my mother's life from the time she met my father on, until 1 about a year before she left.

I must cynically interject here, aside from their wedding picture, there was a minimum of two other people in their "prechildren" photos. Two women. Traveling. Dad and three women. Other random shots that would typically be husband and wife, these other two, unrelated women were in the pictures. Although I do understand that maybe my parents never traveled alone. Although strange, I can accept that, but why not take a few pictures of the happy couple instead of the four or so of them? Dad and the three ladies. A husband would not fancy his wife bringing two friends everywhere, and they were possibly friends of the couple, but the pictures mostly show mom on one side and these two or three on the other. Weird.

I am not aware of any photos of my mom from the time my youngest brother was around one and a half, maybe two years old. An odd but true fact. Were there just none? Or is there something in them that no one should see? The last picture I have of her, actually the last one that I am aware that exists, she is perfectly "healthy". There is a gap of about a year where no pictures exist of her or us. What in the world was going on in my home?

My mother wore dark sunglasses, most of the time. In today's day and age, there would be an assumption of something there, but I will leave that alone. I have several pictures in that box of her with them on. As I rummaged through the boxes, I see pictures and memories that I have seen many times before throughout my life, but not since my childhood memories surfaced on October 6, 2018.

It had been 6 or 7 years since these boxes had been in my possession. I thought they were gone forever. That would have been a reasonable assumption, considering the storage unit story I told in a previous chapter.

They seemed different this time for many reasons that align with my discoveries over the past two years. Some definitely grabbed my attention and were worth a second look. I had a different set of eyes this time. Clear view, clear understanding, no more lies and deception. I am no longer that little girl that believed everything the grownups told me to be true. They didn't know truth. They knew how to twist things to look as though reality was something other than it truly was. Quite on the contrary. I over analyze everything, especially with those closest to me.

Time was limited, but I was determined to finish this task before I left. Again, I can only chalk it up to Divine Guidance, intuition, and support. For some "divine intervention" reason, I decided this time to use my phone to take pictures of the pictures. Only a certain few. All of my mother, some of my grammie, her mother.

I also stumbled upon grammie's watch. Without a thought, I threw it in my purse. Before long, I was repacking these age old boxes into newer more sturdy boxes, and they made their way up to the attic. My brief interaction with these albums, loose pictures, and dusty memories, would prove to more validation for me, in their own way. In a way I can't explain. But I needed to see them that day.

And...............the article! The one missing when I was writing about my father being an exorcist was in one of those boxes! I had found it and added it to this book.

As I always say, "you can't make this shit up!"

FINDING GRACE ~ The rest of the story ~

An unseasonably warm October day in New Hampshire, I had traveled up with the sole intent of a physical search for my mother, like on the ground, door knocking search.

Driving around Hampton, NH ~ I went to all the family houses. My grandfather had built several houses there and we would live in one of those houses until my father got married and we had to move from our childhood home, a mile away to a "better" home.

There were three of them in a row, and other than a little paint color difference on two of them, not much had changed. A few years ago, I had gone to my childhood home when it was for sale. This would be not long before I retrieved my memory. I remember going in and thinking that I should have felt much more joy. I thought it would bring a childhood excitement. Fond memories. Life as it were in a simpler time. Not only did it not do all of that, but I left there with a knot in my stomach. Looking back at that day, I can understand the physical reaction I had in the house. This would be another time that I would "check the box" and chalk it up to "my mother died when I was 5." Which had been my typical response to anything sad, confusing or unpleasant. I thought about it for a while that evening. I am sure my inner child was reminding me that it wasn't a pleasant time in that house. It was a scary time. It was a time that would shape my adult life, my relationships, and my physical health.

The houses were just that, houses. I drove around Hampton a bit and began to feel joy as I went down to Tuck Field. One of my favorite spots when I was young. A short bike ride from my house would bring me to a magical place where no one understood my attraction and desire to be there.

Was it the penny candy store that stood there for a short time? The one room schoolhouse that I would spend hours staring at or hang out in if it were open. OR was it the fact, that the Hampton witch Goody Cole's memorial stone was there. I'd guess the latter, although all of the above were quite intriguing.

The school where my mom had spent her youth was for me known as the Hampton Academy Jr High. Although it has grown in size, it still stands in the same spot. Strategically placed across the street from the cemetery in which my family rests, including Brayden.

Most the colorful autumn leaves had fallen from the trees by the time I slowly made my way into the cemetery. I'd again be the only car there. The fence and trees in front, now all removed made a clear view in from the Jr High. In the years of my school days, that probably wouldn't have been good for me. Having the fence and evergreen trees lining the entire front of the cemetery, kept me from acknowledging what I thought the cemetery represented. "I thought" being the operative words. In my mind, my mom was laid to rest in there. Not because I had any evidence of that, but because after all there was a stone with her name on it.

The stone, the names, missing names....

I started with Brayden. His resting place is super simple. The road into the cemetery leads from the very front to the very back. This road was in the same state of disrepair as it had been for the 52 years that I had been traveling it, by foot, bicycle, car and I believe even roller skates, although looking back that may not have been a wise or safe idea, considering the cracks, frost heaves and potholes.

It once brought me peace to sit there with him. Talking to him about the goings on of our children, asking him to keep them safe, yelling at him for making me a single parent in the deepest sense of the words. As in life, he didn't mind the yelling at his stone as long as he was getting attention.

But now, it's not the same. Both his parents passed away over the past few years and are buried at his feet. The plot above him, reserved for our oldest son. But not long ago somehow, someone managed to put the remains of a high school friend of his smack dab to his left. To this day I don't know how that happened, other than when I spoke to the cemetery foreman, he said that he was told that I had approved it.

The whole area seems crowded now. Maybe because I am sensitive. Maybe because I am a Medium and feel all their energies. Or maybe it's just too damn crowded now where Brayden is laid to rest.

As a Medium and in doing this work, my brain knows he's not there. It knows he is walking with me and our children and grandchildren. There are days, I'm sure, that he really has his work cut out for him. There are days, he probably wants to retire. But he signed up for this, that day he became my knight in shining armor, and protected me from evil. Something that no one, no man or family member had done for me in my 20 years of life, until that point.

My visit with him was short, but sweet. I moved up the street a bit, to my right and then a left. The same roads I'd traveled many, many times, to visit the place where I believed my mother lay in rest. The only difference being that since 1998 I've had a stop on the way. One I never in my wildest imagination, would have believed I would be making.

Hampton is a small town. A reported population of 15,600 in 2020. Just over only a 600 person increase in population since 2010. Not a whole lot of growth. Painfully known for the riots of 1964 where up to 10,000 people gathered at Hampton Beach in an effort to create mayhem. The Casino being a longstanding landmark of Hampton Beach, was a target as they attempted to burn it down. As I write this, my mind reflects on the events of just this past week, where the US Capitol was infiltrated by mobs, leading to a major breach in security, many injuries and deaths. The ability given to the public through social media in this current era of standing up for "rights", to commune and raise hell in different places, especially in this past year, was not something afforded to folks in 1964. But still they rose. And still they raised hell. In my town, at my beach, when I was barely past my first birthday. Lack of police education to respond to this type of attack, is sited as a major downfall in protecting my town during this time.

Hampton is also synonymous with the Pamela Smart case. That whole situation not only took place at our high school, but Brayden was a juror in the trial when our kids were young.

I approached the family plot, passing by the stones of many well known Hampton residents. This time it would be different. This time I'd know that it was never what I thought it was. I stood once again disappointed that my older brother's name had still not made it onto the Kendall stone, although we are fast approaching the 13th year anniversary of his passing. My father's date of death from the following year is there though, as well as his second wife's name. Odd but I have no explanation for any of it.

Blah, I don't feel much when I am there. I miss my brother, desperately. And I am seriously bothered by him not being recognized in on the monument of his resting place. It's kind of blasphemy in my mind. So, I traveled on.

*UPDATE ~ April 5, 2021 ~ I am up in New Hampshire working, seeing clients and made my visit to the cemetery today. Brayden's stone is starting to look so old, the flower box unkempt with one plastic Paw Patrol Easter egg in it. It's been 23 years, unbelievable.

Following a brief visit with Brayden, I made my way to the Kendall stone. I stopped and looked, and immediately said to myself, "something is not right, what is different?" I parked the car, and as soon as I stepped out, there it was, thirteen years after his death! THIRTEEN!! A flat stone lay positioned off to the side of the Kendall stone. An ear to ear grin took over my face, and I instantly forgot how long it took someone to put it there.

The ear to ear, all teeth showing, grin was quickly soaked in tears as I read the stone. "Beloved son, husband, and father", was the inscription on the newly placed stone. I grabbed my phone, took a picture, and proceeded to text a family member; my heart shattered into pieces. It appears that I am the ONLY person who didn't know the new stone had been put there just weeks after my last visit in October! I am also apparently the ONLY person who noticed it doesn't say BROTHER on it!

Afterall, I AM only just the one who pulled glass from every inch of his body that night at my father's house when we were young! That incident being just one of the times I rescued my brother.

I AM the ONLY one who was alone by his side when he passed, because the rest of my family had things they had to do that morning. (Sound familiar??)

I can deal with it not saying "Uncle" BUT.......... "Brother"??? Some may call it trivial. But considering the fact that I had written earlier in the book about how sad it made me that his name was not on the stone, this was a kick in the gut. And yes, there is plenty of room for the word "Brother", it is a full "in the ground" headstone. If it were the inscription cost, I would have paid for the extra 7 letters, to acknowledge his three siblings. I am broken.*

A few twists and turns on cemetery roads, and I would be at the Howes stone. So many people there, some I have met, some I haven't. Some I remember, many I don't. The ones I remember, other than Grammy and Auntie, I don't remember them being too fond of me. Of us. Gracie's kids. I would never have understood all that back then. But it makes so much sense now!!

My grammie's energy makes me smile, although the time we had together was short, just 10 years, she is a happy memory to me. Other than that, and my little Auntie, my mom's half-sister, who was a teen when mom was born, I don't feel much there either.

I would then travel past our homes. Three of them nestled pretty close to each other, childhood memories both horrific and happy, if that's even possible, came rushing in like the waves of the Atlantic Ocean down the street from my childhood home.

I took some pictures of the back of our house. I sent them off to two of my student / friends. Separately they would have visions of the horror that took place in that home. So much that they were having a hard time relating what they had "seen" in their mind's eye. It's okay. I heard a great phrase which I will get into more, later in the book: "the devil is in the details". I don't need to know. I already know what I need to know. What brought me to this place. Why there is a book.

I tried really hard that day to have some innocent, sweet, fun memories. They didn't come.

In leaving the cemetery earlier, I remember calling out to my father in spirit and saying, "if you are sorry, sorry, like you said to me before taking your last breath, then you need to help me now. I want to find my mom. You took her away. Do this for me. Show me where she is." I asked. I believed.

There are just a few what we would call "nursing homes" in my hometown of Hampton. Today, they have nursing homes, assisted living, memory care, elderly housing and several other places where the seniors can live the remainder of their life. Back then we had nursing homes.

Ironically, but maybe not so ironically, once a month or so on Sunday afternoon, we would have to go to these places in the area and sing church songs, hymns. I still to this day can visualize the interiors of all these facilities that were filled with "old people" when I was young. My innocent child mind would often wonder why there were "not so old" people in those places. I'd ask but never got a real answer. Now I know.

I didn't that day, and will never, need GPS to get to these places. Most accessible from main Hampton roads, I knew the back way in. And that is the way I went. The names of the roads won't be stated to protect the privacy of the residents and staff in these places.

I went down the way I knew as a kid to get to this one spot. I pulled in and observed the windows, many happily portraying rainbow pictures done by children. These folks hadn't had an in person visit in over 6 months at this point. Covid has separated them from their families. Many have passed, not from covid, but most likely from broken hearts.

I looked, I meditated. I sat. I spent nearly the entire day at this one facility, leaving only for short periods of time to drive to and visit other facilities, in Hampton and the surrounding towns. I visited nothing short of a dozen locations, but they weren't it. I didn't feel it. So, I temporarily paused my search to grab a bite at the local haunt.

Lamie's is a Hampton Landmark. I love everything about the nearly 300 year old building. Built in 1740, it was a visiting place at Thanksgiving in the year of my birth, 1963, to President and Mrs. Dwight Eisenhower, while their grandson was a student at the neighboring town of Exeter's, Philips Exeter Academy.

No, Lamie's is not seeped in childhood memories, as we were allowed to dine out only four times a year. On our birthday we each got to choose where we had dinner out. I have no idea why I always chose Burger King, because now this fancy connoisseur of fine dining, wouldn't step foot in one. Lamie's is said to be haunted, which to me was just a bonus on the one night that I stayed there. The energy, the history, the food, the people, staff, and customers alike, all make it a warm and cozy place to visit. It is one constant that will probably stay forever in that small town. Hampton has Lamie's and Portsmouth had Yoken's until it closed in 2004 and was later demolished. The infamous "Thar She Blows" sign, returned to its home in 2015, where a shopping plaza now stands.

In 1999, shortly after Brayden's passing, our favorite restaurant, the Old Salt, at Hampton Beach burned, on June 16th, what would have been our 15th anniversary. Just two short years later, after spending some time in a local spot at Hampton Casino, the Old Salt would open in none other than, Lamie's Inn, after the Higgins family purchased the historical Hampton landmark.

Today would be about me. It would be about feelings. When I arrived, I parked the car only just to gaze in front of me and see a vanity plate on the car parked in front of me to be, MADRE, a Spanish word, meaning mother. Lunch would just feel so comforting. I ordered a sandwich, a light martini, and some peace. It felt good.

I was replenished, refreshed and renewed. Ready to take on the rest of the day. Between travel, emotions, memories, bad and good, this day had proved to be quite exhausting. Already. But the strong woman, carried her inner child throughout the weekend with a goal of finding her mom.

Then I made a brief visit back to the facility that felt like a place where my mom was or had been, based on the references of information that I had been given by several mediums. I realized I was done for the day, and ready to wait for my Medium student / friend to arrive after a flight delay that made her arrival a day late.

# EVERYTHING FOR A REASON

I rested peacefully that night, feeling that soon I would find my mom. I believed she was alive; I knew this would be the time.

I calmly went through my morning. I journaled. I meditated. I was at peace. I waited for my student to arrive. I picked her up at the airport. Feeling guilty for slowing things down, which truly was not the way it happened, she was ready to go search. Suitcase and all. I wasn't ready. I took her back to the hotel so she could check into her room. I chilled. She checked in. She came to my room, again ready to go.

"Ya know what? Let's just meditate, set our intention. Connect with those who are going to help us." I swear her eyes rolled back in her head as the anticipation of the day was almost overwhelming for her. Looking back, I think we knew in our heart of hearts that this wasn't going to be a waste of time.

When it was time to go, I could feel it. "Okay, I'm ready, let's do this", I said.

I took her on the tour. Not just the facility location tour, she got the full on Hampton Tour. Approaching my childhood home caused her a physical response that she has since shared somewhat with me. The cemetery tour, I think may have bored her, and by the time I took her down to see Goody Cole's stone, she thought I had taken a leave of my senses.

As the tour went on, her patience growing thin, I finally made my way to the first facility. At the moment thinking it would be the only place we would need to go. My gut thought this was it.

As intuitives we often "can't see our own shit" as we say in the biz. So, the vibe I felt at this one facility was real. I could feel it, I saw many, many signs, but I still wasn't sure. I couldn't see my own shit.

I don't know if I was more excited to see her face when she realized I found it or knew that she would confirm this was it and have ideas on how to validate it all.

A college professor and interim dean when I met her, Joy was "just a client", and has since become a friend.

There was this hot day in Florida. I was there to do sessions. My normal gig in the Fort Myers area is to see as many clients in a couple weeks as I possibly can. Her session was just that, a client session. Her late wife came thru and yes, I actually remember this, because the energy shifted, and her wife was telling her it's time to have more fun.

What do you do for fun? I jestingly asked. "oh, I don't know." A humble yet telling response. "I go to circle and work on my own intuition." "WHAT?"

I consider myself very aware of other intuitives when they are sitting in front of me for a session. But this one went right over my head. But for good reason. We can't see our own shit. Her session finished; I believe it was the last one of the day. Her quiet announcement put a quick idea in my head.

Throwing myself back in my chair, as has been done so many times to me, "read me! ", I jokingly said. But I really wasn't joking. Not one bit. And oh, she knew it. She totally knew.

I had been told several times prior to this that my mother was alive. Let's see if my client now turned medium had any inkling. After the color came back into her face, she agreed to give it a go. She connected with my mom, saying things like "she's waiting for you to find her". "She's sorry about what I have had to endure. She talked about being taken away." My client turned medium was blown away. At herself, at the story. So much so, that even as she made her way out the hotel room door, she turned and thanked ME for letting her do that.

My mom knew she had a good connection here with my newfound medium. A connection she wouldn't let go of.

To relieve any confusion, a psychic medium also connects with the living energy. That includes those who may not know they cannot connect, so they do. In other words, my mom sought out Joy. She made a great decision in doing so.

Joy took this role very seriously and still does to this day.

The best part of her connecting to my mom is how much she surprises herself. How she knows she is doing good and making a huge difference. But she is still surprised. But then again, I surprise myself daily.

After a quiet several minutes in the parking lot of what I thought would be my "home run" spot on, good hit, location.......... In this tiny little voice, I heard Joy say, "I'm sorry but I don't think this is it." Trying to catch my breath, without showing an iota of disappointment, I sat. My stomach in my throat, "okay well there are more. It's okay" I ran the "evidence" through my mind. After all, I've been doing this a long time. She is a "student". But hey whatever. I was extremely attached to the outcome, but I think less attached to how we got there than I originally believed. Afterall, my journal and my photos still had the evidence, for when we'd come back, after she realized her mistake. I had rationalized it all in my brain.

As Mediums, we hold ourselves to a higher standard. As a teacher and mentor, I hold my students to a high standard. "But I am scared to death" they cry, as I push them out of the nest, quite often right into giving messages in a Mediumship Gallery that they are attending, or a session that I tossed in their lap. I always tell my students; "you cannot screw this up". Spirit has your back. Spirit makes no mistakes. Therefore, you won't make mistakes. If you listen and interpret, you cannot and will not "mess up".

Ahhh the lessons we learn. The hard lessons to "practice what we preach". If I believe in the work that I do, if I believe in the power of connection with spirit and our guides, and that this is 100% real, then I am being called to task to remember that this student had completed my mentorship program swimmingly and I had no doubt that she was a gifted psychic medium. I must trust her message. If this is real, and it is, then who am I to pick and choose what I want to hear and what is right and wrong, and what is accurate. She is telling me the truth.

One more spin around, just in case. Just in case she wants to change her mind. Oh, I definitely make a horrible client.

The silence was eventually broken with "I think she's been here, but she's not now." "Oh, thank God. I can now let Joy back into the trust tree", I chuckled to myself

The next place we visited in the same small town, was a newer place. Pulling into the driveway we could see two people having socially distant cigarettes. Employees of some sort. Joy was not afraid to just ask. "Why not? What are they going to do?", her response when I questioned her about why she would do that.

During this adventure, I said several times, "We aren't trying to kidnap a grown human. These aren't daycares where we could stuff a teeny child into a car. We provide no threat or harm to anyone." We surely appear harmless, as well. Two grown ass women, riding around in a rental car trying to find a 90 year old woman. I was not sure if we looked more our own comedy show or a mental health documentary. But we continued on. Unconcerned by our appearance, we had a job to do. Afterall, she had named this "Operation Find Grace".

She rolled the window down, without a care in the world. Like we had a missing persons case. We did. Driven by gut feelings. Driven by intuition and many clear mediumship messages, we were on a case. Only this forensic case was the most important case we'd handle, ever. This was my life. This was 50+ years of not knowing what happened to my mother that day. This was everything to me. And because it was everything to me, it was everything to my friend. She'd stop at nothing to reach our goal. "Finding Grace."

Traveling through my hometown for a while, although time was passing quickly, with zero frustration setting in, total peace was my vibe. The distance from my hometown to where we would go next was not far, after all, I had ridden it a few times on my bike as a kid.

Arriving in the next town, after driving past my brother's house, and other homes of significance, sent chills down my spine. Joy had goosebumps. "We are either close, or she's here", she said. "I have a plan, was my response."

The building had an uncanny resemblance to the first facility in my hometown. The one I had spent so much time at the prior day, waiting and watching for signs. The layout almost identical, barring any newer additions. I knew this place. I'd been here before. A family friend once worked here, and in my days with the Red Cross, I also had reason to have been here. But today was different. Today, and for the past several months, a pandemic has kept all visitors away.

Not having access to the inside would be a major challenge. I mean, how do you find someone in a building, without going in?

"Park somewhere", she said. "I want to walk around." "Oh no you don't. You are crazy". "What are you going to do, just take a stroll?" I asked. Snow hadn't fallen yet, but it was not a warm day by any means. So, fortunately the Floridian had brought her sweater. As we planned and schemed, schemed and planned, suddenly, as if in a scene from the Alfred Hitchcock thriller "The Birds", a swarm of birds circled the facility. It was either get our attention or cause a distraction. But either way, it was working. "Holy shit, it's the birds!!" I yelled. "Always watch the birds", is a phrase I have shared with many intuitives and clients. I believe they are around at important times.

None of them strayed. Like a high school band in the Macy's Day parade, they created perfect formations, as if music was guiding their rhythm. Although it was hard to look away, we needed a plan. I was still unsure where she was planning to walk, to but hey, what harm could she possibly bring?

As if on a mission to find something, she began her walk. In awe I watched those birds circle over her head. They were guiding Joy, guiding us. I could feel their energy, their story. They knew more than us. They always do. After a stroll around the front, Joy returned to the car. I shook my head and asked her, "you have no fear, do you?"

Had the tables been reversed, I surely would have done the same thing. But it feels different when it's my own gig. When I feel like one wrong move, and we are done for. Banished like a drunk patron, starting a fight at the bar.

But in a 'power move' type of way, it also felt like we were doing our work. Like we needed our energy there, to mesh with the bird energy. And if my mom was there, we were 100% going to find her.

"I think this is the place", Joy said, face lit up like the sun. "Wait, what?" It's all fun and games till the intuitive you trust implicitly says "we are here". Thoughts, emotions, fears, I simply don't know how to describe the next few moments. In the moment I wasn't trying to remember every thought and feeling to put in my book, but just to focus and feel.

Vying now for our attention, the birds landed on the back pitch of the building. It was hard to focus, I didn't want to take my eyes off the birds. "Here they come!", I blurted out. The birds swiftly headed to the driveway, and towards the facility sign. Stunned, we both noticed the name of the facility. It was the same name as the other one! Same business, same building, different town. I didn't really know whether I was going to puke or cry. Armed with notes from the intuitives who had done several of my readings, the building and the location "checked the boxes". "This is good", I said. "But now what?"

"She knows you are looking for her. She knows. We are close. We have to do something." Joy cried. Easy for her to say, I was becoming paralyzed, emotionally and physically. Always the organizer, forever the planner, but no plan. Not this time. I hadn't practiced for this moment. I had no clue what to do.

Trust was all I had. Trust that what the Mediums had told me, the notes I had, even just the trusting the fact that my mom was still alive. That was all I had at this moment in time. No plan. Just trust.

"Do you think we should go out back?" She asked me. I don't know how long I had been silent for, but it felt like an hour. If you were to ask me what was going through my head at that moment, I wouldn't have an answer.

"Okay well, here's what I do know", I said, "we can't go inside. Not to ask, not to sneak around, we literally cannot go in past the front door, so that's out of the question."

Slowly reversing out of the parking space, sure that someone had to be watching our escapades by now, I crept up the driveway, 1 MPH max.

I don't know where it came from, but with no doubt that we were going to get the job done one way or the other, and knowing my friend was able to connect to my mother's energy, "tell her to just bang on the window, so we know it's her!" I shouted. "With all these people in all these rooms, how in the world will we see in each window if we drive out back? Tell her to bang on the window when she sees us!" Without hesitation, she did. She connected to my mom and told her. I watched her intuitively do it.

Now I was charged. And in charge. Or so I thought.

Behind the facility, was the employee parking lot. It was just about shift change for second shift, and several employees made their way from their cars, while others leaned over and gave their loved ones a kiss goodbye and watched them drive away.

"Great, of course we have the whole staff out here. We are going to get caught." I whined. "Doing what though? We aren't at a daycare trying to kidnap a child. Okay let's make a plan. Again." One plan to drive out back, and another plan would be needed now that we were out there. These are some of the thoughts that go through your head, when you feel that you are just moments and feet away from seeing your mom for the first time in 50+ years.

As we rounded the corner to the back lot, a woman had come out from inside a little courtyard sitting area. A two foot tall, white wooden fence surrounded the sitting area, clearly for aesthetics, not to keep anyone out. Even I could have jumped the fence if need be. "Although in what instance would I need to jump that fence?" I wondered.

The young woman had just visited a loved one, in what is so widely known now as a "window visit". Conveniently, she left the little swinging gate open. Although it had no lock and had a teeny, little latch. Covid had made "in person visits" come to a screeching halt, six or so months earlier. Little did I know that seeing this woman would get our wheels turning.

"I wish we could just talk to her!" I said, seeing a young nurse, in her neatly pressed blue scrubs, with auburn hair halfway down her back, stroll to the entrance. She appeared to have a lot on her mind, and things she would rather be doing. Before Joy could spot her, she was in the building. Just another day at work for her.

"We just need to ask someone, someone that looks nice. She looked nice. I want to talk to her." I whined.

As I watched Joy "tap in", she smiled. I knew she was connecting with my mom. She always has a sheepish grin when she does. This time was no different. Since the first day Joy outed herself, the look has been the same.

Concocting a plan was as difficult as planning a bank heist must be. Although I have never robbed a bank, nor have any desire to, the energy we were expending had to be similar. "There she is! There is the nurse!" I'm sure the slap to Joy's upper arm left a bruise, but I was surely not thinking about that at the time.

"We are definitely busted", I was sure of it. For what? I have no earthly idea. Blue scrubs, auburn hair, young and definitely sweet looking, I noticed her side eye peering into the car, but then not. I'm going to talk to her I said. "Who??" Joy asked. "That nurse!" Before Joy could respond, with my window rolled down, it was too late to turn back now. "Hey, do you work here?" Asking as if I hadn't noticed the scrubs, or the fact that she had come out of the employee door. "Yes. No sorry, I thought you were my friend who works here, she's inside, but she has purple hair too." I would definitely have to compute that sentence later. Right now, I had other things on my mind. Clearly the nurse did too.

"I just came out to move my car from the front lot, out here to this parking lot". That sentence, I did have time to compute. I'm sure that Joy and I had the same thought. "Girl, you've literally been here less than 10 minutes, why didn't you just park back here to begin with?"

I know why. I knew why. Because it was divinely orchestrated. This poor child had no idea she was a divine player in the big plan to find my mom.

When you are in the passenger's seat of a sedan and someone is close to the driver's window, pretty much all you can see is their torso. I'm sure from where Joy was sitting, all she could see was blue scrubs. Intent on drawing Joy's attention to the name tag I had just set my eyes on, "well, PATIENCE, (*note* her real name was even more divinely fitting) may I just ask you something?" I asked in a clear concise voice, making sure that Joy was hearing the CNA'S name loud and clear. "Sure, what is it?" "Well, I'm fairly certain HIPPA prevents you from telling me if you have someone as a patient in there." "It does", she said, her face slowly turning from a smile to sadness.

She knew. She knew if I was asking that question, there was a reason, and it was probably heart breaking. Patience knew. She was sent to the window of my rental car that day to remind me to "accept the things, I cannot change, the courage to change the things I can; and the wisdom to know the difference. "

"Why?" She asked. 'Deep breath, Karen,' I reminded myself, while Joy sat motionless in the passenger's seat, still trying to wrap her head around the kind nurse's name.

"Well", I thought, "I could tell her the whole damn story, but I am sure her superiors would notice her missing before night fall." "You see, Patience.......」 at this point I was just absorbing the energy of saying her name. "my mother was taken by someone when I was just 5 years old. Not kidnapped, taken by a family member. I was told she was dead since I am just five." Tears in her eyes, I knew we had connected. "Well recently I was told she is alive and is either here or another facility nearby." "WOW!" she blurted out, "Who told you she was here?" "Several reliable sources", I retorted in a firm but gentle manor.

Everything I told Patience that day was the truth. I may have forgotten to tell her that the reliable sources were Mediums, getting their information from somewhere in the ethers, but hey, why confuse things at all?

"What is her name?" "Well, Patience, here's the thing. Her name is Grace, she is ninety years old. She would definitely have had someone who put her here, but most likely under a different name. No definitely under a different name. "

"Oh my god, I wish I could answer your questions for you, but I'd lose my job. I do hope you find her though." "Patience, thank you. I believe I already have," I whispered. She turned to walk away. As I thanked her and looked over at Joy for a response, we realized that her unspoken words, combined with her spoken words, Patience didn't even realize she had given me an answer. Maybe not clear to the layperson, but Joy and I both knew; my mom is in that building.

Without a second thought, and after Patience safely went into the building, Joy said, "I am going over there to look". The courtyard had some chairs and benches, a few plants that didn't make it through the first frost were set here and there and probably brought a lot of color to the unused sitting area, in the warmer seasons. Another special place that had been ripped from the residents, thanks to a global pandemic.

The gate was open, and Joy was going to walk through it. I watched her till I really couldn't see what she was doing anymore. Like the getaway driver at a bank heist, I checked my mirrors frantically, thinking "this is it, we are going to jail". I'm not sure what the charges would be, but nevertheless.

My job as watchman / getaway driver came to a screeching halt as a beaming face yelled to me, "Karen, come here. You must meet this woman!" "What woman????" I yelled. At this point I thought she had lost her damn mind. Caught up in the moment and unable to form a sentence, I just got out of the car. I never looked to see if anyone was coming, or if we'd get caught. The beam of light coming from Joy's face, said it all.

The little gate still open, I made my way into the courtyard, as Joy made her way towards me. "Karen you are not going to believe this! I came in here and there are all these windows of patient's rooms, and I HEARD BANGING ON THE WINDOW! Just what you'd told me to ask your mom to do! She was standing in this window here like she'd been waiting for us! Then she started banging."

Through my sheer excitement, terror, elation, I looked over at the frail, yet energized, 90 year old woman standing in the window. Tears rolling down her face, she blew me a kiss. Focused solely on me, with my purple hair and all, a mother knows her daughter when she sees her. She knew me. She knew her daughter. If nothing else had happened following this very moment, it still would have had the same amazing impact. But that wasn't the end. Not even close!

"What the hell, ……………..??? How did this, I mean how did you, I mean what the hell is happening?" I tried to say. Unable to form a complete sentence, time was standing still. Yet moving so fast. I was looking to Joy for an explanation of what was happening, yet I am sure she was just as frozen as I was.

The impulse to just hug my mom was thwarted as I snapped back into reality. It was a pandemic and the sign so skillfully placed there in the courtyard, reminded me of that. "All visitors must check into the office." Oops! Well, there is no turning back now.

I didn't care. So caught up in the moment, someone could have driven away with the rental car, and I wouldn't have even noticed.

"Karen, I shit you not, I walked over here, and she was banging on the window and clapping! Banging like I had asked her to and clapping as if we had won a gold medal. It's your mom! I know it!" she cried. "Only this is more precious than any medal." While writing this, a song sung by Whitney Houston, at the 1988 Summer Olympics in South Korea plays over and over in my mind. I remember it bringing me to tears back then, but on this day, the day I laid eyes on my mother for the first time in almost 52 years, I was motionless, emotionless. Not void of emotion, just unable to describe this feeling. Seeing her through the glass. A reunion, one that I could never have imagined in my wildest of dreams.

"One Moment in Time" – a Newsweek article written by Tufayel Ahmed, quotes Narada Michael Walden, the song's producer. "'One Moment in Time' says it's okay to take this moment to love yourself, go beyond yourself. It always comes down to love", Walden said.

Two days ago, I wrote in my journal, "It is always about love". No coincidences.

At the end of the day, it's always about love, and the love a mother has for her child remains throughout life, and into the afterlife. Today I saw that in my mother's eyes. No circumstances, history, lies, stories, deceit, or confusion can take that away from her. Or from me. It is a knowing. She knew. Joy knew. I knew.

# ONE MOMENT IN TIME – WHITNEY HOUSTON

Each day I live
I want to be
A day to give
The best of me
I'm only one
But not alone
My finest day
Is yet unknown

I broke my heart
Fought every gain
To taste the sweet
I face the pain
I rise and fall
Yet through it all
This much remains

I want one moment in time
When I'm more than I thought I could be
When all of my dreams are a heartbeat away
And the answers are all up to me
Give me one moment in time
When I'm racing with destiny

Then in that one moment of time
I will feel
I will feel eternity

I've lived to be
The very best
I want it all
No time for less
I've laid the plans
Now lay the chance
Here in my hands

Give me one moment in time
When I'm more than I thought I could be
When all of my dreams are a heartbeat away
And the answers are all up to me
Give me one moment in time
When I'm racing with destiny
Then in that one moment of time
I will feel
I will feel eternity

You're a winner for a lifetime
If you seize that one moment in time
Make it shine

Give me one moment in time
When I'm more than I thought I could be
When all of my dreams are a heartbeat away
And the answers are all up to me
Give me one moment in time
When I'm racing with destiny
Then in that one moment of time
I will be, I will be
I will be free

FREE! That is it! I am free! No longer did I have to wonder where my mom was. No longer did I have to wonder, is there a chance that several Mediums from all over the country, made the same mistake? I expect people, my clients, to trust me daily. To trust that the words I deliver are true. Who am I to ever question the validity of their readings? I believe. And this day is my one moment in time. I was racing with destiny. My mom is 90. Time is running out. I am FREE!

The clapping and banging on the window continued. I didn't mind, I just didn't want it to end. Not again. Not like when I went to bed as a normal 5 year old, and woke up to find my mother gone, 50+ years earlier.

"We were clapping and happy and I knew she knew. She stood here with this one blind ¾ of the way up, but then after a minute of excitement, clapping and banging on the window, she put the blind all the way up, and went to the window beside it, and put that one up too. She was looking for someone. She was looking for you. She could see me in front of her but needed to put the blind up to see you! That is when I came to get you." Joy told me the story, over and over. I couldn't get enough. I still can't.

"There will be long windows on a brick building when you find her" one of the Mediums told me a year ago. "She will be waiting for you." "There will be a gate. It will be open." "Also, I see a sunflower."

Although random, but where we were parked, behind the car, next to the shed, there stood a single sunflower, that had looked much brighter in its day.

I watched the tears run down my mother's face as she stared at her daughter, a moment still so surreal, that I will never forget. "I miss you" she said through the window glass.

"Joy, did you see that? She said I miss you." I yelled. "I saw that", she said. "I saw it."

We both noticed that it was as if Joy wasn't even in front of my mom anymore once I made my appearance. She never took her eyes off me. Well at least not yet. I was so grateful to have Joy there. Not for a witness, I didn't need a witness, because this is my story, and I am not attached to who believes or doesn't believe it. But more so for someone to replay the whole reunion for me. Someone who would remember the little details that may soon leave my memory. Memory loss is definitely a symptom of trauma. I had a lifetime of the ability to block things out. I would never block this day out, but my brain fog definitely had the ability to kick in at any given moment. Joy was meant to be there.

I was meant to meet her in Florida, a few years ago, however that happened. That was the day that her wife, in spirit, nudged me to ask her what she does for fun or what brings her joy. She shared she was intuitive. She told me my mom was alive that day. Without fear. She read for me, for her Medium. She took my Mediumship Mentor program. She was intrigued with forensics. She helped me with some missing persons cases. She offered to help me find my mom. She flew up. She showed up. And now it all made sense. From the day I met Joy, it was all part of the grand plan. The divine unfolding of clarity. Who knew?

Tears still streaming down her face and her hands over her heart, my mom mouthed the words, "Thank you, thank you, thank you." Joy watched in awe. A mom found her child. A child found her mom.

Freeze frame. If only I could hold this moment forever. If only the world could stop turning. If only. I will never forget her face. The emotion that welled up inside of her. The sheer joy and peace that passes all understanding. The conversation, albeit unspoken aloud, that had happened between the three of us, will carry me through for the rest of my life. My mother's eyes spoke volumes. A small scar on her head, extremely noticeable to me, caused me to wonder later on, when my objective mind returned, what had happened to her. I saw the look of a saint; one I had seen only once before. She had "his" same eyes.

I remember it was a warm day in 2019, on the island in Hawaii. The angel man I refer to as my Hawaiian energy healer, let me know that my mom was alive and that I would find her. "You came here to do this work." He said. "Here to earth, or here to Hawaii?" I asked. "Both. There is ancestral healing that needs to take place. This is your job. It's why you are here." He replied. It was not only his words that stuck with me, but his eyes. I've seen those eyes only once since then. My mother. Not way back years ago when she was able to be a mom to me for 5 short years, but on this day. It would be the one physical feature of my mom that Joy and I would both notice and later discuss.

I had two sessions on my last visit to the island. We had a lot of work to do. This type of energy healing needs to happen more than once a year. In the other session he would take me through a visualization that would help me forgive my father. He described him to a "T" in his mind's eye. I needed to pack all that away for another day.

I kept looking back at Joy to be sure she was taking all this in. She was. Absorbing it all as if it were her own miracle story.

From joyful, excited and loving, the smiling teary face of a mother who just found her child, suddenly went blank. Just as quickly as we had found her, something shifted. In a split second, she blew a kiss, and waved goodbye, somehow knowing she would see me again. My mom had no fear that this was the end and no second thought. The window blind in front of her dropped down. She reached over and dropped the other blind. It was as if she had seen a ghost.

"Jesus, Joy what do we do now? What happened? Is someone behind us?" I cried.

I have never had good peripheral vision, and today was no different. Side to side I looked, as did Joy. Trying to use those eyes I've told my kids and grandkids that I have in the back of my head, I saw nothing, yet felt something.

"Okay well she's gone," I said, "something spooked her." Feeling defeated at the moment, we turned and walked back to the car. There was nothing to do but sit there. Silent. For a minute, neither of us had anything to say. Until we had everything to say. As quickly as we had found her, she was now out of sight.

"Wait, what the fuck just happened??? It's her! I know it's her! Did you see her say, 'I miss you'?? She banged on the window! She banged on the fucking window, just like I asked her to! Did that really just happen? Wait, what? Oh my god. It's her! She's here! We found her! But……. I dunno, just now what?"

I was unsure if Joy could even compose a sentence. Because I sure couldn't. I took a breath and gave her a chance to speak. Not much of a chance. But a chance.

"Karen, when I walked over, she was banging on the fuckin window. Banging. Banging and clapping. So, I mimicked her. Like we were playing some sort of game. But that didn't last. As soon as that other blind went up, she was looking for someone or something. She was looking for her daughter! She was looking for YOU!!"

"Wait, tell me what just happened again?" I said. I'd imagine when the numbers of the winning Megabucks ticket that match your numbers are read, or having a gold medal placed around your neck, is not far from what I was feeling at that moment. Elation doesn't cover it. You might

331

ask, "but how are you okay not seeing her in person, not hugging her, and with no actual legal physical proof that it is her?"

A mother knows their child. A child knows their mother. If you have not experienced being misplaced or having misplaced a parent, then it would be a difficult concept to understand. You just know. She knew. I knew.

At this point I had known my mom was alive for two years. All leads did not lead me to her. However, strong, strong intuition and several gifted mediums did! "You cannot make this shit up", will always be my motto.

Let me just say that I am so grateful to Joy for absorbing all that happened that day, for many reasons. For the book. For the story. But most of all for assisting in finding my missing mom, against all odds.

Bigger than my finding my mom, was for my mom to find me. She couldn't use social media, like so many. She couldn't search. She was in a home, and on lockdown.

Twenty years ago, she called me, twice. She heard my voice. I heard her's. She knew I was alive. But I had told her she was dead. She didn't know. There is just no way she had known that I was told she had died. But who stopped her from calling me those two days? Who had stopped her many times before? Who hung that phone up on our conversation in 2000? Were they alive now? Were they dead? Did their death allow me to find her?

From complete and fulfilled happiness, to hysteria in less than 2 minutes, I tearfully gazed over at Joy in the passenger's seat. A happy, tearful, joyful, ecstatic face looked back at me. "Joy, what happened? Why did she so quickly close those blinds?" I cried. "I thought for sure there was an employee behind us and that was it, we were done for."

I didn't fear 'getting in trouble', being removed from the property, or even a potential encounter with the police. My mind wasn't so much in that place, but more of in a place of, "shit, if we mess up, that is the end of this moment in time, and we walk away only with what we have."

"Oh my God, it was my father! She saw him! He must have come up behind me in spirit. That was the chill I felt!" I screamed. I feel it now actually, not in a bad way, as I sit on my sofa, typing away, waiting for the sun to come up. "Not in a bad way though", I said. "I bet he came in to support me. To help me. To validate this reunion. He's on the other side. He's done his work. He is forgiven, by me anyway." I say that now still with conviction on this chilly Sunday morning. I hadn't forgiven him because I found my mom, I found my mom because I had forgiven him.

Forgiven for the abuse. Forgiven for the lies. Forgiven for taking my precious mom away from me when I was only 5 years old. It's not for me to understand. Maybe it was her idea? I will never know. But I do know a healing took place on this autumn day, October 24, 2020

"That's it! She saw him and got spooked. After all, does she know he's dead? Does she think he was really there? Joy asked. "I don't think he meant any harm. I don't think he meant to scare her. He was here for you." She said.

"The least he could do", I said, the cynicism seeping from my pores.

I will never, ever know the circumstances in which she was taken from me, so many years ago. I don't really need to. It doesn't change the story at all. It may make for a better "made for TV movie" but again, as my therapist Dr. Fenton said, "the devil is in the details".

Completely stunned as we sat, trying to figure out what happened. Who spooked my mom? It had to have been my father. The look on her face was as if a human who would have been upsetting to her, was standing right behind me. I know it was him. It's just a knowing. But validated later on by another Medium.

My mom had seen him, she blew me a quick kiss, as if we had a long standing goodbye process, then she waved and closed those blinds, to keep her from seeing what was behind me, and in her mind, to keep what was behind me from seeing her. This kind of thing is unexplainable. Science couldn't touch it. Speculation could create an assortment of scenarios that had just happened. But I know what I know, because I saw what I saw and felt what I felt. No explanation needed.

"Okay now what?" I asked Joy. "We just come back later", she replied. And that we did, only to find the blinds still closed. Through our entire 'window visit' earlier, I had kept one eye on her and one eye in the small hospital type room in which she so boldly stood. Her room door was open, I could see straight into the hallway. Not a human in sight, inside or outside. What or who she had seen that had spooked her earlier, was not in living physical form. I was convinced of that fact, and still am.

Slowly making our way out of the driveway, having a hard time taking my eyes off her window, while trying somehow to wrap my head around what had happened, I just wanted details told to me over and over. My brain was kicking in and not computing. So, I asked Joy to tell me again what went down.

I write this, trying to remember how long we were there. Time stood still. I have no idea. It truly doesn't matter.

"So, I walked over, and heard this bang, bang, bang on the window. Just like you asked for. I looked and there she was, standing there, banging, clapping, and looking. Looking for you. She didn't want me, she wanted you, that was extremely clear." Joy recalled.

Listening to Joy, while concocting a new plan, I yelled, "I just need a sign, a big ole sign!" "Okay so banging, clapping, saying she missed you, blowing kisses, all that, that isn't enough for you? Say nothing about the fact that you have the exact same facial structure! Her facial structure is identical to you AND your grandmother, her mom." She replied.

Although I have been doing this Mediumship work a long time, "acknowledge the signs and trust", is something that habitually rolls off my tongue. Easier said than done. I trust this work implicitly, or I would have never made the trip up there. I knew I'd find her, but I didn't know I'd find her. That makes zero sense, but it is the only way to describe it.

I had to be the client here. Not the healer, not the teacher. The little girl, who through some sort of inexplicable miracle, just found her mom. I needed to drop my defense, drop my leadership and just allow.

I wasn't letting go of needing a sign of validation. I have always taught my clients and students; "you have to ask for what you want. If you want a sign, tell your guides and angels, what you want."

I asked for banging on the window, and I sure as hell got it.

"Please, just one more big sign" I begged. That was my last bargaining attempt of the day.

Most the leaves had fallen, peak leaf peeping season was over, although off and on a bright orange, yellow or red tree would appear. It was warm at high noon and a chill in the air by evening. Nothing had changed in New Hampshire in the year and a half that I had been gone.

I knew these roads like the back of my hand. I was raised in Hampton, the next town over and raised my kids here. I was traveling the same roads we traveled when they were in car seats.

Leaving there, I decided to clear our palettes and stop at a couple other memory care and nursing facilities, "just in case". We had already found my mom, so I am not entirely sure why I thought this was a good idea that would support our objective in any way. Some sort of weird proof, I suppose. Proof that I didn't truly need, but I am human.

Our mind needs validation. The high vibing spiritual mind says, "here we are with my mother, she banged on the window, clapped, said thank you, and I miss you. I look like her, although she is 90. And so it is, period. Done and no explanation needed."

The one piece a logical mind cannot unravel, is the uncontrollable tears that flowed when she saw me. A reaction only a mother would have. No confusion at all. As if this was all aligned in our energies. As if it was part of the divine plan. A well scripted movie. And I was the lead role. It was, in fact, all of that.

"Yup, I am holding out for a big sign!" I boasted. Although I was definitely playing with Spirit and my guides at this point, I wanted what I wanted.

Taking the back way out to the main road, was not my plan, but after all I really didn't have a plan. A left onto the main road, and "DID YOU SEE THAT?" I screamed. "What??" Joy asked. "That sign, back there, did you see it??" Truly on a level of awe that I have never experienced for myself or even with my clients, I have no recollection where I even spun the rental car around.

We looked up at a business sign that doubles the size of any other sign on this road.

Having lived in this town for 15 years, I know signage is a huge deal with the Town officials. This sign didn't seem to fit their parameters, but that was long ago, so what do I know. But it was big, real big, is the point I am trying to make here.

Large, bold, yellow print on a black background, no one could deny what it read. Definitely not a skeptic and certainly not me.

"GRACIE'S", was what it said in huge letters on this huge sign! I was now officially blown away. That's the only way to describe this "sign" that was an actual "big sign" that I had needed or demanded. I don't remember much after that; I think looking back I may have been on "overload", in the best way ever!

"We haven't eaten" I said, as I began to come to my senses. I had no clue what time it was, as time had been standing still. And certainly, food was not on my mind. I was having what I can best describe as an out of worldly experience. That may be a bit dramatic, but I am definitely trying to hit a point home here, for you, the reader. Not to get you to believe my story. Your belief of my experience has no bearing on me. I want you to feel what I was feeling. Experience what I was experiencing. To imagine what this was jaw dropping experience was like for me. Also, how it was for Joy. To this day, she glows when she recalls the events of that weekend. She will likely never have another experience that compares.

I am one who has for many years depended on the sun for time of day. I am not sure when or where I started doing this, probably something I mastered during countless hours of being in husband number three's big truck. Although a difficult time for many, many reasons, I saw the entire country during that part of my life. It might have gone whizzing by the passenger's window of his Peterbilt, but I saw it. Felt it. Experienced it. I am blessed to have experienced the vast beauty that is missed when folks don't have the privilege of seeing the country this way, or in any way. I will never discount that time in my life. It was part of my awakening. A huge part. Therefore, I am incredibly grateful for those years.

Everything we experience in life, every relationship, whether with a spouse or partner, every friendship, happens for a reason. A reason or a season. Quite often, both. There may be times in your life that were hard. Times that you may remember and say, "so glad that is over". But without those times, how would things have played out for you? Good, bad or indifferent, each chapter has its place in your life. There are no mistakes. Heartaches, yes. But no mistakes.

Imagine one chapter, one relationship, one person being ripped out of your book of life. What would be different? Would it be better? Would it be worse? We won't know. We can't speculate. We only have trust that the chapter was there for a reason. Maybe a season. But definitely a reason. I have no regrets with any relationship I have been in. Including the violent abusive one as a teen. Without that relationship, I wouldn't have met and married the father of 3 of my children. That's huge. Imagine life without three of your kids, and if you are blessed enough have them, 6 of your grandkids. I'd prefer not to. I am content. Each chapter had its reason. Including the one where their dad passed when they were young.

After a late lunch we circled back around to the facility. Blinds still closed, we left and headed back to our hotel.

"Tell me the story how we found my mom again?", I asked, now behaving like a 4 year old wanting to hear the story of her amazing birth for the 15th time, simply to stall the bedtime process. Joy was so patient. Not to put words in her mouth, but there had to have been an anticipated reaction when we found my mom. I think that didn't happen. Although we have never openly discussed it, I think she was probably expecting me to be a blubbering fool. But I don't recall a tear. The entire weekend. She may tell the story differently.

Shock is the only way to describe my response and subsequent behavior.

Shock, but as I think more about it, I think I primarily behaved as if I was expecting it to play out this way. Like this was the intent we set, we knew we were in her energy, why wouldn't we find her?

Morning came and I calmly did my journaling and meditation, as if it were any other day. Joy, right ready to get back at it, knocked on my hotel room door, we set our intention and we were out the door.

"Do you realize that had your plane not been delayed, and you had come in the night before, as you were 'supposed to' have, yesterday would not have played out as beautifully as it did. We would have gone out yesterday morning, nothing would have lined up, not the banging, no nurse Patience, no woman just finishing a 'window visit'. THAT is divine timing. Although you so heroically ran through that airport, you weren't meant to get here that night. It would have messed everything up." I told her.

Likewise with our little tour of Hampton. "I could see you coming out of your skin, just waiting and wanting to get on with our search, yet I was just dilly dallying." I told her. "Timing was perfect. It all was perfect."

The drive thru breakfast line seemed to be taking forever. I'm okay if I am the one in control, but when I have no control over the drive-thru line, and it is slowing me down, that's another story.

But the slowdown was fine, the timing was again perfect.

Parking again behind the facility with the mission at hand, we had a plan, but really no plan. "What shall we do today?" I asked Joy. "We should get out of the car and go to the window," she said. "You go!" I responded, with a chuckle. I don't know why I was so nervous, like what would anyone say to us, "are you trying to kidnap the elderly through their window?"

We had gotten a late start, and it was noon before we reached the facility this time. Joy wasn't out of the car but a minute, before she turned and said, "Karen come here, she wants to see you!"

Wondering how she knew that to be true, I remembered Joy is psychic. She had a connection to my mom that truly allowed her to "speak to her". This phenomenon has happened many times in my Mediumship practice.

Although they were not physically there when I found my mom, the Mediums in my life all had a huge part in this story. Specifically Mary, who lives in NH, over near Manchester. We would gather in circle at the beautiful home she shares with her husband. She was the driving force behind all of this. She never once waivered in her belief that my mom was alive. Not for a minute. She gave me some of the validation in my readings that I have referenced in the book. I am so grateful for her constant support, although our paths don't cross nearly enough since my moving to Myrtle Beach.

I have purposely kept this massive discovery quiet over the past 3 months. *As of the current time that I am editing, it now has been over 6 months* I have done that for several reasons. If someone who was aware of my plight asks, I will answer them kind of brushing it away with the phrase, "it's all in the book". I do this for several reasons. First because the story is so unbelievable, I don't need bits and pieces getting out there, without the whole story as I experienced it. Second, some people are twisted. I don't know who I can trust, so why not just be safe?

I have only just this month told my oldest daughter, and her shock was so emotional for me. She trembled with tears in her eyes, sitting there in disbelief, as the details unraveled. "Let's go get her" she quietly yelled, so as not to alarm her family. "We can't", I said. "Why not?!?!" she retorted. This child is 100 percent mine. A carbon copy. A "take action, why are we still sitting here", attitude.

"We can't just go get her. She has lived this life, whatever it has been, for over 50 years." I said. "I am honestly afraid that it would be like taking a child away from a family that adopted them. You just suddenly show up and remove all they know from their life and expect that will bring them joy. I found her," I continued. "That's really all that matters. I had the ability to find her, and other than the phone calls she made 20 years ago, she had no way to get to me. I had to get to her. I did. It was worth it. To take her, I would have to find a way to legally get her. I could fight and fight, and then what if she dies in the process?" I asked. "Or maybe she doesn't want to leave there. It's not for me to decide. I have to trust my gut with this. My gut says, I got what I needed, and she did too. I don't need to prove it to anyone. I didn't need to find her for the book, the book was happening either way. I needed to find her to let her know that I am okay, and that I had done all that I could to get to her". "But.." I said, "that would not have happened without the gift of intuition. During that visit she did have an opportunity to ask me to try to come take her. She didn't. She was happy. Beyond happy. Her tears of joy are ingrained in my mind forever."

Rolling down the window (well pushing the little button) while noticing Joy's beaming face, "are you sure?" I yelled. "Yes, just come here, she's looking for you!" she yelled back. In the only easy chair in her room now facing the window, so as not to miss her daughter's next visit, there she sat bright eyed, thrilled again to see me. As I got closer, Joy went back to the car. "Where are you going?" I asked. "It's not me she wants to see," she reminded me.

With no one in sight, I went right up to her window this time. Her lunch tray, most likely filled with some of her most favorite things, was definitely the second highlight of her day. A small thin woman, she didn't look like she ate much, but she appeared to be enjoying this meal. She looked at me with a huge smile and lifted the tray slightly, with the face that read, "do you want some?" In a way, I know she was serious. Why wouldn't a mom want to share a meal with her child? I would call that natural human instinctual behavior. It was all so emotional and so touching, and this was one of my favorite parts of the weekend. I wasn't just there randomly. I wasn't just anyone. Joy was right, she didn't want her, she wanted me. Without me actually being able to hear her, she was telling me that I can't come in. She wanted me to, but I she knows that I can't. A mom, my mom, consoling and explaining. She may not have "done mom things" for 50 years, but it never left her.

I love that my mom was just so comfortable with my presence that she kept right on eating. It was adorable. That is, until something came over me and I remembered I had my phone in my sweatshirt pouch. Lunchtime is a perfect time to take a walk down memory lane.

The door to her small but comfortable room was open, so my third, no fourth or fifth eye was watching that door. I gazed all over that room while she ate. It was very simply decorated, but not much decor to speak of.

Not one plant, balloon, card, nothing to represent visitors, in there. Although it's pandemic time, there is still mail deliveries, and things from pre-covid, nonetheless. She didn't seem to have much. Her choice? Maybe.

But most importantly, not one framed photo, no memorabilia, and absolutely no sign of a family. Not on the wall, not on the nightstand or dresser. An observation that I was not to have missed. The fact that she was eating, gave me an opportunity to look around and soak up everything I possible could about her current life. The first day, I couldn't take my eyes off of her, while noticing how much I looked like her.

I wondered about the walker beside her bed, because from the moment I met her, she definitely had no issue moving around. Case in point when she flung those blinds down as if she had seen a ghost. As well as the 10 or 12 times she had tried to slide open the windows to talk to me while I was there. A small oak tag dangled from the top rail of the walker of course facing the opposite direction. It's okay. If I was supposed to see it, I would have.

Oak tag?? Did I seriously just type that? I don't even know what oak tag is. I do know it is a word(s) used in grammie's house often enough that I just wrote it. But then I just had to Google it. I haven't said that word since I was a child. I looked it up for two reasons, was it oak tag, oattag, oaktag, I don't know. My laptop didn't underline it as if I had made a mistake, so the spelling has to be correct. But what in the world is oak tag. In Googling it, the first photo that came up on my cell phone, was exactly what was hanging from her walker, oak tag. I can't remember the first 6 to 10 years of my life, but I just pulled that phrase out of nowhere, or somewhere. It's the little things, isn't it?

Suddenly, in my mind's eye, ie: my memory, I am standing next to grammie's piano while she teaches one of the neighborhood children their piano lessons. Resisting the temptation of the M&M's in the small clear custard dish, placed ever so strategically on the side of her upright piano.

When my mom wasn't carefully placing her pasta on her fork, she was watching me, watch her.

Out came my cell phone. I couldn't help it. My trembling finger swiped quickly to the slightly faded picture of the black and white wedding picture. I don't know why my hands were trembling the slightest bit, most likely adrenaline. When I found this picture earlier in the week, I had zoomed in on my phone, which resulted in cutting out my father from the screen, and based on the previous day, that was a good move on my part. All that could be seen in the screenshot was a clear black and white picture of grammie and my mom. In the picture, my mom was wearing the same wedding dress that I wore down the aisle when I married my knight.

Thank goodness she didn't have a mouthful, as she took ONE LOOK at this picture, gasped, covered her mouth, uncovered it, and gasped again. Her long thin piano playing pointer finger, pointed straight in my direction and then back at her chest. "You and me?" She mouthed clearly. What would you have done?

I told her yes, I shook my head yes. She recognized my grammie (her mom) to be her, which the resemblance is uncanny, and she thought she was in me, in the picture. It's fine. The important thing is that this picture of her and her mom, took her breath away. She was not confused. She was not looking at it like it was simply picture day. She knew. She may have misplaced her mom for her, and her for me. But she knew in her soul, we are her family.

I don't know what I was expecting, but that wasn't it. It was more, so, so much more than I could have ever expected. Till the day I leave this earth, I will never ever forget the look on my mother's face when she saw a picture of herself as a young, seemingly happy, Grace.

She clapped again, looked me straight in the eye and said, "I missed you. Thank you." She was not but a total distance of 2 feet from me, and I could just feel the mother's love through the glass that separated us.

343

I had more pictures. I swiped quickly to find the next picture, as she sat perched in her chair, waiting patiently, seemingly now uninterested in lunch. I had zoomed in on a familiar picture on the stoop at my childhood home in Hampton, where she sat with three of us kids, me standing up, hands on hips, in a dress, and mouth wide open. Again with the gasp. "Me?" She asked. "Is that me?" "Yes, yes it is you." I said. She knew, again, she knew. My heart was ready to bust. I wanted time to stand still.

There is no way to describe the emotion, elation, or euphoric feeling that comes over someone at a time like this. I have literally nothing to compare it to. Nothing. I'd imagine it to be similar to finding a sibling that you were separated from at birth. Or a child who had been missing. I don't know. I truly don't know. If I could have bottled up the feelings to take with me to revisit when I got home, I would have. But for now, all I have is the memories, and for me, it is enough. Well, actually the memories as well as the picture that Joy took of my backside while I was talking to my mom at the window. Private indescribable moments between a mom and a child. It is truly that simple.

I had never had this kind of time with her. If I did, I don't remember. This was precious. Genuine. Something that could never be made up or planned.

The next picture, the full picture on the stoop with the older three of us, as my younger brother must not have been born yet, would be the final picture. Keeping in mind that we were there without permission, and more importantly, that my mom had only been aware of me for 24 hours at this point.

Eyes welling up with tears, she knew. She knew me, she knew herself, and I know she recognized my siblings, two of her three other children, only two of which are still living. She stared at me, she stared back at the picture.

Soon I felt our visit coming to a close. I had a feeling in my gut that it was time to go. No specific reason, just time. I glanced at her, I looked one last time at her perfectly made, unwrinkled bed, her sparsely decorated home; her room, and motioned to her that I had to go. She blew a kiss, and waved goodbye. I'm forever grateful to Joy for taking a picture of me at the window that day. It won't leave my memory, but it reminds me that this really truly happened. That I saw my mom. Again.

I can't begin to compare this time to anything other experience in my life, so I will take it and hold it dear, as one of the best experiences of my life, short of giving birth to my children. It is a true miracle.

Her flight was early, so I took Joy to the airport the following morning, and then went back to my room to just ground and feel. All kinds of emotions had come up over the past 48 hours, and I was needing a little balance. Once grounded and journaled up, I would make one last visit to my mom.

The energy would be different this time without Joy there. But it would be exactly how it was supposed to be. This time, without a plan in place again, I would do it alone. Afterall, it wasn't Joy she wanted to see. It was me. Having Joy there gave me more confidence, as well as having a look out, for whatever it was that we were doing wrong.

My third visit there. She knew when I was coming, by day three she was not at all surprised. The blinds in her room wide open, late morning sun had not made its way to that side of the building and there was a little chill on this autumn day.

There she was, just a mom, by the window waiting for her child. When I think of my lack of preparation, and planning, I surprise even myself. What if? What if someone else did show up to visit her? What if someone, a staff member inside the building, came out to see what I was doing.? What if a nurse or aid walked into her room? The door wide open to the hallway again, I had one eye on the doorway for the entire visit. In my heart I know that the Universe would not have let anyone, or anything interfere with what was happening on this October morning. As I gaze over on my laptop, I realize as I write this chapter,

I found my mom exactly 3 months ago today. No coincidence there, as I complete the story of our visit.

Hmmmm, I thought, what will we talk about today? Her room still the same, she was dressed in a blue top yet again. Same color but different shirt all three days. Looking at her, I could feel her desire to look nice. She may be 90 years old, but she wasn't about to lose touch with her appearance.

The room still looked the same, until I spotted a Nike shoe box on her bed. It was placed there so intentionally, clearly lined up with the lines of the bed, as if she had taken measurements to get it squared right in the middle. An obvious inherited trait I admittedly had received from her. The walker relocated now in front of the window, oak tag dangling and turned away. It was hard to take my eyes off of hers, but this would be my last visit, so I just wanted to take it all in.

I think she enjoyed show and tell. Today would be no different. On the drive down, a good 30 minutes or so, I passed a dump truck that was sitting on the side of the road that said Timothy down the side of the dump. Well, there is no coincidence there. My brother, her oldest child was with me.

Halfway there I remembered Grammie's watch in my bag. Although Grammie's wrist was ½ the size of mine, the expandable band allowed it to slip over my hand. No more pictures today. I felt she had had enough. Although I could have been 100 percent wrong. I just wanted her to never ever forget our connection and try to stay in the moment.

The sun danced on the silver watch band ever so slightly, as I slid the sleeve of my sweatshirt up just enough to expose the watch for her to see. The now familiar gasp and her hand over her mouth, took my breath away, again. There is no doubt she knew it was her mom's as she stared at it, looked at me, looked again at the watch. Tears in her eyes, she said "thank you".

Out of the corner of my eye, I couldn't help but focus on that box. The box itself, was not old. Maybe a couple of years? It was in perfect condition, as if it held someone's brand new sneakers. Men's size, as the box was too large to be a woman's shoe. But what was in the box? And why was it placed so neatly on the bed.

Did I even want to see what was in there? How would it affect me? Was it pictures of some family I was not aware of? Was it our family? Was it journals that would explain where she had been for the last 50 years? Was it information that would explain the nearly two inch scar on her forehead, or the certain glow, seen only in the eyes of someone who has had some Electroconvulsive Therapy, or ECT? Which is a form of treatment of mental health conditions, most popular in the 1950's to the 1970's. Or whateverthehell they were using back then. Although my research has been focused on ECT as the more common form of brain altering therapy in those days, and the lifetime effects it can have on the eyes.

This box was not tattered and torn. It did not have the wear and tear of a box that had been lovingly carried around for 50 plus years. On the contrary, it didn't appeared to have been opened but a couple times. There it sat, trying to get my attention, while leaving all kinds of questions in my mind.

Perhaps intuitively, logically, or emotionally, I knew it was family photos. It would only make sense. After all, during our visit the day before I had shared pictures of us with her. Why would she not have some to share with me? Obviously, she knew I was coming. She had to have known. That is why it was placed there.

It is impossible to describe the way my mother looked at me, a manner in which I don't ever recall anyone looking at me, ever. I know Joy saw it, especially that first day. She could probably describe it best from her position of observer.

During my visit to New Hampshire in August, I had begun to feel a helpless feeling. An emotion that I definitely needed to work through, but how? I mean, I had gone this long without knowing her. Would my world come to a crashing end if I didn't find my mom? Would it mean that the Mediums were not right? "Dear God, why didn't the Mediums tell me over the last 10 years?" I wondered if no one noticed that my mom had NEVER "come thru" from the other side during my readings?

I had always wondered, but I think I had just resigned to the fact that Brayden will always crowd out everyone who tries to connect in Spirit.

So in August, alone in my room, near the Seacoast of New Hampshire, I had a great idea.

The tattoo parlor was clean, bright, and colorful. The energy felt great. I knew I had made the right decision. I have had several tattoos over the last 25 years, in several states in this country. But when in New Hampshire, I would always go to my favorite haunt in Portsmouth. This time I just wasn't feeling it, and I quite honestly don't even know if Hobo's is still open.

It didn't matter, I was here now. I felt safe. Although I don't know why I am addressing this, but considering the timing of this book, I may as well, everyone was masked up and the smell of hand sanitizer was far more prevalent than the familiar smell of tattoo ink. That ink smell is a natural high in and of itself.

What's it like to get a tattoo? I can best describe it as something you don't do just once. You can get addicted to it. Hence some of the amazing body art you see these days. It is a euphoric pain, that causes an adrenaline rush. So why wouldn't you go back for more? I always will.

The young artist with the thick accent, in his best creative cursive writing, carefully designed the artwork that would soon be on my wrist. When he was finished my eyes welled up with tears. "Grace" with a small heart above it, sat perfectly on my wrist in plain view, and with no explanation to the artist, I paid his seemingly inexpensive fee, and added a very grateful tip. I was complete. For the time being.

"Well then, why not show it to her?" I was asking myself. "Show her, her name. Maybe she doesn't know it." I thought. "She knows us though, she knows her children, me, her mother, herself and her mother's watch. Would I trigger something? Arrghhh, what to do!"

"Trust Karen, trust your gut", I heard. "Ah, why not?" I am a risk taker and I had to trust she would be fine.

The slightest chuckle left her distinctive Howes shaped mouth, the inherited small mouth with too many teeth that forced me into 8 extractions before getting braces.

Her eyes lit up. She looked at the tattoo, and looked at me, a little less confident than with the photos. Her finger again pointed at her chest, "me?", she asked. "Yes, you. Grace, that's your name." As if prompted, she responded with "I'm ninety"! "Yes you are," I said. If you, the reader, had questions left as to the validity of my claim that this was in fact my mother, I'm guessing you are now aware that it was. If not, you may need to open your mind a bit, as to the fact that everything is not what you have been told it is. And I will leave that right there, as I know what I know, and whether you know it or not, has no bearing on me. And my life, my life was in fact nowhere near what I was told it was.

I loved this dialogue, I had either become an extremely good lip reader, or I could actually hear her. I still, three months later, have not determined which. Her head tilted, her eyes dimmed just a bit, "I love you" fell out of her mouth. There is no mistaking those words. No matter who you are. Frozen in time, I looked at her and said, "I love you". I am trying to find words to describe feels. I have none. So I will leave that to your own imagination. "Bliss" does not describe it.

We were quickly jolted out of this mesmerizing moment in time, by a shadow. It was moving, above me. Was it a low plane? No, it was THE BIRDS!!! My back to the parking lot, my eyes fixed on my mom, her eyes fixed on the birds, she said, "the birds, oh look at the birds. They come here every day. There they are. The birds. Watch them!" I know mom, I know. "It's always the birds, watch the birds."

I've been watching the birds since they alerted me to the Boston bombing. Since they, by his own admission, alerted my brother, warning of trouble, the day before he woke up blind. Since the day they circled above the location of a missing person. And several times circled in the sky above the resting place of a missing pet. If you know me or work with me, you have heard me say more than once, "watch the birds, it's always the birds, they know stuff." Today would be no different. From the time Joy and I sat and watched them land on the roof of the back of that facility on the first day, till this very moment, it has been, "the birds."

Could we have possibly been more unified at that time, short of a physical embrace? I don't think so. I couldn't ask for more, I wouldn't. I am complete.

And with that, I said, "I have to go." A slight sprinkling of rain had begun to fall, and I took that as my cue, that this last visit had ended. I didn't care about tomorrow. I didn't care about yesterday. I cared only about this one moment in time. Nothing else mattered. Nothing.

The routine we had created two days prior, again in full force. She blew a kiss, said "thank you", "I miss you" and waved goodbye.

350

Headed back down the winding back roads to my hotel, a peace came over me that I had never felt before. One I would never feel again.

As I write this part of my story, on the couch by the living room window in my Myrtle Beach home, I hear the call of one of my totem or spirit animals. I look out and circling above my yard is a red tailed hawk.

It's always the birds. They always know. Or to put it in my words, "you can't make this shit up"!

That feeling when you want to drive by your ex's house just one more time, just in case, just to see? That is how I woke up the following day, the day I would be driving back home. "Well, one little detour isn't going to hurt," I said. I debated for close to an hour. It somehow didn't feel right, but also didn't feel bad either.

My car headed east, I soon arrived at the facility. As I had done the three days prior, I parked facing her window, at about the same time as the previous days, only to discover both blinds closed. I took a picture, although I am not sure why. Why would the blinds be open? Somewhere in time and space, somewhere in our energy, we had planned this. We planned 3 days, three visits, 1,2,3. The blinds weren't open because it wasn't part of our plan.

Stopping for the night in Virginia, I scrolled through my pictures to remind myself this weekend, this visit with my mom, was really real. I had the one picture that Joy had taken of my backside when I was talking to my mom while she had lunch. I had old pictures. I had a picture of a huge sign less than a mile from the facility that read GRACIE, in no uncertain terms. And I had a picture of us. My mom and me.

The last day we were together, I had my phone in my hand, and my mom had thought I was showing her another picture. With a glare on the screen, she squinted, as I hastily pressed the buttons that would save this one moment in time. This picture will never be released. I respect my mother's privacy. She never asked for any of this. Why would allow this book to upheave her life? Not now. Not ever.

It was late, but suddenly I was a detective. Putting the picture of us side by side, with the picture of grammie, (identical) with the picture of my mom when she was younger, pictures of me, of course, but the clincher, was when I put the picture of my mom's face next to that of my younger brother's. There was no denying, he is the child of this woman. His face a bit swollen from chemo treatment for his NMO, didn't effect at all the similarities with the nose, mouth and jaw area. I couldn't see the eyes, as he too, now had to wear the dark sunglasses, even inside. Just like her, just like his mom.

I hadn't looked at the last picture until that moment. Two orbs. One at the top of the evergreen, I knew to be like an angel on a Christmas tree, my brother Timothy. Then one at my height, I can imagine to be my father. Was three days of visits the plan? Or had she seen him again while she was waiting for me? I will never know the answer, but either way, the ever so slight gap in the middle of the blind, tells me she knew I was there. Maybe she just didn't want to say goodbye. I sure as hell didn't.

The skeptic here would interject and say, "Okay, how do you know? This seems like wishful thinking. Or perceiving things how you want to perceive them." I am sure that I have thought of just about everything a skeptic may say or ask. In writing a book like this, it is only going to be natural to want my story to be believable. Not only this portion, but the other traumas as well. "Maybe I will even give in to the temptation to provide proof." I often think. It has been a constant battle for me. "No one will believe me." I think. "Joy is just repeating what Karen told her to say." They might say.

Oh, I have played out the scenarios over and over again in my mind, only to come to the conclusion that I don't care. I truly don't. It's not a matter of whether you believe me or not, my story of the lies, deception and abuse, in a home that had been revered as sacred. This is also a story of hope, a mother's love, and survival. How I survived, how she survived. The last words my father said to me were, "I'm sorry." People do not apologize on their death bed, unless they have something devastating to apologize for.

Maybe he was apologizing for lying about the fact that even when we were younger, he was bald. Yup, no one knew. We had seen the 'wig like' screen behind his pompadour on the top of his head. Curious kids, we would ask, "is that a wig or your real hair?" He never even told the truth about his hair. He lied about something so small. But I truly don't think that is what he needed to apologize for on his deathbed.

Lockdown. Quarantine. Pandemic. Covid 19. Corona. For many, those frequently used words in 2020, brought them so much heartache and pain. For me, I feel so blessed. You see, without the world being on high alert, and no visitors allowed in any health facility in the country, there would have been no "window visits". At a senior health facility, a window visit is walking up and having a conversation with a family member through the glass, instead of going inside the actual facility to visit in person.

Not one person noticed my window visit with my mom. For that, I am grateful.

Had I gone into the facility at a time when it was possible, I would have gotten stopped in my tracks, spun around and sent back to South Carolina. The pandemic that rocked the world, changed my life, as well. I found my mom.

For those who lost during this time, I send my deepest sympathy.

Finding my mom? All divine, timing, intervention, creation, alignment, guidance. I must believe that the brain can't decipher any other explanation. Although it tries.

**Here is an excerpt from my journal, the morning after we found my mom.**

"I found her! We found her! I found my mom! I know it's her! The story is long, but there were birds, there were tears and there was clapping. I just can't wrap my head around this. I am still trying to figure it all out. I just feel so supported, but so alone. Joy is here, she witnessed it all. It is a true miracle. To the point of where it is almost unbelievable. But it is her. This is the beginning."

## JOURNAL ENTRY ~ OCTOBER 26, 2020 ~

It is starting to hit me. She was like a small child. She had a smile as big as the window that she stood in front of. She waved only at me, as if Joy wasn't even there. She smiled. Then she cried. She clapped. Then she looked at me and said, "thank you". She tried so hard to pull open the window. Then just blew me kisses. Not Joy. None of this was for Joy.

But then........she looked past me. What did she see? She closed the blind of the window she was standing in front of, then quickly closed the other blind. As if she had seen a ghost. Did she? Was my father standing behind me in Spirit?

The second day 10/25, Joy went into the courtyard. There she was watching, waiting, in the same long window. She waved gently at Joy and stared. As if looking for someone else. So Joy came and got me in the car. She said, I miss you, I miss you!" I was wearing grammie's watch and showed it to her. She gasped and covered her mouth. She knew exactly what it was.

I then showed her a picture on my phone from her wedding of just her and grammie. She pointed to me and then to herself twice and asked, "you and me?" I just shook my head yes. The fact that she knew. After all she had been through, she knew who it was.

10/26, the third day I went alone. Joy had gone back to Florida. She was waiting in the window. 52 years apart and she and I had a connection where she knew I would be back. She looked at her mom's watch on my wrist again and laughed out loud. I was able to hear her laughter through the window. She put her hand against the window. I met her's with mine. It was a scene from a movie.

Then the birds came. I heard her say, "look at the birds. Every day the birds come here!" I watched her put her hands in the praying position and say, "Thank you god, thank you god, thank you god" as she looked up to the sky. She showed me her hand. The last digit on one of her fingers was bent over, just like grammie's hand. Exactly like her mom. She had long piano fingers. I was always told I had piano fingers. She is at peace when I am there. She never asks who I am. She recognizes me. She knows her child. Her look is the look a mother gives her child. There is no question. I look at her barren room. The bed made with precision, is eerily familiar. There is a nearly new shoe box placed with perfect alignment on her bed. I know there are pictures inside. I don't need to see them. I know.

She looks at the watch on my left arm again. I flip over my right arm and pull up my sleeve. "Grace" it reads. She laughs and covers her mouth in surprise. Grace, you are Grace. Oh but you already know that. Tears in Heaven start falling from the sky, we blow a kiss goodbye. For now? Or forever?

**\*UPDATE ~ APRIL 5, 2021 ~**

I just got back from trying to see my mom. My gut told me over and over not to go. But it's hard to stay away when I am up here in New Hampshire. The small white fence with the little gate, has now been replaced by a 5+ foot fence with a large gate with a large lock. Her blinds were closed on one side and barely open on the other. Clearly, she wasn't expecting me. I don't even know if she is still in there. I am sure this is all coincidence and she's fine.

My gut says that the one weekend that I did see her, would be the one and only time. My "One Moment in Time". UNLESS, when this book comes out, someone steps up and gives me the evidence that I need. My heart hurts, but I will always hold out hope that someone comes forward, and I am able to hug my mom, like I've dreamed of for so long. I am so grateful for the picture that Joy took of me talking to my mom thru the window, as well as the one I took of us with my mom inside the window, and me outside. To protect my mom, those pictures will never be produced. In addition, I cannot help but wonder if my October visit with her is what spawned the new high fence, with the large gate and the large lock. I will never put my mother in jeopardy, even if it means that I never get to lay eyes on her again. I have had my "One Moment in Time".

# CONCLUSION –

Not knowing your mom really is alive doesn't hurt, until you know she is. Fortunately for me it took only 2 years, almost to the day, to find her. For 50+ years I had missed and grieved the mom I never knew. I thought of her every day. Through pictures I had a memory. That's truly all I had. Finding out she was alive from several trusted sources, brought a new level of pain from the lies I had been told my whole life. But it also brought hope. I knew I would find her, I knew it. I told several people that I would find her. I was right.

People have told me things about her my whole life. There was so much that I didn't trust, and I didn't believe. One doesn't just drop their wife off alone at a hospital in New Hampshire, for whatever it was she was supposedly having done, if she was truly as sick as some say she was. If she had a medical condition that allegedly made her hair fall out, that would end her life in less than 45 minutes, they never would have let my father just leave her there and go to work. Although, he did have an attendance record to uphold of not missing a day of work as an English Professor. That was super important to him. I am not exaggerating. He eventually did tarnish that record though, either when he was sick with a kidney stone or a heart attack. I've forgotten which was first. Kidneys = fear. I will leave that right there.

She was "so sick for months" is what I have been told. I don't know. Was she? Or was she like me? Or I am like her. Was she gifted but treated as if she was sick, or possessed? I have one memory of her on

357

the couch, that's it. The rest of my memories are from pictures. I knew only what I was told. I do know that there are doctors who can treat bacterial endocarditis. Yet she had no doctors' appointments, ever. Yes, I am being cynical, I'm angry.

Why was she kept from having medical treatment if she had a fatal illness? No doctors? No tests? Till the day he took her and "left her at the hospital for a test ", and she supposedly lived less than an hour?

I've had that question answered 100 times and the answer is always the same. "He trusted his God to heal her". Although, I know now that death wasn't what happened that day, I am fairly certain that "God" may want folks to have the sense to also use medical resources.

Was it coincidence that she hadn't been treated by a doctor, but the one time she was taken from the house, she didn't come back? If he had taken her an hour later, she would have "died at home." So no, I have never believed this story. Hence the black sheep position I proudly hold in that family.

One simply doesn't speak to a group of women on Graphonalysis, **and** stay around to "answer questions", according to the newspaper article I recently found, the night before your extremely sick wife is going to the hospital. Or any night that your wife is hours from her "death". Especially not with four children ages 3 to 9 at home with her. If she had in fact, died from bacterial endocarditis, as I was told, she didn't just succumb to the illness in the 45 minutes it took him to get from the hospital to the college in Massachusetts. His story was that she died before he got to the college. At the time there was no cell phones but he "had a message at the college, that she had died."

Although hesitant to write this, I also find a very interesting connection with the woman who was standing in my living room, when as a 5 year old I made my way down the stairs, only to learn my mother was "dead", and the fact that this was also the married woman that he maintained a daily routine of 2 to 3 hour "counseling" sessions with on the phone. The calls that we were not allowed to interrupt. Imagine thinking ANY phone conversation takes priority over your now "motherless" children. I tell my adult children quite often, "it's not what it is, it is what it looks like it is, that people will believe."

ALSO, hair loss is NOT a symptom of bacterial endocarditis. Yet I was told "she was so sick her hair fell out", implying that was the reason for her wigs. Nope, I don't believe it. Two things: a) many women wore wigs in the 60's. b) Hemochromatosis DOES cause hair loss, see my explanation below.

About 15 years ago, my younger brother was diagnosed with Hemochromatosis, a disease where the body creates too much iron. His treatment was weekly to monthly bloodletting, phlebotomy, to remove the iron. Not like when you or I donate blood, but a lot of blood.

When he received this diagnosis, I of course associated it with his past issues. That was until I mentioned it to my doctor, several months later. "Okay" she said, we need to test you today. You probably have it too!" "You see", she explained, "in order for your brother to have it, "both your parents would have to have the abnormal gene. Those who inherit one of the abnormal genes, won't develop hemochromatosis. They would have to inherit the abnormal gene from BOTH parents. So both your parents have it or had it, in reference to your mom. One parent would typically be asymptomatic; one parent would have symptoms. "

I ran to my father with this information, which he naturally laughed at. Unfortunate for him, I was his transportation to his oncologist the following day, which always consisted of a lab visit.

Yes, even after all I have shared about my childhood, I was a caretaker to him during his last year or so. As well as my sister and his wife. But I did most of the doctors, labs, and chemo transports. But also remember, I was completely unaware of the trauma and life of lies at that point. I had blocked every bit of it out. I am still stuck with huge blanks from my childhood. He's been gone twelve years. I have known the secrets for two.

The blood test was positive for Hemochromatosis. He was asymptomatic, which means my mom had the symptoms. That would 100 percent explain her hair loss when I met her in 2020, as well as the yellowish skin. Although, if she has been in a facility for the whole 50+ years she's been gone, I am sure she has had great medical care.

That would be a reason why back then she would have had hair loss, if she really did. Not bacterial endocarditis. I told my family. They don't believe me, because the same story that I was told, is the story we were all told. It is what they believe, and I don't care. What other people believe or don't believe is none of our business.

I proved my mom had Hemochromatosis and it didn't fit with the "story". So I guess that was on me, not the medical information I was providing.

Would I have found my mother without help from the Spirit world? Absolutely not! She was right there under my nose for many, many years. It wasn't time. I wasn't meant to find her. SHE put the wheels in motion 20 years ago, when she called me. Back then my brain said it couldn't be her, and family members referred to the caller as a crazy woman. "Wait what? So the elderly are out prank calling people?" I asked them. She was 70 at the time. My gut knew it was her. I didn't take action then. It wasn't time. It had to play out in Divine timing. There was no other way. It lined up perfectly.

Her voice. I can never forget the sound of her voice on the phone that day. "Karen, this is your mother."

The last time I visited her in October, I was right up against the window and was talking right to her. It was the same voice, no doubt in my mind.

So yes, anything is possible, if you believe. Even when it feels like it can't be real. Can we raise people from the dead? No. But if we have no actual proof of their death, like visual proof, and not some hokey pokey document, and we have only the stories we have been told of a death, we absolutely can challenge it. As a matter of fact, I implore you to challenge it.

If your gut tells you that you are adopted, have another sibling, have a different parent, or a loved one is NOT dead, challenge it.

Believe you will receive the answers. The answers will either come to you in meditation and journaling, or perhaps through an intuitive, such as myself. I have intuitively told people that they have a sibling and had them leave their session thinking I was nuts. Only for them to contact me 6 months later after meeting their brother or sister for the first time. If I was told my mom was alive over and over in the past two years by trusted Mediums, and chose the lies and brainwashing that happened in my first 50 years, then who am I to do this work? I surely cannot expect my clients to trust me and my connection to Spirit, if I don't do the same. Yes, I waivered a few times. I am human. Well, maybe many times. And you will too!

Many of us have been programmed to believe this or that to benefit someone else. Not for our greatest good and well-being.

Sometimes you might be like me. Although in October I saw my mom, and she cried when she saw me. She said, "thank you" and "I miss you", within TEN minutes of seeing me in person for the first time. It was her. She banged on the window, exactly how I had requested not even 5 minutes earlier. But when we pulled out of that driveway, I still had the fear that it was all a dream.

50 years of lies, how did I just find her so easy?? Because Divine Intervention. Because I was supposed to. Because she knew I would come. I bet she waited by that window. Was it enough for me? Nope. I still asked for a sign, "a big one". I got it! Not ten minutes later we passed that huge sign that read "Gracie"!

Trauma. Trauma doesn't define you. It happened to you, some say it happened for you. It molded you in a way that neither you nor I will ever be able to wrap our heads around. It's not meant to be understood, so don't try. That won't speed up the healing. Do I wish I knew what really happened in my childhood sooner? I don't know. I have to trust that it was all orchestrated this way. It is not up to us to decide.

As a child, I was mad at God for making my mother die. That's when all this heaven and hell stuff began to sound silly to me. I was mad at everyone when my kids' dad died. I saw him dead, I won't ever forget.

But that anger brought me to where I am today. I don't agree with a lot of "religious ideologies" based on MY experiences only. I don't believe in forcing your beliefs down anyone's throat, yet at every twist and turn, yet I have people doing that to me. I have been told that I am a "false prophet"! Really? Who gets to decide that? "Who made *you* into the God that you profess to believe in?" I would ask. I don't knock on doors with religious paraphernalia and push it into a stranger's hands. Or leave bibles in weird places. Those who desire a higher consciousness and spiritual journey, will be lead in that direction. I don't need to stuff anything down anyone's throat like they do mine. And neither do you. I know what I know, and I believe what I believe. It is my journey.

I also believe the word God in Spirituality is used to define a higher conscience. Source. Spirit. The Universe. I tell many people ~ "your higher power can be a slice of toast, but just believe in something higher than yourself." You don't have to walk this road alone.

I believe this book will land not only in the hands of those who need it, but specifically the hands of those who were conditioned (a soft word for brainwashed) by those affiliated with a religious group or organization and need some help. Or those who were sexually or emotionally abused by their church members, or minister, not just solely priests. Or those who, God forbid, the abusive minister was the parent. This book is for those who are drawn to read it. This book is meant to be passed on to those who are hurting.

To those who are healing. This book is a tool. It was "given" to me as a gift, much of it written in my meditations. I hope it is a gift to you as well.

Brainwash ~ Wikipedia ~ "make someone adopt radically different beliefs by using systematic and often forcible pressure"..... "persuasion by propaganda or salesmanship."

Whispererpedia ~ Brainwash ~ case in point, "forceable pressure" ~ fear of going to hell as a child, instilled by a parent or person of authority, i.e.: minister, deacon, etc... in order to gain some sort of sick control of the child, emotionally, physically, or for any other reason.

"Persuasion by propaganda or salesmanship" ~ Propaganda = printed information handed to you or forced on you. Media information, i.e.: "A Thief in the Night".

"Salesmanship" ~ Well let's see.........(this is my opinion only and does not have to align with yours, it's okay). I go into a building, a person tells me his or her interpretation of a book that they say they abide by and believe in. Although quite often their "real life" is the exact opposite. Then they pass around a dish for me to give them my money. Then the church gets fancier. Please don't bother contacting me on this one, I have said this same thing since I was a child, and I speak only for myself. Keep in mind that I am the daughter of the minister who received a new car as a gift from the church one Christmas when I was a child, although he had a full time position as an English professor, and already had a perfectly good car. Oh the mouths that kind of money could have fed, and the local children that could have been clothed.

This is my last point on this subject. Afterall, this IS the conclusion chapter. But you didn't expect my book to follow guidelines, did you?

The "offering plate" discussion ~ and I will close with this. I was taught to give 10% of everything I earned to the church. It's called tithing. I was repeatedly quoted the scripture that said God wanted me to do this. And we all know what I was told by my father and the church, if I didn't do what God wanted me to, I'd be on a fast track to hell.

I was not taught to give to the poor. I was not taught to donate to charity. I didn't even know what philanthropy was, until I volunteered for the Red Cross as an adult.

Now I give nothing to the "church", that is MY personal choice. Again, to each their own, but I do all I can for those in need. Financially, and in kind of goods and services. Do I keep track and make sure it is 10%? Never. Who decided that number? It's actually probably more than 10%. I give what is needed.

If I see an "ask' that resonates with me, I give. My missing pet services are 100% gratis. As well as all of my Forensic Mediumship cases, which are often months or years of work, completely free of charge. That includes homicide cases, whether for the family or for law enforcement. Missing persons cases as well. I cannot imagine being contacted by a frantic parent and saying, "oh yes I will help find them, but it's $200 an hour."

Again, give what you choose, where you choose. Neither me, nor my spiritual beliefs will tell you what to give and where. I believe it is a personal choice. I do not judge anyone for who or what they believe in. I have an open mind. I trust the reader of my book does too. I don't expect to receive hate mail, judging my point of view. That would be a perfect example of fear based beliefs being shoved down my throat. Oh, as well as the fact that judging me also a sin.

Someone asked me what my fears are around releasing this book. I have a few.

- Will someone try to find my mother, and upset her life?

- Will someone go after one of my siblings to get their side of the story? I have nothing to hide, nor do I care about their view of my childhood. Because they don't know. And their 'not knowing' doesn't make it not true. I just don't want them bothered.

- Will this affect his widow in a negative fashion? Although I have no intention of legally researching and proving that my mom was taken away and I was lied to. It does technically mean he was still married (unless there is a divorce somewhere. Quite honestly, at this point, nothing would surprise me.) I want no harm to come to her. I am sure there are more lies.

- Will this affect the other unnamed men and their families? No, I haven't even come close to naming them.

- And one of the biggest fears is ~ Is someone going to read my book, and contact me to tell me they were abused in his church too? Although it is a "fear", *I want anyone* who was abused in my church to please come to me. Or in any church for that matter. My goal is to start a community once I hear from you.

"Two roads diverged in the wood, and I, I took the road less traveled...... And that has made all the difference".

I will never stop taking the "road less traveled".


## ~ THE END~

# EPILOGUE ~

As I lay down my pen, on this the eve of the death of my first husband, the light bulb on the lamp next to me, has just blown. Although the finish date was set at what I thought needed to be 2/21/21, in therapy we found a new date, due to other things I needed to address before editing this book. 3/3/21 ~ or 2+1 is also 3. 3/3/3 ~ It is 5:33pm! I sh*t you not!

My therapist sent me this yesterday. "The number 3 in numerology is all about creativity and communication....... It encourages us to think outside the box. We will receive a double dose of this energy........It makes it a perfect time for tackling our goals with a creative flair. Three also represents free thinking. But it is heavily focused on communication."

I ordered lightbulbs yesterday. They arrived an hour ago. "This little light of mine. I'm GONNA let it shine..............Hide it under a bushel. NO! I'm gonna let it shine."

"Cute trick Brayden! But I was one step ahead of you this time."

I do understand the reference though of the light going off. The book is done.

*"A portion of the proceeds from this book will be donated to the New Hampshire Coalition Against Domestic and Sexual Violence. The Coalition is a statewide, nonprofit agency that works to help amplify the voices of survivors of abuse in order to build safer communities across the State and Nation."*

# ABOUT THE AUTHOR ~

Karen Whisperer is a renowned Psychic Medium. She has clients all over the country and around the world. Growing up in New Hampshire she often spent time alone as a child. She didn't know then what a huge impact that would have on her gift of intuition as an adult.

Since she was a teen, Karen has always wanted to write. She would write short prophetic stories in her journal and from there began her first book. Many, many revisions and title changes later, the book has changed themes several times.

Karen is a mom of four adult children, and a gamma of 6 grandchildren. She made a move from the cold New Hampshire winters to Myrtle Beach, South Carolina in 2019. Karen also makes her home on the island of Molokai, Hawaii. A place she manifested for herself, after her first visit there in 2017.

Currently working on her second book about amazing readings from beyond, Karen also has a cookbook in the works.

# FINDING GRACE ~ ABOUT THE BOOK

Several years ago, I started a book. It consisted of throwing some neat information together as a potential self help book. After years of seeing clients, I felt I had received so much information intuitively, as well as channeling and through readings, that someone out there "surely could be helped".

I recently found in an old box, an index card from a workshop I attended 10 years ago. We were instructed to create our future on the cards. This card had my amateur drawing of a book, and on the front of it, the title "Gracie's Pain". As I looked at that card, I wondered, "what was I thinking?" What IS/WAS the pain part? What did I subliminally know back then?

Over the past three or so years, I myself have received several messages from other Mediums regarding my past, my mother Grace, and several things in my life that simply had not added up. Two years ago, I awoke to some horrific memories that shook my world. I switched gears, and so did the book.

This book will take you through the pain. My pain, my childhood, and a whole lot more. Finding Grace is based on a true story of deception, religion, addiction, confusion and a childhood of loss and lies. It begins when at age 5, I woke up to find my mom gone, forever.

But it is also a tale of survival, growth and life beyond the lies. It is about Finding Grace, no matter the life you are handed. I have put my blood (yes I got a paper cut from the manuscript when I printed it), sweat (don't get me started about my bright ideas to write outside in the sunlight and humidity), and tears (and there were enough to mess up my keyboard) into it. This book is a labor of love. Self-love, which is what I am mastering now, love for my ancestors, and love for my family. Also, love for you, the reader.

In my work, I often incorporate humor during sensitive topics. I tried to weave it into my book, as well.

Please read, read again, and then pass this book on. My goal is to get the message out there, to let you know there is help. And that you are not crazy, I am not crazy. It is about getting the message into as many hands as possible. You can make that happen. I am grateful for everyone who reads this book, then passes it to someone who may need it. Be blessed.

Printed in the United States
by Baker & Taylor Publisher Services

Printed in the United States
by Baker & Taylor Publisher Services